D0976073

The
Obama Gang

How Barack Obama, through his post-presidency foundation, assembled, launched, and wages the new assault on American law enforcement

STEVE POMPER
National Police Association

ISBN 978-1-09835-525-8 eBook 978-1-09835-526-5

Contents

Introduction

Decriminalizing Crime and Criminalizing Law Enforcement

Those who can make you believe absurdities can make you commit atrocities. —Voltaire

The National Police Association (NPA) exists to teach people how best to assist the nation's law enforcement officers in completing their public safety mission and to help the public understand the true nature of police work. The NPA does this, in part, by publishing an informative website (nationalpolice.org) where people can access information, articles, and videos regarding current issues affecting law enforcement and learn ways they can better support their cops. People may also make tax-deductible contributions to help the NPA continue its important work.

As an example of this work, the NPA has filed complaints against prosecutors who refuse to prosecute criminals or falsely prosecute cops. Also, the NPA has filed several amicus briefs to support police officers across the nation under attack by anti-police mayors, city councils, and prosecutors who have attempted to fire them or even to put them in prison just for doing their jobs.

The NPA also keeps people apprised of what's happening in the law enforcement world through articles written by its staff of contributors, which includes writers from around the nation who are retired law enforcement professionals with diverse experience. This guarantees experienced perspectives affecting a wide array of American law enforcement issues.

When considering all the anti-police individuals and organizations in existence, the NPA realized how so many of these Obama-connected entities intertwine, collude, and collaborate in their mission to eradicate traditional policing in America. The organization also realized these people and groups appeared organized and that the verbal attacks against the police seemed coordinated, often proliferating the same words and phrases in a manner resembling propaganda.

The NPA noticed the anti-police factions seemed to be a part of a larger "family" or "gang" of wealthy and radical individuals and organizations. With former President Barack H. Obama at the top, they seem to operate similar to an organized crime family—on the periphery of civil society.

From the bottom up, the organizational chart begins with the "soldiers" on the streets, who caused such visible destruction during 2020, and climbs the crowded pyramid to the top. This "family" (not to be taken for the president's personal family, who are lovely) or gang of individuals and organizations are now working together like never before to collapse policing in America as we know it—to collapse America as we know it.

At the other end of the organizational chart, similar to Mafia families, is Don Obama. And, in keeping with the allegory and establishing a proper ambience, perhaps it's time to start referring to Obama as the Boss.

The Boss is at the head of this anti-cop gang, using the Obama Foundation (Obama.org) to destroy law enforcement. Next comes Obama's caporegime, his captains, who run and deploy his soldiers. These soldiers are people who hit the streets to protest. However, many also commit violence, directly challenging (even injuring or murdering) police officers. Also important, but more tangentially "connected," are the gang's myriad associates.

These individuals and organizations assist the family in achieving its goals. This comparison obviously isn't identical because crime families are comparatively small. The anti-cop, anti-traditional-America mob, on the other hand, is a diffuse conglomeration operating in a massive fog of political (and actual) war. The comparison, nevertheless, is apt—and kind of fun.

It's important to note that, unlike the less-bulky Mafia mob families, many of these Obama-connected groups and individuals have served in multiple capacities at various levels of support for years. For example, the Washington Examiner reported[1] about two Brooklyn attorneys who qualify as typical Obama supporters and would normally be seen as associates. However, because the police arrested them for firebombing an NYPD car during a riot in May 2020, they also qualify as soldiers. Some people have started in one category and later moved into another, through promotions or de facto transfers.

This shifting of positions also makes these people and operations even more nebulous. In fact, you'll see that some of these organizations have former convicted terrorists as heroes or even members and directors. It's hoped that people can use this book as a jumping-off platform to do their own research and reach their own conclusions. While efforts have been made to point out the massive weblike connections that exist in this realm of political intrigue and possible criminal behavior, it's impossible to venture into every single proverbial nook and cranny. This is especially true with the gang's shape-shifting nature. At some point, it's necessary to escape the maze, stop consuming additional information, and disseminate what's been gathered. Still, as readers choose which links to follow, like one of those photos of multiple mirrors into infinity, one will lead to another, which will lead to.... There's the idea.

With the massive amount of information in existence, the NPA has done its best to provide readers with legitimate evidence and solid sources for readers to consider and judge for themselves the validity of the people, events, and materials offered as evidence. Note that these gangs of shadowy people and organizations frequently delete posts, remove pages, take down websites, or even shut down and reorganize entire organizations just to hide what they are doing. The Boss's former ACORN is a good example.

As another example, in September 2020, the Black Lives Matter organization scrubbed[2] from its site information about its connections to Marxism and its desire to eliminate the nuclear family from American culture. Keep this in mind if a link fails to deliver you to your destination. Also, remember that simply not agreeing with or not liking a bit of information is not "proof" the information is wrong. As we say in law enforcement, follow the evidence to where it leads, even if—especially if—it leads to an uncomfortable place.

OBAMA GANG ORGANIZATIONAL CHART

BOSS
Barack H. Obama
Obama Foundation

CONSIGLIERE
Eric Holder
(Wingman)

UNDERBOSS
George Soros
(Bond Villain)

CAPOREGIMES	SOLDIERS	ASSOCIATES
Media	Antifa	Social Media
Governors	BLM	Wall Street Banks
Mayors	Media Matters	Lawyers
Prosecutors	MoveOn	Corporations
City Councils	Transition Integrity Project	
ACLU		

Chapter 1

The Anti-Police State

The nationwide onslaught against law and order and law enforcement is not the result of an organic popular uprising against corrupt and abusive American police forces. Each of the jurisdictions most hostile to the police did not just happen independently upon their organized, systemic hostility toward cops. The current offensive against the police is a part of a larger agenda perpetuated by an alliance of radical leftist groups to transform drastically what we have known as the United States of America. The major political parties are no longer flip sides of the same coin—the loyal opposition. They now seem more like two separate coins.

One major component of the anarchists', socialists', and Marxists' plan to eradicate traditional America is to eliminate the cops first. Police officer boots on the ground are the mechanism by which civil society will defend itself and return to normal, and after which the insurrectionists can join other leftist radicals in well-deserved historical obscurity.

Ronald Reagan, in a speech[3] to the British Parliament in 1982, put it best. "What I am describing now is a plan and a hope for the long term—the march of freedom and democracy which will leave Marxism-Leninism on the ash-heap of history as it has left other tyrannies which stifle the freedom and muzzle the self-expression of the people." It is for no less than this ideal that people who want to keep the true American Revolution alive now strive. Today, Americans find their gun rights threatened by this same radical faction. They want to take away the people's most effective means of self-defense (against them): firearms. Ironically, they've always said, "People should rely on the police." What, then, should we conclude now that they want to get rid of both the police and your guns?

Where does that leave the individual American regarding his or her God-given right to self-defense? Not in a good place. However, a disarmed populace combined with a "re-imagined," "re-envisioned," or "re-combobulated" "police alternative" corps of "violence interrupters" loyal to the Left makes it much easier to rule over rather than serve under the people. To paraphrase Seinfeld's Soup Nazi, "No more self-government for you!"

So, who is doing all this? Glad you asked. A lot of people—an awful lot of people.

The Obama Foundation sits atop an organizational, institutional, and political structure, with alliances both tacit and explicit, that operate much like a Mafia crime family—I was going to add, "without the violence," but that would be inaccurate, wouldn't it? After all, the Boss was encouraging the mayhem when he said, "I want you to argue with them and get in their faces."[4]

Just ask the people who live in Portland. In late August 2020, a Joe Biden supporter, Michael Reinoehl, an Antifa member, allegedly shot and killed Donald Trump supporter[5] and Patriot Prayer member Aaron "Jay" Danielson on the street. Reinoehl also supports Black Lives Matter (BLM), reportedly having a BLM neck tattoo. The killing was captured on video.[6] A few days later, deputy U.S. marshals shot and killed[7] the alleged murderer when Reinoehl reportedly drew a gun on federal cops, as the fugitive task force attempted to arrest him on a murder warrant.

Back to the issue at hand. Is it fair to compare the Boss's anti-police movement to the mob? Here, it seems so. Anyone who seeks to "reform," defund, or abolish law enforcement, especially in a systematic and even violent way, is engaging in organized crime against civil society. In other words, the anti-cop political leaders have put a contract out on traditional America, and they're trying to have law enforcement *whacked*!

When you have several like-minded, loosely affiliated people heading in the same political direction, that's one thing. But when you have an official 501c3 nonprofit organization (Obama.org), complete with loyal captains, obedient soldiers, and useful associates, that's another thing entirely.

There are people engaged in an organized effort to manipulate the national discourse and public policy by getting politicians to swear a loyalty pledge, known as "omerta."[8] This promise commits them to destroying traditional American institutions, especially the police. How do we know the Boss is anti-police? Well, we can look at what he's said and done to weaken law enforcement, law and order, and equal justice in America.

First, there is what the Boss said and did, pertaining to police officers, while in office, and what he's been involved in since leaving the presidency. We'll begin with an off-the-cuff remark the Boss made regarding a police incident about which he admitted he did not have all the facts. He said, "The Cambridge police acted stupidly...." Shouldn't a president of the United States give the police the benefit of the doubt—at least initially? That seems fair, right? But he chose not to do that. Instead, he chose immediately to disparage the police, thus inciting an anti-police sentiment in America that would grow and eventually rage out of control.

This single incident has been chosen for chapter 2 to start this examination of the Obama Foundation's anti-cop agenda because it happened in 2009, only six months into the Boss's first term. It serves as a bit of table-setting for the president's obvious hostility toward law enforcement.

During his presidency, he would insult law enforcement in many head-on and oblique ways, including by refusing to light[9] the White House in blue to honor fallen police officers. He had previously lit the White House in rainbow colors[10] to celebrate the Supreme Court decision favoring same-sex marriage. It would not have been a difficult gesture. Why such reluctance? On the other hand, President Donald Trump has bathed America's house in blue[11] repeatedly.

Despite what the Boss and his defenders have said to the contrary, Obama's presidency was filled with, at best, apathy, and at worst, antipathy for cops. His singular pogrom against law enforcement demonstrated this when he, along with his "wingman"[12] Eric Holder as attorney general, weaponized the Department of Justice (DOJ). With that, they launched attacks against several American police departments and inflicted on them bogus consent decrees.[13]

Incidentally, the Boss's close association with Holder makes it appropriate to give the wingman a new title: Consigliere. Of course, Valerie Jarrett comes to mind as a more literal consigliere—advisor to the Boss. But for these purposes the term is being applied more as an allusion than literally. Holder and the Boss's relationship seemed more public, with Jarrett's and the Boss's seeming more private. Besides, it's just a device to advance the allegory, so *fuhgeddaboudit*.

As mentioned in my book *De-Policing America:*[14] *A Street Cop's View of the Anti-Police State* (Post Hill Press, 2018), "According to Newsmax. com's Sean Piccoll, former U.S. attorney Andrew C. McCarthy, who prosecuted the criminals of the 1993 World Trade Center bombing, says, 'They've [DOJ] had their thumbs on the scales from the beginning.' Piccoll continues, 'McCarthy cited a string of federal civil-rights investigations into some 20 police departments, including Ferguson, Missouri's, which he said the Justice Department has approached with a presumption of racial guilt.'"

McCarthy was right and still is. Exploiting high-profile use-of-force incidents, in which most officers have been cleared, the Boss/Consigliere DOJ inflicted protocols on the police that, pardon the pun, has handcuffed them. The Boss/Consigliere DOJ never met a police department it didn't think was "systemically" abusive and corrupt.

This attitude is at the heart of the Boss's antagonism toward law enforcement, which, as we will discover, did not end with his presidency. In July 2020, the Boss delivered a eulogy[15] at the funeral for civil rights icon John Lewis, a Georgia representative from 1987 till his death. As occurred with former President Bill Clinton before him during Minnesota Senator Paul Wellstone's funeral[16] in 2002, in 2020 the Boss hijacked the Lewis funeral to deliver a painfully partisan and inappropriately political speech.

But because it was the Boss and he was enmeshed among his adoring syco-phants, he got away with it—as usual.

Only by ignoring the obvious video and eyewitness evidence can anyone buy into what people like Rep. Jerry Nadler (D-NY) have called a myth[17] (note: YouTube has taken down this video), referring to reports of violence occurring during Antifa riots. They are no myth. Ask the myr-iad cops who have been assaulted. Or, better yet, Nadler should ask fellow Democrat Keith Ellison. Ellison is a former deputy chair of the Democratic National Committee (DNC) who resigned over sexual assault allegations.[18]

By the way, Ellison's anti-police qualifications are well established. About sexual assault investigations, Ellison said, cops "shouldn't respond to 'sexual assault' calls if the assailant ran away." Sean Hannity of Fox News reported that Ellison elaborated, "If you're a woman who's been a victim of a sexual assault, and the assailant ran away, wouldn't you rather talk to somebody who is trained in helping you deal with what you're dealing with, as opposed to somebody whose main training is that they know how to use a firearm? Right?" Wrong! That is an ignorant insult against police officers.

Ellison emphasized his obvious view of the police when he posed with the Antifa: The Anti-Fascist Handbook[19] and tweeted, "I hereby declare, officially, my support for Antifa." So, how did Minnesota voters punish Ellison for an alleged sexual assault that caused him to resign his DNC position and for supporting a violent anarcho-communist group? They elected him their attorney general—the state's top law enforcement official.

Rep. Nadler could also ask Adam Haner. He's the man whom a cow-ardly militant named Marquise Love kicked in the head[20] in Portland, after other brutes had beaten him. Haner had gotten out of his truck to help a transgender woman[21] who was being robbed by mob thugs. Still, Haner was not the only person[22] an Antifa or BLM rioter has kicked unconscious in Mayor Ted Wheeler's utopia, otherwise known as Portland, Oregon. As one of the Boss's captains, Wheeler was doing his part to keep America chaotic, hoping it would hurt President Trump's chances for reelection.

Through initiatives such as My Brother's Keeper Alliance Pledge[23] (MBKAP), the Boss is cajoling his capos, mayors, city council members, and prosecutors to pledge to introduce drastic "reforms" to their police departments. In fact, a story at BET.com is titled[24] "Obama Demands Every American Mayor Review Use of Force Policies." *Demands*. Reform was the ostensible goal. Well, "reform" is how it started. Now, the Obama Foundation and its allies have transitioned to "defunding" and even "abolishing" the police (and eventually the courts and jails too).

It's no accident that terms such as "systemic racism," "police violence," and "de-escalation" have proliferated across leftist-run jurisdictions and news media in recent years. The immediate, visceral response to "systemic racism" is this: the Left *is* the system—and has been for decades—in the cities that complain the most. "Police violence" is a euphemism for not liking how cops do their jobs when they must use force—even when they're doing it right. And anti-cop critics use the word "de-escalation" when they need to blame the police for a use-of-force against a resisting or violent suspect.

There are always some violent people who will not agree to de-escalate. In uses of force, the bad guy gets a vote, too. Just because you don't like how police do their work, that does not make what they are doing wrong. If there is a magic word someone can give the cops that will calm a violent criminal who does not want to be calm, no doubt the cops would love to have it.

This notion recalls the story of an American politician at the start of World War II. He reportedly said, "If only *I* had spoken to Hitler…." This is not a comparison of anyone to Hitler. This is a comment about the type of person who thinks he, of all people, could have talked Hitler out of his evil.

Again, don't think the Boss packed up his antagonism toward cops when he left the White House. Since his presidency ended, he has been busy lording over a large group of loosely affiliated and tacitly allied organizations committed to ending policing in America as we have known it.

While the Boss and his gang's ultimate stated goal has been to "fundamentally transform the United States of America," one of their ancillary missions necessary to accomplish their goal of creating a socialist state is to eradicate federal, state, and local law enforcement, who are the only people, outside of the military, who can physically stop them.

The radical far Left counts among its allies a major political party, the mainstream news media, academia, Hollywood, and, increasingly, large corporations. And let's toss in various militant anarchist, socialist, and Marxist groups such as Antifa and BLM, who serve as foot soldiers for the Obama Foundation and other leftist organizations' insurrection.

Incidentally, as alluded to earlier, could another reason the radicals want to dismantle the police be because law enforcement is one of the few remaining conservative institutions in American government? It's worth considering. After all, the radicals' condemnation of the cops, to one degree or another, is universal. As the radicals have coined, ACAB: All Cops Are Bastards/Bad. This sentiment has not been condemned by many politicians on one side of the aisle.

While some in law enforcement leadership, especially police chiefs appointed by leftist mayors, may lean left politically, most street cops, patrol sergeants, detectives, and management (lieutenants, captains, majors, and so on) tend to lean right politically. Politics often drifts left as ranks increase. However, there are some outstanding police chiefs, such as Loren Culp[25] (who ran for governor in 2020) in Washington State and Chief James Craig[26] in Detroit, Michigan. And don't forget about Constitution-loving sheriffs like Scott Jenkins[27] of Virginia and Adam Fortney[28] of Washington State.

While he was in office, and since he's left, the Boss has put a virtual contract out on cops. He has been merciless in attempting to whack American law enforcement. With multiple serpentine appendages, the Obama Foundation's anti-police agenda is reaching into every crack and crevice to extract equal justice so his minions can replace it with social justice. Isn't it time to dismantle the police departments' dismantlers and find out just what the Obama Foundation is up to and how its godfather, the Boss, and his mob are destroying American policing?

Chapter 2

Obama's Early Hostility toward Cops

"The Cambridge police acted stupidly." Most people likely recall the Boss's slur against American law enforcement uttered in July 2009, early in his first term as president. For the police, the comment is etched into *every* cop's memory. Police officers share a sense of abandonment when the president of the United States, the nation's top law enforcer, is not just ambivalent toward law enforcement but shows outright hostility. Without knowing all the information, the president's instinct was to criticize the Cambridge, Massachusetts, police officers.

This incident, occurring early so in the Boss's term, betrayed what cops could expect from their president for the next four—and then eight—and more years. For leftist cop-haters, he did not disappoint. For cops and their supporters, the highest law enforcer in the land did nothing but disappoint. Let's look at the evidence.

Our 44th president, without knowing even a small fraction of what happened, insulted the Cambridge Police Department, who were just doing their jobs. What we know is that Cambridge police sergeant James Crowley arrested Harvard professor Henry Louis Gates Jr. even after the sergeant knew the professor owned the house. But that was not the full story. That's only as much as the Boss knew before he criticized the cops.

We now know Sgt. James Crowley arrested Gates for disorderly conduct (M.G.L. c. 272, § 53[29]), not burglary. Apparently, the Boss did not know about the professor's alleged behavior that led to his disorderly conduct arrest. The president's comments gave the impression Crowley arrested Gates specifically for breaking into his own house—because he was black.

Yes, to make matters worse, both Gates and the Boss immediately inferred racism against the cops—with no evidence—as a motivation for the arrest. Jumping to a racist conclusion is not fair to justice, and if a U.S. president is not aligned with ensuring equal justice for all citizens, including the cops, then he is abdicating his duty as the leader of this great nation.

The Boss admitted he didn't know the facts[30] before he made his acerbic anti-police comments, but he made them anyway. In response to a question from the *Chicago Sun-Times*'s Lynn Sweet, the Boss said,[31] "I should say ... Skip Gates is a friend, so I may be a little biased here. I don't know all the facts. What's been reported, though, is that the guy forgot his keys, jimmied his way to get into the house—there was a report called into the police station that there might be a burglary taking place. So far, so good.

"At that point, Gates is already in his house. The police officer comes in. I'm sure there's some exchange of words. But my understanding is that Gates shows his ID to show this is his house. And at that point he gets arrested for disorderly conduct—charges which were later dropped."

Then the Boss cites the "long history of African Americans and Latinos being stopped by law enforcement disproportionately"—again, insinuating racism into an incident where no evidence of racism exists. The former president seems to expect racism[32] from police officers, especially those who are white.

According to Boston.com, Gates, who comes off in public as a very pleasant man, has never apologized for his alleged behavior and denied calling Crowley a racist.[33] Did the Boss, or anyone else, truly believe Sergeant Crowley asked Professor Gates for his ID, and that, after the professor showed it, the sergeant just arrested him? As they say, that doesn't pass the sniff test.

The public can only judge Sgt. Crowley based on what he has said and how he has behaved from listening to and watching him on TV. This brief incident, during the "Beer Summit,"[34] informs us about Sgt. Crowley's character. While the Boss walks ahead toward the cameras, apparently unmindful of his friend's physical limitations, Sgt. Crowley instinctively helps Professor Gates,[35] who walks with a cane, down the stairs.

Sgt. Crowley's and Officer Carlos Figueroa's police reports,[36] which are evidence that can be relied on in court, show that Gates is the one who inserted racism into the incident with his very first words. This is not surprising if you read what Lisa Miller wrote in Newsweek[37] back in 2011 about a new NPR series on race. "Henry Louis Gates Jr., known to all as 'Skip,' remembers the day he became obsessed with the subject of race." It was when he was nine years old.

According to police reports, Crowley called into the house to a person who turned out to be Gates. The sergeant informed the professor he was there to investigate a burglary. Reportedly, Gates replied, "Why, because I'm a black man in America?" Remember, it was Gates's neighbor who called the police. Gates's alleged comment rings true for cops who've been on the receiving end of such tirades. And, since he's been "obsessed with race" since he was a 9-year-old, is that surprising?

Shouldn't Gates—and the Boss—have been happy that a concerned neighbor called 911 to report a burglary at the professor's house? According to the report, later in the incident, Gates mentions that his door had been damaged during a previous burglary attempt, which is why he had to break in.

In his report, Crowley writes that he initially believed Gates was the homeowner, so that was not the problem. Had the professor not allegedly continued to harangue the sergeant, this incident would have been over quickly. According to the police reports, Gates seemed intent on provoking the police officer—using race.

The next high-profile person to insert race was the Boss when he said, "Now, I don't know, having not been there, not seeing all the facts, what role race played in that. But I think it's fair to say, number one, any of us would be pretty angry. Number two, that the Cambridge Police acted stupidly in arresting somebody when there was already proof that they were in their own home."

The Cambridge Police acted stupidly.

Remember, Gates's reported anger came before the arrest. In fact, it appears his alleged anger caused his arrest. There was zero evidence race was a factor. However, the Boss said, "I don't know … what role race played in that." He assumes race had a role solely because the cop is white and the professor black. Isn't that assumption racist?

Critics, such as at the Associated Press (AP), as reported by Fox News, said a study concluded the incident was "avoidable,"[38] and the sergeant should have *de-escalated* (remember this word; it'll be repeated often). But, according to the police reports, the professor immediately began berating the sergeant when, allegedly, he immediately replied to him, "Why, because I'm a black man in America?" Remember, *obsessed since he was nine.*

In the report, Crowley writes that he asked Gates to speak outside. Gates replied, "Ya, I'll speak with your mama outside." Crowley also reported Gates spoke so incessantly and loudly that the sergeant needed to go outside so he could hear his police radio.

Now, let's step back from the racial politics inserted into the incident by Gates and later by the Boss and consider how Gates could have, and perhaps should have, viewed events. Gates had been out of town. His neighbor, Lucia Whelan, was apparently looking out for the professor's home when she saw two people with backpacks trying to break into Gates's house.

Also, the professor allegedly accused the sergeant of racism when what he was doing was investigating a possible burglary at Gates's home. Does Gates believe Crowley is psychic? Does he think the cop magically appeared at his house just so he could harass a black man? No; Whelan dialed 911, and the dispatcher notified officers of a burglary in progress. Sgt. Crowley, who was in the area, volunteered to take the call. No good deed goes … well, you know.

Gates's political leftist bona fides include serving as director[39] of the W.E.B. Du Bois Institute for African American Research at Harvard. Du

Bois was an admitted Communist[40] who lauded the Soviet Union, to which he traveled, and he applied for membership in the Communist Party USA[41] (CPUSA) in 1961.

This Cambridge incident revealed the Boss's apparent deep-seated enmity toward law enforcement. And, it appears, this hostility did not end with his presidency. It continues to this day through the Obama Foundation. But, rather than with words and policies as president, the Boss remains engaged in tearing down traditional policing in America by having returned to his roots as a community organizer.

During a speech given in early June 2020, only a few days after the George Floyd rioting had started, "Don" Obama addressed his "soldiers" personally. According[42] to NBC News, the Godfather "calls for police reforms, tells protesters [soldiers] to 'make people in power uncomfortable.'" He offered "advice to demonstrators [soldiers] during a virtual town hall … in his first on-camera remarks, as growing unrest against police brutality[43] continues across the country."

The Boss has assembled a powerful collective, has fabricated an effective media and public policy strategy, and is fully involved in continuing his plan to *fundamentally transform* (destroy) law enforcement in the United States of America.

Chapter 3

What's Wrong with the Police?
(They're in the Way)

W hat's wrong with the police? *Nothing.* At least, nothing that continually striving to improve, which law enforcement agencies already do, won't fix. There is no other occupation in this nation where more people not trained to do the job believe they know better than the trained professionals how to do it.

If a teacher is accused of fondling a child at one school, there are never calls that "teaching needs to be reformed" nationwide. No graffiti declaring "ATAB: All Teachers Are Bastards." No threats shouting, "What do we want? Dead teachers. When do we want it? Now!" And no calls to defund or abolish teaching.

One thing people must do when investigating individuals and organizations hostile to the police, such as the Obama Foundation, is to investigate the lies they tell about the police and why they're doing it.

For example, look at the accusations the critics make against police, and then dissect their assertions. Most of the time, the reason they don't like a police tactic or strategy is simply because *they don't like* a police tactic or strategy—period. Or they don't like any use of force by the police, no matter which technique or strategy a cop uses.

It's important to remember that it's not necessarily about people who are ignorant and believe stupid stuff but could eventually return to their senses. Now, these folks may also be ignorant and believe stupid stuff—in fact, they probably are and do. It's about people who must be treated like the radical true believers they are. Unfortunately, by either committing violence or condoning it, they have moved out of the realm of political opponents and into the realm of sociopolitical enemies.

If someone tells you they believe in socialism, in Marxism, in a revolution to collapse capitalism, believe them. Who cares that socialism has worked nowhere on earth? Who cares that Europe, contrary to leftist talking points, has no truly socialist[44] countries? Who cares that socialism is objectively, demonstrably, and historically not the answer to society's ills but often the cause of them?

Every generation of neo-lefties believes *they* will finally be the ones to implement socialism correctly—*this time—for sure—wait for it—you'll see.* When they tell you, or show you, that they are violent socialists/anarchists/Marxists who want to overthrow traditional America by any means necessary, believe them. Remember, they're assaulting, severely injuring, shooting, and even killing people in the streets, *right now*—including police officers.

During World War II, would it have been prudent for American soldiers to have treated German soldiers as if they were just misled or misinformed and would eventually reclaim their sanity? No. In fact, most German soldiers did eventually return to a normal, sane life. However, while they were pointing guns and shooting at American soldiers was not the time to try to understand them or their reasons for trying to kill Americans; it was the time to fight them.

Doesn't this describe the current situation in this struggle for traditional America? Traditional Americans are facing a sociopolitical, cultural enemy who knows what they want, and they will tear down American society to achieve their goals.

Just ask them.[45] As mentioned previously, a BLM and Antifa supporter allegedly shot and killed a member of the Trump-supporting Patriot

Prayer,[46] a conservative Christian group. Fox News reported[47] that a Marine Corps veteran said he heard gunshots from his Portland home and then heard the rioters "celebrating" the death of the Patriot Prayer member.

Miranda Devine of the *New York Post* wrote,[48] "It's spine-chilling to hear activists in Portland cheering about the cold-blooded murder of a Trump supporter[49] Saturday night." If there are still those who resist ascribing to BLM and Antifa the mantle of Nazi Brownshirts,[50] they have no arguments left. History informs that the similarities are unavoidable.

To illustrate the warped priorities of the cop-hating mayor of Portland, Ted Wheeler, he repeatedly refused federal assistance even with well over 100 straight days of rioting. He also blamed the federal government for "enflaming" the riots even though the federal officers were there only to protect federal property. In fact, it's a congressional mandate that the feds protect federal personnel and property.

However, after refusing and blaming the feds, Wheeler finally agreed to allow the U.S. Marshals Service to deputize Portland cops assigned to the riots. Why would he reverse himself so suddenly? This is pretty funny. Two reasons: one, he says he thought the federal deputization would only apply for the weekend. And two, because that weekend there was a planned Proud Boys counterdemonstration.[51] Ironically, the moronic mayor thought he could use the federal authority to charge and prosecute the Proud Boys. Good one, Mayor Wheeler.

So, let's get this right. Wheeler wanted no federal help to arrest left-wing rioters who caused mayhem daily for five months straight. But he wanted to use the same federal authorities to toss right-wing counterdemonstrators, who demonstrate infrequently and do not riot, into jail and then chuck the key into the Columbia River. A fascinating study in hypocrisy and stupidity.

Wheeler was openly disappointed that, unlike Antifa and BLM, the Proud Boys committed no violence. As written in an article at NPA, "after well over 100 days of straight far-left extremist rioting, local media delivered this hilarious opening comment: 'A national call for far-right extremists to descend on a Portland park Saturday did not result in the extreme

15

violence[52] with counter-protesters that state and city leaders feared.'" Since when did Gov. Kate Brown and Mayor Wheeler fear "extreme violence"? They allowed it to occur in Portland every day for nearly half a year.

Obamaland looks on leftist radical Marxists and anarcho-communists like BLM and Antifa as beloved cultural crusaders—supposedly idealistic youths building America by tearing it down. Simultaneously, they accuse right-wing, conservative organizations such as Patriot Prayer and Proud Boys of being "white supremacists." The groups insist they are not[53] racists, and they seem to have obvious proof.

Also from the NPA article above, "It appears city officials allowed the deputizing[54] because of an upcoming Proud Boys demonstration.[55] Now, that 'white supremacist' group, headed by a black Cuban man[56] and which has black female members, the district attorney would prosecute for spitting on the sidewalk."

Concerning police uses of force necessary to deal with this violent insurgency, unfortunately, civilian and police leaders don't do their officers any favors. They should know better than to issue knee-jerk responses to the media after any high-profile police use of force incident. What's wrong with saying something like, "Based on what I know now, I stand behind my officer and his actions"? Why is that so hard to do for so many chiefs?

You know why? Because it's so much easier, in the short run, to appease the radicals than it is to stand above the fray and maintain the dignity and integrity of your police department and its officers. That's how it is when it's about the chief's career and not the officers' well-being. Leaders should teach the public why the officer's action was right (if it was). Don't tell the public that what the officer did, which was how his agency trained him, is now somehow "wrong" but only *after the fact*. Chiefs and sheriffs who do this are emulating the Boss's "the Cambridge police acted stupidly" remarks.

Now, let's tick through a brief list of concerns and allegations police critics make that cause police work to be more difficult and more dangerous for cops.

Use of Force

One element that separates law enforcement officers from other public employees is the authority to initiate force when suspects refuse to comply with a cop's lawful orders. Officers' use of force is necessary in some circumstances. Some bad guys guarantee that. Sadly, organizations such as the Obama Foundation and the various associated groups have been working diligently to weaken a cop's ability to use force even when it's necessary. This puts law enforcement officers and the public at risk.

De-escalation

One tool cop-haters have intentionally misused is the term "de-escalation." Cops operated on a "de-escalate first" basis even before it was mandated in formal police training. That's because de-escalation, when it is possible, is common sense—something cops have in abundance.

So, it is insulting that anytime an officer has to use force, it is the cop who failed to "de-escalate" the situation. It doesn't matter what the suspect does. If the suspect fights, and as a result the officer has to fight back and injures the suspect, it's *always* the officer's fault. For example, the feckless capo Lt. Gov. Mandela Barnes of Wisconsin accused the officers involved in the Jacob Blake shooting on August 23, 2020, of failing to de-escalate[57] the situation before shooting Blake.

In fact, Barnes made this absurd comment: "The irony isn't lost on me that Jacob Blake was trying to de-escalate a situation in his community, but the responding officer didn't feel the need to do the same." What a horrendous comment. Lt. Gov. Barnes was referring to an erroneous report that Blake was attempting to resolve an argument between two women over car keys when, it appears, he was actually attempting to snatch the car keys from a woman to use the car himself—with kids in it. Some people call that kidnapping.[58] Lt. Gov. Barnes has not apologized to the officers for taking the alleged rapist's side.

Here is what was actually reported and gleaned from video: Before the shooting, officers knew Blake had an arrest warrant for an alleged sexual assault. Police also knew Blake was frequently armed. Blake had refused to obey lawful police orders, including punching a cop and then overcoming a taser application. The officer didn't shoot Blake until, while continuing to ignore police orders, Blake ducked into a car and allegedly tried to get something (as it turns out, a knife).

Maybe some people believe cops should bet their lives that the suspect isn't retrieving a weapon. But there are some people who don't want police officers to make that bet: cops' families come to mind.

It's convenient that Lt. Gov. Barnes, like the Boss, could package his limited information into a neat little false narrative with which to infect the public discourse involving de-escalation. But that's what these folks do, isn't it? Infect the public with myths and lies about police officers. More information continues to come out regarding Blake's criminal history. His criminal record reportedly[59] includes arrests or convictions for firearms, domestic violence, and rape. Yet people like Capo Barnes continue to paint Blake as a victim of police brutality. Democratic vice presidential candidate Kamala Harris even told Blake she was proud of the alleged rapist.[60]

Chapter 4

A New Coordinated Attack on Cops

Seeking donations from large corporations and philanthropic organizations is not enough for the anti-cop crowd. As written in an NPA article,[61] they not only want to raise money for their own organizations, but they also want to prevent the police organizations from raising funds for themselves. Many police agencies are also beneficiaries of police foundations. They provide support in areas where needs exceed budgets. For example, the Seattle Police Foundation[62] (SPF) has been active for many years, providing moral, material, and financial support to police officers. One example of many is supplying mountain bike squads with police bikes.

More recently, the SPF raised funds to provide protective eyewear[63] for officers dealing with the frequent riots. The glasses neutralize the effects of the industrial lasers with which BLM and Antifa radicals have been attempting to blind cops[64] (and sometimes succeeding). Just think about how barbaric that is. It's shameful that city leaders in Minneapolis, Seattle, and Portland didn't find that tactic against police officers sinister enough to immediately shut down the violence. But, since murder is not enough, blinding cops is obviously not either.

No, these groups, psychic vampires that they are, are not content with using racialist emotional extortion to raise money from some of America's largest and wealthiest corporations and individuals. Today, they are engaged in pressuring large corporate sponsors of police foundations to withdraw their support.

In an article[65] at Politico titled "New Racial Justice Target: Defund the Police Foundation," Zachary Warmbrodt explores this new front in the war on cops. BLM and Antifa want "dead cops," so, to reiterate what was mentioned above, it seems they're obviously okay with blinded, burned, beaten, or otherwise incapacitated cops too.

Politico reports that anti-cop activists have targeted major corporations and Wall Street banks. BLM and Antifa supporters are putting pressure on them "to cut ties with nonprofit police foundations, which racial justice activists say are increasingly funding law enforcement practices that fuel violence against black people." Again, a provable lie.

It's difficult for police foundations to fight against a radical viewpoint hawked as mainstream on social media, in the news media, and by some high-profile political leaders. Promotors of such viewpoints fabricate the definitions of issues, set strict parameters for compliance, and then attack people who don't subscribe to their definitions. For example, a recent news blurb referenced an article about "why police officers resist reform."

By misdefining *reform*, the writer ensures that anyone who disagrees with them is consequently resisting "reform." And to *resist* is to disagree with the fascists' position. Remember, free speech only applies to them. They view any disagreement as hate speech.

The Politico story returns us to those same insidious connections. This is also related to billionaire George Soros's Color of Change (COC), a civil right advocacy organization. COC's senior director of criminal justice campaigns, Scott Roberts, has a goal of ending private donations to police foundations. Scott Roberts's biography can be found[66] at the website of the American Civil Liberties Union (ACLU). One comment is all the introduction to Roberts we need: "fight the way our society criminalizes Black (sic) people." Before the COC, Roberts "worked ... on campaigns to advance criminal justice reform." Progressive t's crossed and i's dotted.

All police foundation donations must be approved by the law enforcement agency beneficiary. However, COC says these foundations "have become a resource for surveillance technology, SWAT team guns, armor, drones and K-9 dogs." In addition, Roberts said, "If the police foundations existed to raise money for the families of fallen police officers, we wouldn't say we need to abolish police foundations. It's the specific work that they're doing that we object to."

And that "specific work" is to equip cops properly to complete their public safety mission as safely as is practical. So, to understand COC's position: it's okay if police foundations support *dead* cops, but the COC is working to prevent police foundations from supplying officers with the equipment necessary to keep cops *alive*?

Who do they think they are, deciding for police agencies how their officers should protect themselves and do their jobs? They are whiny, childish socialist radicals who want their way, and if they don't get it, they'll stomp their feet—*on your head.*

Unfortunately, many CEOs are cowards and too easily yield to pressure. As Warmbrodt points out in the Politico article, some corporations are vacillating. "Wells Fargo says it has paused donations [to police foundations]." He also writes that Goldman Sachs has agreed to negotiate with domestic terrorists by meeting with radical anti-police factions. This is troubling especially when you consider how many bank robberies[67] police have investigated, bank robbers they've arrested, and robberies they've responded to in which some officers have been wounded or killed. When was the last time a leftist radical squared off with an armed bandit—and got shot—protecting Wells Fargo staff and property?

In Seattle, in June 2000, a Wells Fargo bank robbery[68] suspect shot a 45-year-old Seattle police officer—*three times.* The officer suffered wounds to his left shoulder and arm. He underwent surgery, survived his injuries, and continued his career. Wells Fargo, who appreciated the police officer's efforts on their behalf, gave him an award incorporating a model of the iconic Wells Fargo stagecoach to express their appreciation. Now, do they really want to join with cop-haters, not only to defund the cops but also to defund those who help the cops?

Roberts said COC intensified its efforts after the Atlanta Police Foundation disbursed $500 bonuses to the city's police officers to show its appreciation. The foundation did this in response to the officer-involved shooting death of Rayshard Brooks, discussed in chapter seven. The county prosecutor, Paul Howard, filed murder charges against the officer before any investigation concluded—even before it had barely started.

Roberts also attacked what he called the "more controversial aspects of policing." He includes surveillance, an important law enforcement tool; obtaining "militarized equipment"; and "increased presence in Black communities." But what if those are the communities whose residents are under attack by criminals? A recent Gallup Poll showed that 81 percent of black Americans[69] want the same number or more police officers in their neighborhoods.

COC asserts these police foundations act as an "unaccountable back channel" operating outside the "democratic process." Oh, step off the podium. They're charitable community organizations, just like yours are, right? (Except one is constructive and the other destructive.)

Some foundations are hedging in the face of this unreasonable pressure for corporations to "divest from supporting the police." Warmbrodt writes in Politico, "Some foundation leaders tried to distance themselves from groups that have helped arm police." What is wrong with arming police? Is it wrong just because COC says it is? Cops are armed because criminals are armed.

Responding to the assertion that foundations "helped arm police," the chair of the Salt Lake City Police Foundation reportedly said, "I don't know if our board members would be part of the foundation if that was the case." If what were the case? Arming the police? Whether people like it or not, arms play a significant role in keeping cops and communities safe. Fortunately, officers having to fire those arms is rare. Most officers never fire their weapons in the line of duty. Corporations must learn to shrug off the attempts to stigmatize the necessity of police officers carrying and sometimes having to fire their guns.

Chapter 5

Don Obama—The Boss

It would be understandable if the Boss and his supporters took offense at someone alluding to the former president as an organized crime boss. However, if he and his crew are honest, they must realize that, from a cop's perspective, Don Obama has been engaged in (with apologies to Heather MacDonald for nicking the title to her excellent book) a war on cops[70] (Encounter Books, September 2017). And cops view this war as an organized criminal enterprise perpetrating harm against civil society, public safety, equal justice, the rule of law, and the cops themselves. This loose comparison to the mob is one way to lighten what is a very serious situation—and, yes, to trigger the thin-skinned.

The anti-cop factions, including the mainstream media, wish to portray the defund/abolish movement as an organic, grassroots struggle of an oppressed segment of society. But that's not the case. Digging even a little shows deep and extensive connections among the anti–law enforcement forces. And just a glance at the terminology shared by the groups provides evidence of this conspiracy to crush policing as America has known it.

So, if the Boss is the boss of this anti-police crime family, then the leftist governors, mayors, and prosecutors are his captains (capos), and the "mostly peaceful" protesters, community activists, pro athletes, and street terrorists like the Marxist BLM and anarcho-communist Antifa comprise his cadre of soldiers. These acolytes revere our 44th president not because he was our first black president but because he was our most liberal, progressive, socialist-leaning, closeted Marxist, far-left president in history. They went all in to help him fundamentally transform the United States of America. And, like the Boss, they haven't stopped either. They've joined him in this continued assault on policing.

Lumping these folks into the category of "soldier" does not imply they are all violent or are committing crimes. They're not. You can be immoral and unethical without breaking the law. And, as in any other military or paramilitary organization, soldiers do all kinds of jobs. Yes, some engage in violence. But others are involved in logistics, acquiring and moving supplies, intelligence, propaganda, "legal observer," communications, and even first aid.

"Soldier" applies to people involved in all of these activities. When so engaged, they operate at the bottom rung of the organizational ladder even if they are at the top rungs of their own professions or organizations. For example, while LeBron James is at the pinnacle of his profession, he is still, essentially, a foot soldier promoting the Boss's anti-police messaging.

Many people, including conservatives, libertarians, Republicans, and independents who voted against the Boss, tried to look at the positive side when he became president. At least, many said, he will be great for race relations in America. Wow, they sure got that wrong! Race relations are worse now than when the Boss took office.

Black or white or half black and half white—like the Boss, most who opposed him for president didn't care about his racial composition. The Right would have voted for a black man or woman, if he or she were a conservative. Despite the caricature drawn by the opposition, most on the Right don't care about ethnicity, race, sexual orientation, religion, or gender. They care about liberty, freedom, limited government, and free markets—the things that have made America what President Ronald Reagan called "a shining city upon a hill."[71] It's something cops and their supporters believe is still true.

But the Boss has allied with a network of individuals and organizations who care nothing about all that America's founders sacrificed to secure liberty for their posterity—for *us*—and to suggest it to the world. In fact, while overseas in Spain, which never seems to stop him, in July 2020, the Boss defended BLM as riots in America worsened. The Boss said, "And that is sometimes messy and controversial but because of that ability to protest and engage in free speech, America over time has gotten better. We've all benefited from that." But does he believe that?

Americans will not allow Marxist revolutionaries to turn the United States into a tattered hint of what was once the greatest nation ever to have existed on the planet. The American dream will live on, and the nation's cops will continue to protect the people's pursuit of happiness. Even if it's against a former president and his comrades in the corporate boardrooms, ivy league halls, Hollywood hills, and the streets of America.

Chapter 6

Don Obama's 2020 Democratic National Convention Anti-Police Speech—Obama's Eulogy for Civil Rights Icon U.S. Rep. John Lewis

A s they say, that was then, and this is now. The Boss had an admittedly mixed record when enforcing federal law. While he made some efforts to keep criminals in prison and to deport illegal aliens, it also seems he worked as hard in the opposite direction. Examples are the "dreamers" (youth who qualify for the Development, Relief, and Education for Alien Minors Act), Obamacare for illegals, pardoning violent offenders, and granting clemency to nearly 2,000 people, including 330 on his last day in office. Aside from his federal anti-law and order efforts, what is clear is he's demonstrated he doesn't care for local law enforcement—at all. His anti-police comments and his administration's proliferation of DOJ consent decrees inflicted on local police agencies proves this.

Now that he's been out of office for nearly four years, his community organizer cap firmly on his head, he has his social justice laser beam focused intensely against America's cops. He is the only American president not to leave Washington, DC, after leaving the presidency. So, what's so important in Washington? Many people would love to know. He said he stayed in DC so his daughter could finish high school. Makes sense, but she graduated in 2019.

But now is the time to deal with what is known. Aside from his Obama Foundation actions, it is known that his 2020 speech to the Democratic National Convention (DNC)[72] and his funeral eulogy[73] for U.S. Rep. John Lewis, which will be covered below, betrayed the intensity of his hostility toward traditional America, and the police in particular.

The Boss began his DNC speech with laudatory pro-Constitution flourishes his political opponents truly wish he believed, but, based on his words and actions, throughout and after his presidency, they know he does not. For example, he began with, "I'm in Philadelphia, where our Constitution was drafted and signed. It wasn't a perfect document. It allowed for the inhumanity of slavery and failed to guarantee women—and even men who didn't own property—the right to participate in the political process. But embedded in this document was a North Star that would guide future generations; a system of representative government—a democracy—through which we could better realize our highest ideals."

The Boss nails it, regarding the magic of the U.S. Constitution. He looks past the "necessary" inherent, intentional flaws to the document's inevitable promise. Allowing temporary slavery made passage possible and the eventual abolishing of slavery inevitable. Frederick Douglass was a former slave, scholar, abolitionist, and friend of President Abraham Lincoln. He had a similar view but seems to have held it in his heart, rather than, as the Boss apparently had, as some kind of oratory bait and switch.

Constitutional scholar and historian David Barton wrote a book titled[74] *Setting the Record Straight: American History in Black & White*. He writes about Douglass's evolving view of the Constitution as a "pro-slavery" document to one that is a vehemently anti-slavery—one "through which we could better realize our highest ideals." At one time, Douglass believed the abolitionists' "pro-slavery" claims about the Constitution. "His early speeches and writings reflected that belief," according to Barton. However, his thinking changed as he read the Constitution and other writings by its authors.

Douglass explains, "I was, on the anti-slavery question ... fully committed to [the] doctrine touching the pro-slavery character of the Constitution.... I advocated it with pen and tongue, according to the best of my ability.... [U]pon a reconsideration of the whole subject, I became convinced ... that the Constitution of the United States not only contained no guarantees in favor of slavery but, on the contrary, it is in its letter and spirit an anti-slavery instrument, demanding the abolition of slavery as a condition of its own existence as the supreme law of the land." He also states, "I was conducted to the conclusion that the Constitution ... [was not] designed ... to maintain and perpetuate a system of ... slavery—especially as not one word can be found in the Constitution to authorize such a belief."

Barton adds Douglass's conclusion. "The Constitution is a glorious liberty document." He invites people to read the purpose of its preamble. He asks, "Is slavery among them [purposes]? Is it at the gateway? Or is it in the temple?" Further, Douglass writes, "If the Constitution were intended to be, by its framers and adopters, a slaveholding instrument, why neither slavery, slaveholding, nor slave can be found anywhere in it?"

The Boss is a constitutional scholar, but despite his words, he apparently has not reached the same conclusion Douglass had—or he has and rejected it. Infamously, the Boss referred to Douglass's "Glorious liberty document" as "a charter of negative liberties. It says what the states can't do to you. Says what the federal government can't do to you but doesn't say what the federal government or state government must do on your behalf."

Heather Higgins, writing for *U.S. News & World Report*, commented,[75] "He [Obama] believes—and he's right—that changing this [belief the Constitution means what it says] is the way to bring about 'redistributive change.'" Indeed, it is. And, along with his anti-police efforts, his desire to redistribute American wealth from the productive to the unproductive has not diminished. This is also being realized in the new "de-fund the police" movement, which redistributes funds from the police to leftist community organizations.

Another black scholar, classicist, and political philosopher, Harvard professor Danielle Allen, came to similar conclusions as Douglass when writing about the Declaration of Independence in her wonderful book[76] *Our Declaration: A Reading of the Declaration of Independence in Defense of Equality*. Prof. Allen begins her close reading of the Declaration with a prologue. She writes:

> The Declaration of Independence matters because it helps us see that we cannot have freedom without equality. It is out of an egalitarian commitment that a people grows—a people that is capable of protecting us all collectively, and each of us individually, from domination. If the Declaration can stake a claim to freedom, it is only because it is so clear-eyed about the fact that the people's strength resides in its equality.
>
> The Declaration also conveys another lesson of paramount importance. It is this: language is one of the most potent resources each of us has for achieving our own political empowerment. The men who wrote the Declaration of Independence grasped the power of words. This reveals itself in the laborious process by which they brought the Declaration and their revolution into being. It shows itself forcefully, of course, in the text's own eloquence.

The point of including scholarly writings about the Constitution and Declaration in this work is that they show there are very intelligent, thoughtful, critically thinking people whose work shines light on those, like the Boss, who are wont to indoctrinate people with a partisan ideology that smears our founding documents as "white supremacist."

Consider this point: When was the last time you heard someone on the Left tell people to do their own research, read original sources, and come to their own conclusions? Not anymore. The Left now ignores or distorts history and exclusively drives people to specific websites, books, and other publications that will corral them into ideological pens from which they may not stray. And those on the Left, those who do this, are mainstream progressives.

One prominent conservative example, and the antithesis to rigid leftist orthodoxy, is Glenn Beck. For years, back to his time at CNN and then at Fox News, Beck was famous for encouraging his audiences to "check my work," "not take my word for anything," and to "do your own research." He was emphasizing the importance of independent and critical thinking. Beck still does this on every TV and radio show he does.

The Boss's "preamble" at the DNC continues lauding the Constitution until, at least for his opponents, there is an almost audible "thud" on stage. It happens when he disparages President Trump and, poorly, attempts to convey confidence in his former vice president, Joe Biden—a man the Boss, until close to the 2020 DNC, refused to endorse for president. The Boss continued to speak projection gibberish about Trump. Honest critics can say a lot about President Trump, but "not putting in the work" isn't one of them. The president, objectively, is probably the hardest-working president America has ever had.

The Boss goes on to regale the audience with string after string of the supposed virtues of the Democratic presidential nominee. He does the same for VP nominee Sen. Kamala Harris, the first major Democratic candidate to drop out of contention due to a precipitous fall in polling from Democratic voters (whom she argued were racist[77]).

The Boss tells the DNC audience that he can understand the white factory worker dealing with declining income and jobs being shipped overseas (said with a straight face—who did that, Boss?) and "why a Black (sic) mother might feel like it [government] never looked out for her at all." But he was president for eight years. And, apparently, he was ignoring fifty years of President Lyndon Johnson's "Great Society," which ostensibly existed to help that mother.

Then the Boss makes this audacious statement about Biden and Harris, with which most everyone would agree, at least publicly. He says, "They believe that no one—including the president—is above the law, and that no public official—including the president—should use their office to enrich themselves or their supporters." Ah, sweet projection arises once again.

At any rate, the Boss and his obsequious capos, soldiers, and associates had better hope this is not true, or they may be in a truckload of trouble. Then again, this illustrates a long-held tenet, which former NYPD cop and U.S. Secret Service agent Dan Bongino[78] is fond of saying: "If you want to know what the Left is up to, just listen to what they are accusing the Right of doing." This is such a dependable formula. Consider the evidence put forth so far about Don Obama's alleged gangland-like efforts to interfere with a presidential campaign and then overturn a legitimate presidential election. This matters to cops because it points to a violation of the rule of law, ignoring equal justice, and because the effort is being done to return anti-police politicians to office.

The Boss wrapped up his DNC speech with this unusually honest statement:

> You [young people] can give our democracy a new meaning. You can take it to a better place. You're the missing ingredient—the ones who will decide whether or not America becomes a country that fully lives up to its creed. [Is he talking to the young people rioting in the streets?]

> That work will continue long after this election. But any chance of success depends entirely on the outcome of this election. This administration has shown it will tear our democracy down if that's what it takes to win [remember, "what they are accusing the Right of doing"]. So we have to get busy building it up—by pouring all our effort into these 76 days, and by voting like never before—for Joe and Kamala, and candidates up and down the ticket, so that we leave no doubt about what this country we love stands for—today and for all our days to come.

What exactly has President Trump actually done, specifically, to "tear our democracy down"? And, even worse, what did the Boss say about the police during his impious John Lewis eulogy?

Among other highly offensive comments the Boss has made in the past against law enforcement officers, his cop-hating during this eulogy may be the worst, especially considering it was such an inappropriate venue. The Boss said,

> Bull Connor may be gone, but today we witnessed with our own eyes police officers kneeling on the necks of black Americans. George Wallace may be gone, but we can witness our federal government sending agents to use tear gas and batons against peaceful demonstrators.

Think about a former U.S. president uttering such a vicious lie, a slander against police officers and federal agents. He pluralizes "police *officers* kneeling on the *necks* of black Americans," as if it is a common occurrence when he knows it's not. Even more vile, the president accused federal agents, people who used to work for him, of using "tear gas and batons against *peaceful* demonstrators" (emphasis mine). Law enforcement does not use force against peaceful protesters. *Period!* And the Boss knows it, and his comment is disgraceful.

A former president of the United States went in front of the American people and, using a funeral as his venue, lied to their faces about law enforcement. And he did this during a time of momentous civil turmoil in our nation. If he truly wants to put out the national inferno, jet fuel is not what he should have poured on the flames. Infernos are consuming his country and his fellow Americans. But putting out the fires is obviously not his goal; providing fuel for the fires is his obvious goal.

Even the media continue to refer to "mostly" peaceful protesters, even as flickering flames in the background eerily silhouette CNN[79] and MSNBC[80] "news" reporters. You can add "peaceful demonstrators" to the list of euphemisms used by the Don and his gang. They also use other inflammatory terms like "de-escalation," "police violence," and "demilitarization." And instead of "defunding" or "abolishing" the cops, they say "re-imagining," "re-envisioning," or "re-thinking" the police. Once again, for the record, local, county, state, and federal cops have not used and do not use force against *peaceful* demonstrators. To say they do this is a cold-hearted lie.

Chapter 7

The Obama Foundation—My Brother's Keeper Alliance Pledge

It's no secret that American law enforcement officers know the Boss was associated with a war on cops as president. It's no mystery because he didn't hide his animus toward law enforcement officers. While he was reportedly friendly and civil in person, his words and actions as president, and now as the Boss, tell the truth. He's not just associated with the war on cops; he's leading it.

The initial idea for this book about the Boss's continued efforts to upend the American criminal justice system came about by accident after NPA President Ed Hutchinson happened upon a Twitter post [81] from the Fraternal Order of Police Lodge 27 (FOP 27,)[82] in Delaware County, Pennsylvania. The @FOPLodge27 tweeted, "Less than 48 hours after this valuable, multi-purpose vehicle was utilized in rescues during the tropical storm flooding, the administration in Upper Darby felt it necessary to remove this asset by flatbed. It will never be used by UDPD again." Why take away an important asset that had just proved its value beyond its military/law enforcement applications? We'll get to that in a moment. But, first, is a community safer without what the Left calls the "militarization" of the police? It doesn't seem so.

The key here is that the armored vehicle is truly "multipurpose." It's hard to imagine, while sitting in the comfort of your own home, why any community would need an armored vehicle. But people may recall an incident in 1997 where two heavily armed men robbed a bank in North Hollywood. They had ballistic vests and automatic weapons, far outgunning the cops. Bet the cops would have appreciated a bit of "militarization," whether rifles, Kevlar helmets, or armored vehicles, that day. This incident is explored further in chapter twenty-nine.

Why should an armored vehicle intimidate any law-abiding person in a community? Are people who live next to military installations intimidated every time a Humvee or armored personnel carrier drives in or out of the base? An armored vehicle is just that. A vehicle with an armored shell that protects the people inside. Aside from its usefulness at incidents such as the Hollywood bank shootout, there are many other practical uses. Rescuing victims during riots, natural disasters, or a tropical storm are a few examples.

Law enforcement agencies in various communities will always have to assess their need for such military surplus equipment. Mayberry's Barney Fife[83] might not need an armored vehicle in a lifetime of copping. Or he might. And that's the purpose of such equipment. It's insurance for what cops call "just in case." It's smart to adhere to the adage "it's better to have it and not need it than need it and not have it"—within reason.

But that's not how people like the Boss, his subordinate disarm-the-police goombahs, and connected associates think. They truly believe in the socialist/Marxist fallacy that a government-created utopia is achievable. Each generation of this collective of comrades believes it will be the one, finally, to do socialism the *right way*.

Amity Shlaes sat for an interview with Peter Robinson of the *Hoover Digest*.[84] Answering a question about why socialism, despite its chronic failures, "is on the rise again," Shlaes answered, "It's idealism. It sounds better to ears that have not heard much history, and this is partly our fault, let's face it. We've failed to teach histories in our schools well enough."

Shlaes explains that young activists, the Boss's soldiers in the streets, don't know about the destruction wrought by socialism or communism during the twentieth century and continuing today in China, North Korea, Cuba, and Venezuela. She points out, "They don't really know what's happening in Venezuela right now in real time—the same tragedy being replayed. The old saying is that socialism is a process, so you can never condemn it because you've never seen the finished product."

That nails it precisely—it's a constantly rolling illusion of a political system with a beginning and middle that refuses to acknowledge that socialism's end is always collapse. The explanation is always that something external sabotaged the system's success. Therefore, once again, there is the "we will be the ones to do it right, this time—if America doesn't get in our way" illusion.

Lara Logan hosted a wonderful special on socialism[85] in America that appeared on Fox Nation. Logan used Venezuela as a recent example of socialist society's collapse. The nation went from the wealthiest and most prosperous in South America to one of the poorest countries on earth within a few years. And who do the Venezuelan (and American) socialists blame? Certainly not socialism. No, they blame the United States.

Back in Upper Darby, a little digging into why officials surrendered such a valuable asset as an armored vehicle links together the Boss and his gang and their destructive anti-cop "reform, defund, abolish, and de-police" agenda.

According to WHYY PBS/NPR,[86] "In June, [Upper Darby Mayor Barbarann] Keffer signed on to the MBKAP," the My Brother's Keeper Alliance Pledge. The specific MBK Alliance webpage for mayors,[87] so presumably endorsed by the Boss, declares:

> More than 1,000 people are killed by police every year in America, and Black people are three times more likely to be killed than White people. We can take steps and make reforms to combat police violence and systemic racism within law enforcement. Together, we can work to redefine public safety so that it recognizes the humanity and dignity of every person.

But this is inaccurate and misleading. This implies that the thousand people shot were innocent by associating them with "police violence and systemic racism within law enforcement." It's misleading because the same source that provides the total number shot, which the Boss uses—the Bureau of Justice Statistics (BJS)—details that the vast majority of those people were felons trying to kill the officers[88] who shot them.

This is also true of the black suspects killed. Even most of the suspects listed as "unarmed" (the *Washington Post*'s Fatal Force database seems to range between eight and fourteen unarmed black people shot by police) were trying to kill the cops who killed them. *Law Enforcement Today* (LET) cites fourteen and provides a solid analysis [89] of the data, so let's err with the larger number. Regardless, neither number represents a "slaughter" by definition and certainly not a "genocide" as Minnesota attorney general Keith Ellison suggests.

About black suspects being three times more likely to be shot, the "three times more likely" is not drawn from the black population at large. Since black males commit crime at a higher rate than other racial groups, it's only logical more black males would encounter police use of force. This is reflected in the statistical analysis.

As Benjamin Disraeli famously said,[90] "There are three types of lies—lies, damn lies, and statistics." True, but statistics result from how one crunches the raw data, such as the misleading percentages used on the Boss's MBKAP website. With raw data, however, the numbers can't lie. If police killed fourteen "unarmed" black people, and, as the *Washington Post* reported in 2019, nearly all of them, according to subsequent investigations, were trying to kill the officer who killed them, that is the raw data speaking the truth. Fourteen is fourteen. Or as sportscaster Vin Scully was said to have remarked, "Statistics are used much like a drunk uses a lamppost: for support, not illumination."

You'll notice something missing from the MBKAP "process for *police* reform." It doesn't include the police. The four steps are as follows: *review* how police use force; *engage* the community for police anecdotes; *report* back what was seen, heard, and said; and then *reform* how cops may use force. This is far from scientific or objective and does not include asking the police *why* they use the specific force and tactics they use.

Officer safety does not appear to be on their radar. They don't consult the very people who depend on reasonable use-of-force policies, tactics, and tools to go home to their families at the end of shift. Rather than what works, these "reformers" base their decisions on how *they feel* about what uses-of-force look like *to them* on TV.

WHYY reported, "Upper Darby's police superintendent, Timothy M. Bernhardt,[91] is fully cooperating with the effort." Sadly, we live at a time where many police chiefs, appointed by leftist mayors and city councils, serve as puppets for the regime, acting more as chiefs of mayor than chiefs of police.

The MBKAP "Commit to Action" information at Obama.org directs "community members" to the Leadership Conference Education Fund[92] (LCEF) at civilrights.org. The first thing that greets folks surfing over to the site is the image of a young man with his hands raised over his head. This gesture is intended to honor the "hands up, don't shoot"[93] myth. A myth constructed from a false police brutality incident in Ferguson, Missouri, in 2014. Police brutality never happened. Who says so?[94] Well, that brings us back to the Consigliere, former attorney general Eric Holder. Holder's DOJ investigated the Ferguson incident, and essentially found Michael Brown was not surrendering with his hands up when he was shot.

As Andy McCarthy alluded to in chapter one, speaking of having a thumb on the scale, the Consigliere just could not let the Ferguson Police Department (FPD) get away with having an officer cleared of wrongdoing. (To summarize, in August 2014 in Ferguson, Missouri, in an act of self-defense, police officer Darren Wilson fatally shot eighteen-year-old Michael Brown Jr.) Despite clearing the officer, the Consigliere's DOJ found the FDP guilty of a "pattern of intentional, egregious violations by members of the Ferguson police department [that] created a toxic, incendiary environment, perfect for the firestorm that followed Brown's death."

There is no way they weren't going to find something. Paraphrasing an old Soviet adage, "Show me the police department, and I'll show you the crime." As is happening now, in a broader manner, the Boss's DOJ provided rioters an excuse to commit mayhem. This laid a solid foundation for the urban violence we're seeing today.

After descending on Ferguson with an army of FBI agents and DOJ prosecutors, the Consigliere finally announced there was no evidence to bring charges against Ferguson police officer Wilson (whose career the Boss and Consigliere helped to destroy). Reportedly, during the investigation, several witnesses, most of them black, confirmed Officer Wilson's account: that Michael Brown, a robbery suspect, had attacked Officer Wilson and tried to take his gun when the officer shot him.

Another prosecutor recently conducted another investigation[95] of the Ferguson incident. He again found no evidence to show Officer Wilson did anything other than his job. Seems voters had elected a new prosecutor with the hope he'd conduct another investigation to see if they could get an indictment—*this time.* Anti-cop activists and groups hoped the result would be different since the new officeholder was black. Fortunately, they accidentally elected a prosecutor with integrity. Does anyone doubt that if Kim Foxx in Chicago, St. Louis's Kim Gardner, Boston DA Rachael Rollins,[96] Chesa Boudin in San Francisco, or Philadelphia's Larry Krasner had been the prosecutor, Officer Wilson would be wearing striped pajamas right now?

This pervasive anti-police faction has proliferated throughout the country and has proven that it will advance its ideological agenda to the point of sacrificing an innocent officer's career—or even life. In Atlanta, Georgia, Fulton County district attorney Paul Howard, who is being investigated for wrongdoing,[97] charged and indicted an Atlanta police officer for murder—for doing his job.

On June 12, 2020, Officer Garrett Rolfe shot and killed[98] Rayshard Brooks, who'd just assaulted him and another officer, stolen an officer's taser, and then shot the taser at Rolfe before the officer shot Brooks. In DA Howard's rush to prosecute, he announced charges even before the Georgia Bureau of Investigation (GBI) had completed its investigation.

But these prosecutors should beware. Americans are smarter than the Left thinks. The incumbent, Howard, who had served as DA[99] for over two decades, lost [100] big in his bid for another term when voters tossed him out of office during a special election. His opponent, Fani Willis, collected 73 percent of the vote. That is a loud and clear statement made by the county electorate on how they feel about his rush to judgment, overcharging, and apparently generally dishonest behavior.

Chapter 8

George Soros—The Underboss

Billionaire investor George Soros, with his omnipresent reach throughout the Leftistsphere's financial and political universe, seems rightfully placed as the Boss's de facto Underboss (although some may prefer *Bond Villain*—or, as Glenn Beck calls him, *Spooky Dude*). The Underboss works in support of the same anti–law and order ambitions as the Boss, which demonstrates the expediency of their relationship. How the Underboss assists the Boss with achieving his ultimate anti-police, anti-traditional American goals (and vice versa) is through a pragmatic and potent kinship.

The analogy of "Underboss" doesn't apply precisely to the socialist billionaire and interferist-in-chief. But, like a malignant Merlin, he provides the Boss—a Bizarro World "King Arthur"—a veritable mystical smokescreen covering the Boss's cop-hating enterprises. The Underboss does this by diverting funds to myriad leftist organizations and then further diluting the transactions through literally hundreds of other leftist organizations, thereby avoiding scrutiny.

Through the Underboss's Open Society[101] platform, funds are distributed to one organization, which are then distributed to another, and so on, before the cash lands in the desired pot for distribution to the chosen disrupters. However, when watchdogs attempt to follow the money, they find it difficult to trace it back to the Underboss or to its original source. This is critical to maintaining a lack of transparency.

The Underboss strives hard to cloak his activities to influence political outcomes and avoid responsibility, and he conceals his veiled activities for a reason. The Underboss, in conjunction or concurrently with the Boss, is engaging in a major campaign against America's justice system.

The Underboss has not only allegedly funded illegal immigration[102] into the United States as well as domestic terrorist organizations, but, as previously mentioned, he is also contributing to the campaigns of anti-cop candidates for prosecutors' offices, such as district attorneys, county prosecutors, circuit attorneys, and so on, across the United States. His malicious handiwork is already coming to fruition and is providing him, the Obama Foundation, and the radical Left with plenty of anti-police dividends.

Often these "dividends" don't work out well for cops. Two examples are Philadelphia municipal government district attorney Larry Krasner (Underboss-funded) and Mayor Jim Kenney. Krasner infamously released a known violent criminal who then killed a cop.[103] On October 26, 2020, Philadelphia cops fatally shot a man named Walter Wallace Jr. who refused to drop a knife. Without any investigation, Kenny, in a statement,[104] said, "My prayers are with the family and friends of Walter Wallace. I look forward to a speedy and transparent resolution for the sake of Mr. Wallace, his family, the officers, and for Philadelphia." What about prayers for the officers who will now have to live with having to shoot another human being? What about the officers who may now be prosecuted, perhaps for doing their jobs, by an Underboss-funded radical DA? What about them, Mr. Mayor?

In response to this incident, of course, the mob hit the streets, and one of the mob drove his truck into a line of police officers, seriously injuring one of them. This was without any investigation as to what happened, which in the vast majority of cases shows the police behaved properly. Then again, why should the violent mob wait for an investigation before "taking sides" when the mayor doesn't?

Just look at what St. Louis circuit attorney Kimberly Gardner, an Underboss acolyte, beneficiary, and Don Obama capo, is doing to[105] Mark and Patricia McCloskey. A violent BLM mob had destroyed a historic, locked iron gate, gained entry into private property, and then allegedly shouted threats to commit arson, rape, and murder. The McCloskeys prudently armed themselves, Mark with an AR-15 and Patricia with a semiautomatic pistol, as protection against a violent mob—a mob they'd witnessed every night on TV news, wreaking mayhem, destroying property, and assaulting people across the nation. However, the activist prosecutor, rather than charging the violent mob, charged the couple.[106] For what?

And not only did Gardner apparently make up a crime out of self-defense, it appears she hedged her bet when she allegedly also tampered with evidence.[107] She asserted Mrs. McCloskey's gun was functioning properly although the McCloskeys, both attorneys, said they'd previously rendered Mrs. McCloskey's pistol inoperative so it could be used as a prop in court. However, in a recent indictment,[108] Gardner added the charge of "tampering with evidence" against the McCloskeys.

Since Gardner was originally accused of tampering with evidence, she seems to be turning things around and is countering that the McCloskeys had disabled the pistol to "avoid prosecution" instead of to use it as a prop in court. If that's Gardner's intention, it would make no sense. Why wouldn't the McCloskeys have disabled both weapons in that case, if they were doing it to avoid prosecution, as Gardner seems to be implying with this new charge? But no one can think anything is beyond one of America's emerging neo-(non)prosecutors.

However, Gardner didn't prosecute any members of the mob (some of whom were reportedly armed) for any of their many alleged crimes. She also hasn't charged most of the rioters who destroyed the city she's supposed to protect from criminals. No, instead, she only charged the McCloskeys, who video evidence clearly shows were victims.

Yes, the Underboss can claim responsibility, along with gullible voters, for such an embarrassment like Kim Gardner becoming the top prosecutor for a major American city. It's been widely reported that the Underboss funded Ms. Gardner's campaign.[109] And she has performed as he expected her to—tearing at the fabric of America's criminal justice system. It's not about equal justice anymore; it's about social justice, now. It's about demolishing the American criminal justice system. Just think about how backward it is for a prosecutor to charge the victims of a crime rather than the criminals who perpetrated it. Kim Gardner did that.

Think about the devastation caused to the American criminal justice system when Underboss-funded prosecutors refuse to prosecute hundreds of rioters who are committing millions of dollars in theft and property damage—not to mention assaults and murders. But these prosecutors now defame cops and fabricate crimes to indict law-abiding people[110] attempting to defend themselves with firearms, as is their God-given constitutional right.

Gardner's flip-flop of jurisprudence is also an assault on the Second Amendment, which includes the people's inherent right to self-defense. The Boss and his gang's hostility toward the people's right to keep and bear arms becomes clearer, now. For years the radicals have told people, "You don't need guns; you have the police." Now that their gun-grabbing efforts are combined with their "defund or abolish the police" movements, the pretense is over. They don't want you protected either by yourselves or by the police. People who dissent from this new orthodoxy are too hard to control if they have police protection or are armed. This is insidious.

President Trump's personal attorney, Rudy Giuliani, is a tenacious critic of the Underboss. During an interview with Martha MacCallum on Fox News, as reported[111] by the *Jewish Journal*, former New York City mayor Giuliani fired barbs at the Underboss. "The president [Trump] should declare them [BLM] a domestic terror organization and then maybe we can stop Soros from giving them $150 million. Soros is intent on destroying our government for some sick reason of his that goes back to his sick background."

Over the decades, the Hungarian-born nonagenarian has diddled his finger in many nations' domestic pies. After he finished his political

and financial mischief in Europe, he turned his sights on America[112]—
he even became an American citizen. At Change.org there is an effort to
"Revoke the U.S. Citizenship of George Soros and Cancel His Passport."
The Underboss reportedly became a naturalized U.S. citizen in 1961.

In 2018, the *Economics Review* at New York University published
a story about "How Soros Broke the British Pound." Devansh Lathia
reported:[113]

> On September 16th, 1992, George Soros made one of
> the most audacious trades in recent times when he bet
> an enormous sum of money against the British ster-
> ling. He pocketed over a billion dollars and brought
> the Bank of England to its knees. Making a billion
> dollars is by all means no small feat, but to destroy the
> monetary system of Great Britain in one single day is
> something else altogether.

These proceeds are a part of the multibillions of dollars he's using to
destroy the traditional American way of life.

His birth country, Hungary, passed a law[114] specifically aimed at
thwarting the Underboss's efforts to fund illegal immigration into that
country. Vanessa Romo at NPR wrote:

> The suite of bills, called "Stop Soros," allow the govern-
> ment to imprison individuals and nongovernmental
> organizations for up to a year if they're deemed to be
> facilitating what it says is illegal immigration by peo-
> ple not entitled to protections, the BBC reported. A
> separate amendment to the constitution declared that
> an "alien population" cannot be settled in Hungary.

But the primary benefit for the Left is the ability for cash flow to
be shrouded within the Underboss's socialist agenda–supporting miasma
resulting from his political and financial alchemy. Directly and indi-
rectly, the Underboss funds over 200 leftist community organizations.[115]
Reportedly, Open Society donates funds to one organization that will in
turn donate to other organizations and so on. This creates an illusion of

support coming from other than the Underboss or whoever else originally donated the funds.

While reprinting such a long list in its entirety may seem cumbersome, the information contained within, and the effect of the sheer number of organizations, impresses upon the reader a visceral sense of how people like the Boss and his Underboss obscure their political financial operations.

In 2018, according to writer Jim Hoft, "Tom Fitton and Judicial Watch announced[116] … the Obama State Department was working hand in glove with George Soros operatives." Hoft added that according to Fitton, "the US State Department spent $9 million in taxpayer dollars to fund Soros operations in Albania." What "operations" seems a good first question. And, "Fitton also reminded his audience that the Soros operatives were harassing and stalking US Senators[117] … on Capitol Hill." This was in 2018—during the Trump administration. But there's no "deep state" still assisting the Boss, right?

Adding to the evidence of the relationship between the Boss and his Underboss, Susan Price, a Gold Star mother and analyst, wrote a piece in America Out Loud titled "Soros, Obama and Hillary Clinton Are the Shadow Party." [118] Price wrote:

> Americans are witnessing the unfolding of the most egregious crimes committed against "We The People" breaches of national security in the name of treason and sedition by the former President of the United States Barack Obama and his "deep state" henchmen.

> It is beyond human comprehension, the level of heinous crimes these people at the highest levels of government have committed against us behind our backs, and now this information is becoming known through Patriots and Pro American organizations, Americans are demanding Justice and Accountability against the Traitors who manipulated the masses and the laws to complete their global take over.

This may smack of conspiracy theory and hyperbole, but, as credible evidence emerges, it's only prudent to consider that sometimes there is a conspiracy. This seems to be one of them. It's worth considering because the anti-Trump conspiracy sits atop the Boss's anti-police agenda partly because President Trump is so pro-police. Another pro-police supporter and author, Kevin Jackson at the Black Sphere, provides a valuable "time-line[119] of Obama's Treasonous Attempt to Get Trump."

And Jackson's not alone. Back in 2017, no less than Rush Limbaugh, according[120] to the Daily Wire, asserted that the Boss's "Deep State" is his "Shadow Government." The radio talk show legend recently reiterated when he told his audience he thought the Boss would run the "resistance" more overtly. Limbaugh explained he was surprised that the Boss has continued attempting to take Trump down but from behind the scenes.

Below is a partial list, as mentioned above, of the Underboss-funded organizations, as of January 2020, published at the *Will County News*, as sourced from the website Discover the Networks via Dr. Eowyn. (Discover the Networks[121] is a project of the David Horowitz Freedom Center). It would be cumbersome to include the entire list of links along with their summaries. So, what follows is an abbreviated list of just twelve of the most well-known of the organizations funded by the Underboss with their summaries.

Regardless, people are encouraged to go to the links provided and scroll down the entire list to absorb the impact of what a mélange of organizations this is and of the far-left issues they encompass. Included in this list is the organization's number as shown on the original list. It should be noted that all of these links have been disabled in this venue since they were originally included in this book. Efforts have been made to provide the reader alternative links.

> 11. American Civil Liberties Union: This group opposes virtually all post-9/11 national security measures enacted by the U.S. government. It supports open borders, has rushed to the defense of suspected terrorists and their abettors, and appointed former New Left terrorist Bernardine Dohrn to its Advisory Board.

14. American Federation of Teachers: After longtime AFT President Albert Shanker died in 1997, he was succeeded by Sandra Feldman, who slowly "re-branded" the union, allying it with some of the most powerful left-wing elements of the New Labor Movement. When Feldman died in 2004, Edward McElroy took her place, followed by Randi Weingarten in 2008. All of them kept the union on the leftward course it had adopted in its post-Shanker period.

22. Amnesty International: This organization directs a grossly disproportionate share of its criticism for human rights violations at the United States and Israel.

42. Center for American Progress: This leftist think tank is headed by former Clinton chief of staff John Podesta, works closely with Hillary Clinton, and employs numerous former Clinton administration staffers. It is committed to "developing a long-term vision of a progressive America" and "providing a forum to generate new progressive ideas and policy proposals."

63. Democratic Party: The Soros funding activities are devoted largely to helping the Democratic Party solidify its power base. In a November 2003 interview, Soros stated that defeating President Bush in 2004 "is the central focus of my life" … "a matter of life and death." He pledged to raise $75 million to defeat Bush, and personally donated nearly a third of that amount to anti-Bush organizations. "America under Bush," he said, "is a danger to the world, and I'm willing to put my money where my mouth is."

121. Media Matters for America: This organization is a "web-based, not-for-profit … progressive research and information center" seeking to "systematically

monitor a cross-section of print, broadcast, cable, radio, and internet media outlets for conservative misinformation." The group works closely with the Soros-backed Center for American Progress, and is heavily funded by Democracy Alliance, of which Soros is a major financier.

129. MoveOn.org: This Web-based organization supports Democratic political candidates through fundraising, advertising, and get-out-the-vote drives.

132. NAACP Legal Defense and Education Fund: The NAACP supports racial preferences in employment and education, as well as the racial gerrymandering of voting districts. Underpinning its support for race preferences is the fervent belief that white racism in the United States remains an intractable, largely undiminished, phenomenon.

145. National Organization for Women: This group advocates the unfettered right to taxpayer-funded abortion-on-demand; seeks to "eradicate racism, sexism and homophobia" from American society; attacks Christianity and traditional religious values; and supports gender-based preferences for women.

148. National Public Radio: Founded in 1970 with 90 public radio stations as charter members, NPR is today a loose network of more than 750 U.S. radio stations across the country, many of which are based on college and university campuses.

149. Planned Parenthood: This group is the largest abortion provider in the United States and advocates taxpayer-funded abortion-on-demand.

184 Southern Poverty Law Center: This organization monitors the activities of what it calls "hate groups" in the United States. It exaggerates the prevalence of white racism.

There are also seven additional organizations listed that don't receive direct Soros funding but are funded by other organizations that do.

Though ostensibly still supporting each other through having similar objectives, Fox News reported[122] that the Underboss has expressed disappointment that the Boss didn't take more financial and economic advice directly from him during his administration. The Underboss said the Boss "was known to take his supporters for granted and to woo his opponents" (apparently meaning Democrat opponents).

The Underboss, who financially supported Hillary Clinton to the tune of millions of dollars in her bid for the presidency, said some two years after she lost the election, "I don't particularly want to be a Democrat." Neither does the Democratic Party, which now identifies as socialist, even Marxist, so why should one of its chief benefactors?

It's stunning to watch the media contorting themselves to help the Underboss obscure his mischief. In September 2020, Fox News anchor Harris Faulkner admonished[123] Newt Gingrich for mentioning George Soros in his comments during a segment. Tucker Carlson, also of Fox News, has had show content[124] referencing Soros censored after posting it on Twitter. And Robby Starbuck at the *Federalist* asks,[125] "Why aren't we allowed to talk about George Soros's plan to remake America?" He continued, "Since 2015, George Soros has pumped tens of millions of dollars into local races in Texas, Colorado, California, Oregon, Washington, and New York, as well as swing states."

After mentioning the Underboss having spent a staggering $1,700,000 to get Philadelphia's non-prosecuting, cop-killer-releasing DA Larry Krasner elected, Starbuck provides this list of Underboss-funded prosecutors who won election, with the following comments:

Although his efforts haven't been universally successful, the vast majority of Soros-backed candidates have won with Soros donations pushing them across the finish line. Here are just a few examples [officials covered in more detail in **bold**]:

- $2,000,000 to fund **Kim Foxx** in her Cook County (Chicago, Ill.) re-election bid.

- $1,400,000 to fund Aramis Ayala's campaign to become state's attorney of Orlando, Fla.

- $1,150,000 to fund Jake Lilly's run to become DA of Jefferson and Gilpin County (Denver) in Colorado.

- $958,000 to fund Joe Gonzales's run to become DA of Bexar County (San Antonio, Texas).

- $650,000 to fund Jose Garza in his Travis County (Austin, Texas) re-election bid.

- $750,000 to fund Joe Kimok in his Broward County, Fla. state's attorney race.

- $583,000 to fund Kim Ogg's run to become Harris County (Houston, Texas) DA.

- $583,000 to fund Parisa Dehghani-Tafti in her race to be Arlington County (Va.) commonwealth's attorney.

- $500,000 to fund Jody Owen's run to become Hinds County, Miss. (Jackson) DA.

- $406,000 to fund James E. Stewart's run to become Caddo Parish, La. (Shreveport) DA.

- $392,000 to fund Steve T. Descano's bid to become Fairfax County (Va.) commonwealth's attorney.

- $275,000 to fund **Diana Becton**'s bid to remain as Contra Costa County, Calif. DA.

- $147,000 to fund Darius Pattillo in his run to become Harris County, Ga. DA.

- $116,000 to fund **Kim Gardner**'s re-election bid as St. Louis circuit attorney.

- $107,000 to fund Raul Torrez bid to become Benalillo County (Albuquerque, N.M.) DA.

- $89,000 to fund Scott Colom's bid to become DA of Lowndes County, Miss.

> That's just a partial list, but it surely corroborates Gingrich's point that Soros "paid for" the outcomes of those elections, notwithstanding [Marie] Harf's unsubstantiated denial [said "Soros doesn't need to be a part of this conversation." Then she denied that "Soros is buying these races...."] In 2018 the *Los Angeles Times* reported that Soros spent $2,700,000 on California DA races alone, and another $16 million on 17 DA races in other states.

Like never before, people are learning how important it is to pay attention to local political races. Whether it's for mayor, prosecutor, or city council, voters must not only take time to learn about where the candidates stand on issues but also to find out who is funding them. People can't rely on biased campaign ads. With people like the Underboss funding candidates in even relatively small local races, his candidates can have great influence if people are not paying attention.

Chapter 9

Governors—Capos

B efore the Boss left the presidency, he began in earnest to initiate Democratic governors into the gang—in essence, to have them "made." In 2012, as Alex Newman wrote in the headline to his article at the New American,[126] "Obama Urged Governors to Celebrate UN Day." In fact, Obama issued a "presidential proclamation" naming October 24th as UN Day in the United States. Newman also reported, "Obama, an unabashed fan of the planetary body that critics refer to as the 'dictators club,' praised the UN and the 'ideals' it purportedly represents."

In 2014, NPR published a recording and transcript[127] of a panel conversation at a fundraising dinner featuring the Boss. David Greene hosted, and Mara Liasson, among others, attended. NPR summarized the premise of the Boss's remarks as accusing the opposition of doing what his gang is doing. Liasson wrote, "Obama told Democratic governors that their Republican counterparts are making it harder for people to get health insurance or exercise their right to vote." The Boss's critics strongly argue both contentions, accusing the Boss of projection, as there was abundant evidence the situation was the reverse.[128] The Heritage Foundation published a detailed study[129] on the issue.

And the claim of Republicans committing voter interference from Obamaland is perennial, with no evidence to back it up. The perennial complaint about voter ID falls flat for so many reasons. To name just a few,

ID is needed for the most basic functions in life: cashing a check, renting a car, and entering the Democratic National Convention. Also, it is the height of condescension to assume black people have a harder time getting an ID than people of other races.

For example, while the Georgia Governor-in-exile, Capo Stacey Abrams, continues to argue voter suppression, statistics showed the election she ran in had one of the highest participation rates in Georgia's history. According to a piece[130] at Politifact, "Abrams lost by almost 55,000 votes in a race with record turnout for a midterm race, said University of Georgia political scientist Charles S. Bullock. Black turnout in 2018 actually slightly exceeded that in 2016, he said." Yet, the claim persists because fellow capos like Sen. Cory Booker (D-NJ) and Sen. Amy Klobuchar (D-MN), as well as friendly media outlets, continue to perpetuate this myth.

In 2019, Julian Zelizer, of CNN, wrote,[131] "Sen. Cory Booker's announcement Friday that he will run for president is not only another sign of the historic diversity of the Democratic Party as it heads into the 2020 presidential primaries. It is a demonstration of the power of former President Barack Obama's legacy in American politics." With the benefit of hindsight, perhaps Zelizer's comments were a tad overstated, but the sentiment was clear—a sycophantic fawning over the Boss.

As for Sen. Klobuchar, her press secretary reported she did not have any "conversations with Obama" about endorsing his vice president. But, on March 2, 2020, NBC News was[132] "looking for Obama's hidden hand in candidates coalescing around Biden." Coincidentally, on March 2, 2020, Capo Amy Klobuchar ended her bid for the Democrat presidential nomination and endorsed VP Joe Biden.[133] The Boss's "hidden hand," indeed.

In reality, Americans saw for themselves on their TV screens the voter intimidation of Republicans at a Philadelphia polling location when members of the New Black Panther Party showed up in black uniforms, holding clubs, allegedly to intimidate voters. It was the Boss's DOJ that dropped a case[134] that had been prepared under the Bush administration and was ready to prosecute.

Liasson noted that at the previous year's event, the Boss pressed for bipartisanship. He said, "And one thing that I know unites all of us and all of you, Democrats and Republicans, and that is, the last thing you want to see is Washington get in the way of progress." If only he truly believed that. Well, that all changed the next year when, as Liasson reported, "White House Deputy Press Secretary Josh Earnest explained the president's message will be [understatement alert] a little more partisan."

Despite the words, based on increasing evidence regarding the Boss's administration's apparent use of federal law enforcement and intel agencies to interfere with President Trump's candidacy and presidency, the Boss was one of the most partisan presidents (and ex-presidents) in American history. The following governors have supported him serving as virtual capos.

Gretchen Whitmer, Michigan

It's difficult to say who deserves the Draconian Award for "lockdown" governors, but Gretchen Whitmer of Michigan and California's Gavin Newsom come to mind. Oregon's Kate Brown, Washington's Jay Inslee, and Andrew Cuomo of New York are also in contention. These governors are 100 percent Trump-haters. Well, maybe not 100 percent, as—credit where credit is due—Gov. Whitmer did send a statement of support[135] to President and Melania Trump when they contracted the CCP virus [136] (Chinese Communist Party virus, otherwise known as Covid-19).

However, she has endorsed VP Joe Biden for president, of course, and, by locking down the state, she is operating in the Boss's anti–rule of law mode. In early October, the FBI announced they'd thwarted a kidnapping plot against the governor.[137] Congratulations to the FBI on their good work, and everyone should be relieved the governor wasn't harmed and is safe. Now she can continue her tyranny, in which she expects the state's cops to assist her. Good luck with that.

Jay Inslee, Washington

More than in what he does, Inlsee's hostility toward law enforcement officers is also with what he doesn't do. Responding to a press question about the debacle that was becoming Seattle Mayor Jenny Durkan's Capitol

Hill Organized Protest/Capitol Hill Autonomous Zone (CHOP/CHAZ), Inslee, looking like he'd just smelled a fart, claimed he wasn't aware of it.[138]

He's the governor of the state, and rioters take over a part of his state's largest city, and he wants people to believe he doesn't know about it? Remarkably, once he did know about it, he continued to allow Seattle police officers to suffer at the hands of poor city leadership. Like too many other politically minded leaders, he refused federal assistance to quell riots that have continued unabated.

Rioters were injuring Seattle's cops in large numbers, yet the governor did nothing. He could have sent Washington State Patrol troopers to assist. He didn't. He could have deployed the National Guard. He didn't. He just continued to stand by and watch the lawlessness and chaos occur in what was once the queen city of the Great Pacific Northwest.

While Inslee was locking down innocent, law-abiding people in the state, he allowed lawless rioters to gather in huge groups in downtown Seattle and in CHOP/CHAZ. The result: assaults, burglaries, robberies, arsons, rapes, and murders, all ignored by Gov. Inslee.

Inslee has also presided over the passage of an anti-cop law that makes it easier to prosecute officers.[139] Washington's "most prominent Democrats," Sen. Patty Murray, Rep. Adam Smith, and Pramila Jayapal, dutifully supported the measure.

Inslee has been a long-time supporter of the Boss. In fact, the Obama-supported Human Rights Campaign (HRC) endorsed Inslee[140] for his reelection. This is the same HRC the Boss addressed at its banquet in 2010. The HRC, which supports Inslee, opposed[141] the confirmation of the overwhelmingly qualified Amy Coney Barrett for Supreme Court justice. Justice Barrett was sworn into office by Justice Clarence Thomas on October 26, 2020.

Incidentally, Judge Barrett has two black children, and some on the Left condemn Barrett for adopting black children from Haiti. They refer to her as a "colonialist" acquiring "props." Disgusting. Meanwhile, Inslee, slinging the same racist excrement, continues to refer to our police-supporting

President Trump, who nominated the mother of two black children, as a "white nationalist[142] ... in the White House."

Gavin Newsom, California

Not much has to be said to validate Gov. Newsom's radical qualifications. Aside from his rigid anti-police stances, he apparently also has a totalitarian nature. After inflicting on Californians one of the most draconian CCP virus lockdowns in the United States, Newsom has found a way to push even that envelope. Though he *grants* restaurants the *privilege* of opening at 25 percent capacity, he is now mandating that customers pull down face masks to take a bite of food and then replace the mask while chewing. That's nuts! If a governor can make people do that, what can't he make them do?

Now, is the governor getting together with his buds, maskless, drinking beers, rolling on the floor laughing at people stupid enough to obey his edict? Or is it time for Californians to introduce a ballot initiative to invoke California's equivalent of the 25th Amendment, so they can boot the nut from office? Whichever it is, it doesn't look like the governor's crazy edicts are about to stop anytime soon. Remember who is supposed to enforce his stupid, unpopular, unlegislated rules: the cops.

In 2019, Newsom, after 150 years, became the governor who struck down the California Posse Comitatus Act of 1872. The act required able-bodied adults [143] to assist officers with arrests or with enforcing other criminal offenses when requested. Essentially, Newsom decided it should not be a crime to refuse to help a police officer in trouble. This is not about the value of such an act, which might be arguable; this is to say, Newsom's action sure wasn't pro-police.

Why Newsom felt that after a century and a half, with all of the state's myriad problems, he had to tackle this nonissue now is up for conjecture. Just one more kick from the governor to the state's cops who are already down.

Kate Brown, Oregon

Oregon's Gov. Kate Brown has proven herself one of the most anti-police political officials in America. After embarrassing herself and her state by refusing federal assistance to suppress the relentless riots in the state's largest city, Portland, she tried to blame President Trump for the violence. If this weren't so unconscionable, people could be forgiven for laughing hysterically. After BLM and Antifa had rioted in Portland for some ninety days, the feds deployed extra personnel to protect federal facilities. After an agreement with the governor, the feds left, and the riots continued. Yet, Gov. Brown again blamed the president for the violence. How is that President Trump's fault? It's not; Brown is just locked into one of her party's talking points.

J.B. Pritzker, Illinois

Gov. Pritzker is one of those governors whose motto is: do as I say, not as I do. This was on display after he locked down the state due to the CCP virus, restricted travel, but allowed his wife to travel[144] to another home they own in Florida. When asked about it, he refused to answer, except to say it was a private matter. How convenient. As for his anti-cop bona fides, upset that people didn't want to follow his edicts and cops refused to enforce them, he resorted to threats.

Rick Moran of PJ Media wrote,[145]

> In recent weeks, enforcement departments in rural areas of the state [Illinois] have indicated in no uncertain terms that they were through enforcing Pritzker's iron will. That brought a blast from Pritzker's office designed to put those [police/sheriff] departments in their place.

Pritzker's new edict[146] threatened to withhold federal funds from law enforcement agencies that refused to enforce his executive orders. Law enforcement leaders from across the state, including the state police and local departments, refused to penalize or arrest violators under Pritzker's rules. Aside from other considerations, Pritzker's "law" held that a business owner could serve up to a year in prison for a violation of Pritzker's CCP virus diktats.

Tim Walz, Minnesota

Gov. Walz is on the anti-police bandwagon with other governors in signing legislation that will castrate law enforcement. Exhibiting his ignorance, the legislation includes banning "warrior-style" training, which is an essential part of an officer's survival tools. Mohamed Ibrahim, for the Globe and Mail,[147] wrote that the new law also "imposes a duty to intercede on officers who see a colleague using excessive force and changes rules on the use of force to stress the sanctity of life." Okay, but sanctity of whose life? Walz doesn't seem to be interested in the sanctity of an officer's life.

So, how does this work on the streets? People should realize the confusion this will cause. Can anyone imagine new officers coming out of the police academy, having been indoctrinated with a social justice–neutered curriculum? What are they going to do when they observe a veteran officer using sound use-of-force techniques, but the rookies decide, based on their social justice indoctrination (and inexperience), that the veteran is using "excessive force"?

Is that new officer supposed to stop assisting the veteran officer, start helping the suspect, alert the media, or just take the veteran officer into custody and let the bad guy go? Remember, the new law calls not for the officer to report what they believe was excessive force (after the fact) but to "intercede." Do these political leaders ever think about how things like this will work in real life?

Tony Evers, Wisconsin

In yet another knee-jerk response from a politician, after hearing about the Jacob Blake shooting in Kenosha, Gov. Evers issued one of the most anti-police statements of them all. In fact, the governor's words[148] can speak for him:

> Tonight, Jacob Blake was shot in the back multiple times, in broad daylight, in Kenosha, Wisconsin. Kathy and I join his family, friends, and neighbors in

hoping earnestly that he will not succumb to his injuries. While we do not have all of the details yet, what we know for certain is that he is not the first Black man or person to have been shot or injured or mercilessly killed at the hands of individuals in law enforcement in our state or our country.

This is an incredibly ignorant and dangerous statement for a governor to make, especially while the nation is on fire. Still, when he found out he was saying this about an alleged rapist, perhaps he reconsidered his statement. Not so much. In fact, his (and his lieutenant governor's) comments were so egregiously anti–law enforcement that Wisconsin's top police chiefs and sheriffs issued a statement of their own.[149]

According to TMJ4 News, the top cops warned Evers and Barnes "to stop making statements regarding the police shooting of Jacob Blake 'until the facts of the investigation are known.'" Doesn't seem like so many adults should need to be corrected with advice every good parent gives their children.

Nicole Galloway, Missouri (Democratic candidate for governor)

Missouri State auditor Nicole Galloway was recently "made" by the Boss. The *Springfield News-Leader* reported[150] that the Boss had endorsed Galloway's "bid for governor Friday as part of his 'second wave'[151] of elections recommendations this year." Second wave? The Boss has been busy cultivating his captains. His first wave[152] of election recommendations came in early August 2020. Including Galloway, the Boss is, as CNBC says, "putting his considerable political weight behind 118 candidates … in 17 states." Galloway lost the election.

Chapter 10

Mayors—Capos

So, how does this semi-open conspiracy (so-called open society) work? Under the Boss, it starts with a list of those who could be considered among the Boss's "capos." These captains are the country's governors, mayors, and prosecutors. They are the people who influence, coerce, and order their subordinates (soldiers), either implicitly or explicitly, to commit direct actions. And while there are only twenty-four Democratic governors, they have many more mayors and prosecutors. This caporegime has proliferated for years in some of America's largest jurisdictions, but this is changing. Today, they're seeping even into rural areas, such as the cultural and political destruction happening in Virginia.[153]

Each of the following mayors has signed onto the Obama Foundation's My Brother's Keeper Alliance Pledge (MBKAP) and are using their offices to push through their extreme partisan agenda. It's the mechanism by which the foundation infects American society with the socialist and Marxist political disease. Many Leftist mayors eagerly serve as puppets for their, as Rush Limbaugh has referred to the Boss, "immaculated" leader.

Mayor Keisha Lance Bottoms, Atlanta, GA

An eager signer of the MBKAP and a big believer in "police reform," Mayor Keisha Lance Bottoms, tweeted, "Atlanta accepts the challenge @ BarackObama. I will issue an Executive Order establishing a Commission of stakeholders and organizers to examine our use of force policies and call upon them to make recommendations accordingly. Thanks for your leadership. @MBK_Alliance" (June 3, 2020).

Mayor Bottoms, who can come across as inoffensive and reasonable, and who wisely called up the National Guard during some of the 2020 rioting, still has a slithery quality. She deflects interview[154] questions about "defunding the police" and instead refers to it as a "reallocation of resources into community development and alternatives to just criminalizing responses to behavior." What the heck is she babbling about? *Criminalizing responses to behavior?* Isn't that what she's doing to her cops? Criminalizing *police* responses to *bad* behavior.

But this shouldn't surprise us. Mayor Bottoms also touted "how the city has gut its corrections budget by 60 percent and is allocating funding to convert the Atlanta Detention Center into a health and wellness center." Well, if you have no jails, you have no prisoners. If you have no prisoners, you have no ex-cons. If you have no ex-cons, you have only law-abiding citizens—and on it goes. Problem solved.

During the George Floyd riots, Atlanta Mayor Bottoms was right there with the mayors of Baltimore, Minneapolis, Portland, Chicago, Los Angeles, New York, and Seattle. They allowed rioters, to quote former Baltimore mayor Stephanie Rollins-Blake, "space to destroy."[155] Americans watched on TV, along with Mayor Bottoms, as militants did their best impression of Union General William Tecumseh Sherman during the Civil War when Union troops tore into the city and set Atlanta ablaze.[156] Today, the city's own citizens are setting Atlanta ablaze.

Mayor Bottoms admits what many people already suspected. As president, the Boss was in the forefront of transferring wealth from the productive to the unproductive. Now, he and his gang can combine their disdain for the police with their penchant for wealth transference. During a city council conference call,[157] Bottoms said, "The intent of this movement [defund police], as best as I can assess, really is about reallocating funds for social services and support and community enhancement initiatives." In other words, transferring wealth from the police and public safety to social justice initiatives and by enhancing or creating new social programs.

Mayor Hillary Schieve, Reno, NV

After signing the MBKAP, Mayor Hillary Schieve tweeted, "We can and will be better to effect change President @BarackObama. Thank you for always inspiring @usmayors. Signed challenge and committed on police use of force policy change @CityofReno. Ask your mayor or council to join us. Obama.org #8cantwait."

The link to "#8cantwait" returns people to a page which exclaims, "campaign to bring immediate change to police departments." And the change always involves weakening the police, doesn't it? Councils, committees, commissions, and other civilians, rather than the cops, decide on the use of force officers rely on to keep themselves and innocent people alive.

Remember, it is this concept of destroying the police that Mayor Shieve and so many other officials have agreed to by signing the pledge—an organized effort to dismantle and restructure a city's public safety apparatus, according to a socialist utopian dream.

Kim Driscoll, Salem, Mass

Mayor Kim Driscoll is just one of the many small-city U.S. mayor virtue signalers who've signed on to the Obama Foundation's MBKAP. Her leftist philosophy mirrors other Democratic mayors in the Boss's pocket.

Mayor Driscall tweeted, "Yes! I pledge to:

1. REVIEW police use of force policies in my city

2. ENGAGE my city by including a diverse range of input, experiences+stories in review

3. REPORT findings of review+seek feedback w/in 90 days

4. REFORM my city's police use of force policies based on findings (June 3, 2020).

This was brought to the fore when an unknown employee used the police department's Twitter account to post a tweet[158] about the CCP virus that included, "So, you [Mayor Driscoll] issued a permit for 10 of thousands of people to protest but I can't go to a restaurant? You are ridiculous." The police department removed the tweet. Still, the sentiment reflects what many people find frustrating about leaders who severely restrict the law-abiding people's liberty but exempt from the edict protesters, and even rioters, who serve their political agenda.

Andy Berke, Chattanooga, TN

Though he came right out against the George Floyd in-custody death, radicals, ostensibly from his side, accused Mayor Andy Berke of hypocrisy, asserting the Chattanooga PD has its "own cases of alleged police brutality." As we cover in more detail below, many of these mayors cling to an illusion that they can allow the mayhem and then also somehow eventually control it. Some have compared it to trying to ride a tiger. Ask Portland's Mayor Ted Wheeler about making conciliatory overtures to the mob. The mob Wheeler had been protecting for over one hundred days of rioting forced him to move out of his condo. However, the mob did sing "Happy Tear Gas to You[159]" on Wheeler's fifty-eighth birthday—the ninety-fifth day of rioting. No candles on a cake, but they attempted to set the building on fire.

In response to what happened to George Floyd, like so many of his comrades, Mayor Berke signed the MBKAP.[160] During the riots, in June, the *Chattanooga Times Free Press* published an article[161] titled "Chattanooga Mayor Signs Obama's Commitment-to-Action, Pledges to Review Police Policies." Of course he does. "Mayor Andy Berke also defends protesters rights to have their voices heard." Again, of course, he does. Aren't these statements a prerequisite whenever leftist politicians mention "mostly peaceful" protesters?

People like Mayor Berke continue to defend the "mostly peaceful" protesters, even though they remain in the crowd after people become violent. The *Free Press* wrote this curious paraphrase attributed to Mayor Berke. "Berke said that interactions between protesters and police this week—which have largely been peaceful, even when Hamilton County Sheriff's deputies deployed tear gas on a crowd of hundreds of protesters

Sunday[162]—demonstrate the culture that he and Roddy are trying to establish in the city's police department."

"Largely … peaceful … even when … sheriff's deputies deployed tear gas on … protesters…." This makes no sense and is another attempt at gaslighting. Don't trust your lying eyes. This cannot be emphasized often enough: *Cops do not use force on "protesters."* Police use force on rioters. And once a protest becomes violent or police declare it an unlawful assembly, if a person remains, the person is no longer a protester; that person has become a rioter.

Which brings the reason for "riot" statutes. They make it possible for police to use necessary force when a demonstration turns into a riot. It is impossible for the police to differentiate the violent from the nonviolent during such mayhem. In fact, the radical insurrectionists themselves state that they depend on "peaceful" protesters to provide them cover for their violence.

Eric Johnson, Dallas, TX

A signatory to the MBKAP, like others in the Boss's extended anti-cop gang, Mayor Eric Johnson is taking an oblique approach in nodding affirmatively at the anti-police mob. When proposing salary cuts for city employees, he wrote in an email,[163] "If Dallas City Hall is going to truly reflect its 'service first' mantra amid the pandemic, your city councilmembers must be willing to look at defunding the bureaucracy"—and note his "twist," as *Dallas Observer* writer Jacob Vaughn called it, "to widespread calls to 'defund the police.'"

In Mayor Johnson's case, he retains the word "defunding" but rather than the "police" specifically, he uses "the bureaucracy." Either way, the result will be the same: a disabled police department incapable of fulfilling its public safety mission.

Steve Benjamin, Columbia, SC

Mayor Stephen Benjamin wants to make the Boss happy. About the MBKAP he tweeted, "Valuable discussions on #8cantwait tonight, thanks to @MBK_Alliance, President @BarackObama & @MsPackyetti it's important to note that @CityofColumbia & @ColumbiaPDSC have already implemented ALL of these policies." Mayor Benjamin illustrates how to micromanage the police with flare. Everyone knows the "knee on the neck" uproar that has now confused a carotid artery (sleeper) hold with a choke-hold. Now, Mayor Benjamin became concerned that, during an arrest, an officer had a knee not on a suspect's neck, but on the back of his lower legs.

This is a common technique for controlling violent or resistive behavior. Does it hurt? It can, depending on the amount of pressure applied, which depends on the amount of resistance offered. That's why it works. What could the suspect do to stop the pain? Stop resisting. It is not, as they say, rocket surgery. When an arrest involves multiple officers, defensive tactics instructors teach officers to control various areas of the suspect's body proximate the officer's location.

London Breed, San Francisco, CA

Emphasizing the alliance between the Obama Foundation, politicians, and media, San Francisco Mayor London Breed sat for an interview[164] with *Vogue*. Here's how André-Naquian Wheeler begins his supposedly objective interview. "Since becoming mayor of San Francisco in 2018, London Breed has simultaneously strived to protect and represent her city's endangered Black community." The only black community members who are "endangered" are criminals who refuse to obey lawful police orders. Nevertheless, the mythology must proliferate.

But Mayor Breed is definitely on board with the Boss' anti-cop agenda. About MBKAP, she tweeted, "San Francisco has enacted eight of the #8cantwait policies, but we know there's still more work to be done. That's why I've signed on with the first group of mayors to @BarackObama's commitment to action on police use of force. Obama.org/mayor-pledge/.

Mayor Breed, who is apparently also psychic, like other Obama-devoted mayors, said in June 2020[165] that "police will no longer respond to non-criminal calls as part of a major reform of the department," according to Fox News. Mayor Breed is apparently basing this on the flawed premise that a dispatcher or officer can know ahead of time that a 911 call will not need an armed response. The calls she's talking about aren't complaints of children refusing to go to bed, do the dishes, or go to visit grandma (yes, cops get these calls, too). The mayor includes in these "non-police" responses neighbor disputes, reports of homeless people, and school discipline issues.

Every cop reading this envisions the irresponsibility of sending unarmed "police alternatives"—what one Minneapolis city council member calls "violence interrupters"—to such calls. Neighbor disputes often become violent, as do calls involving the homeless, including addicts and the mentally ill, which also often involve criminal activity. And, if school authorities (who are half social worker already) who work with kids all day, every day can't handle student discipline in-house, why would social workers do any better?

Mayor Breed apparently resorts to what's become an old standard for anti-cop politicians: if a situation becomes violent, it's *always* the officer's fault. The cop failed to de-escalate. Fox News reported, in a news release, that Breed said, "Police would be replaced by trained, unarmed professionals to limit unnecessary confrontation between the police department and the community." And the insults and disrespect continue unabated. How can normal people think that way? Wait—the answer is in the question, isn't it?

Muriel Bowser, Washington, DC

Mayor Muriel Bowser also tweeted her support, but she is an interesting case. She tweeted, "I am committing to the @BarackObama Mayor Pledge. And while she grabbed headlines early in the riots for her open support of BLM and defiance of President Trump, things seemed to have changed more recently. During the initial skirmishes between rioters and police, Bowser said about President Trump, "He sent tear gas into the air and federal helicopters, too. I knew if he did this to D.C., he would do it to your city or your town." Media showed images of a church burning while still declaring that President Trump ordered officers to use tear gas to disperse "peaceful protesters."

Mayor Bowser authorized activists to paint a massive Black Lives Matter mural on the recently renamed Black Lives Matter Plaza. But she ordered removed a "Defund the Police"[166] mural that activists had added to the original BLM mural. Some BLM activists saw hypocrisy (rather than sanity) in the Mayor's action to remove the mural. They also didn't like what she had to say at the Democratic National Convention (DNC). WTOP News wrote this headline:[167] "Black Lives Matter DC Criticizes Mayor Bowser's DNC Remarks."

After criticizing what she views as the mayor's support for police (which is not actual support but is not as harsh as the radicals want), April Goggans, a BLM DC organizer, said,

> The fact that Mayor Bowser is introducing George Floyd's family is disgusting. And that's where we should be talking. And she did it on purpose, overlooking Black Lives Matter Plaza. All of these things are made to actually distract, make other people who don't earn the right of talking about Black Lives Matter look like they're leading it.

As written in an article[168] at the Mises Institute:

> Revolutions eat their children. This observation, by a journalist during the French Revolution, was only partly true. In reality, revolutions eat their parents. In particular, history's left-wing revolutions eat the left-wing intellectuals who made them happen. By "left wing" here I mean revolutions that explicitly aim to use government power to reshuffle society. To remake society so it matches whatever version of "justice" strikes its promoters as attractive.

Regardless of whether it's the parents or the children who are eaten, history has shown repeatedly that a leftist revolution will eventually turn on itself. In Mayor Bowser's case, the "children" turned on a "parent" quickly. Now that the parents (Democratic Party) have nurtured their spoiled, selfish children, the children are out of control, and the parents don't know what to do. So, as in Portland, Seattle, San Francisco, Chicago, New York, and elsewhere, the parents do nothing as their children try, literally, to destroy American culture. You know—because *this time* they'll get social-ism right.

Sam Liccardo, San Jose, CA

Mayor Sam Liccardo came into office already a sycophant to the Boss who is hostile to the police. According to the San Jose Spotlight,[169] "Mayor Sam Liccardo presented a nine-point proposal for reforming the San Jose Police Department ... , striving to initiate tangible changes to how the city's more than a million residents are policed in the wake of George Floyd's death in Minneapolis."

Think about that. After signing the Obama Foundation MBKAP, this mayor has mounted a full-on "reforming" of the SJPD over a contro-versial death in police custody two thousand miles away. Only because of the exploitation of a crisis by the Boss, his Underboss-funded allies, and BLM and Antifa soldiers is any of this destruction of traditional polic-ing happening.

Mayor Liccardo's tweet of support is positively saccharine. "I've signed on to former President @BarackObama's Mayoral pledge & commit to review, engage, report, & reform common-sense limits on police use-of-force. #notonemore." The obligatory hash tag was a nice touch.

Aside from banning crowd-control tools necessary for the police to conduct their public safety mission safely, Mayor Liccardo wants to "shift more power to the mayor to hire, fire and direct" the police chief. He believes he should be able to "act without a City Council vote." Whenever anyone tells you the goal of leftists is power, believe them.

Michael Venezia, Bloomfield, NJ

Mayor Michael Venezia signed the pledge and tweeted, "I signed the mayor's pledge, and I'll work with the community to review and reform our policies. Commit to action: Addressing police use of force policies. Together, we can work to redefine public safety...." Again, a euphemism for reforming, defunding, or abolishing the police. Don't be fooled. "Redefined" may sound like a tame phrase, but it betrays yet another mayor who has bowed down to the altar of the Boss, his guys, and the war against law and order.

Bill Peduto, Pittsburgh, PA

Mayor Bill Peduto is not as well-known as his far-left colleagues Ted Wheeler, Jacob Frey, and Lori Lightfoot, but he is every bit the anti-cop radical they are. In mid-August 2020, as riots continued to rage in many American cities, Mayor Peduto could not care less about the affront to the law-abiding people of his city or about the crimes committed by militants. No, Mayor Peduto got upset with—who else?—the cops.

According to a report[170] on MSN.com by CBS Pittsburgh, Mayor Peduto commented on what he called a "disturbing arrest." Peduto tweeted,[171] "It is hard to find the words for how livid I was after seeing the online videos of the disturbing arrest at Saturday's protest. I have taken the time to review all the video and information that has been made available to me." He's "livid" at the officers but not "livid" at the rioters wrecking his city.

Reportedly Hizzoner didn't like plainclothes cops driving unmarked cars and arresting violent rioters. After the massive destruction caused by these vicious mobs, this Boss's MBKAP disciple is worried[172] about cops doing their jobs—the way *he* thinks they should do them. Hey, Mr. Mayor. Believe it or not, it's hard to sneak up on criminals while in uniform and driving a marked patrol car. No, really; it's true. Some criminals are actually able to figure out that those guys wearing police uniforms and driving marked police cars with light bars on the roofs are cops. Clever, eh?

CBS reported, "The mayor said he won't tolerate this tactic in the future." But, apparently, he will tolerate the violent left's tactics of destroying his constituents' property, including by arson, and also injuring police officers. He also tweeted, "As Mayor, I will never tolerate these tactics being used at peaceful protests again." There they go again with the "peaceful" protests. If they were peaceful, the cops wouldn't be using "these tactics."

Why do they never show video of cops using force against actual "peaceful" protesters? Because it so rarely happens.

This is irresponsible and unconscionable. What he calls "these tactics," in the real world, is called good police work. The problem is, these Obama mayors must have assigned a new definition to the word "peaceful." Rioters can hurt cops, hurt bystanders, and steal, burn, and destroy property, and magically, according to America's leftist mayors, the destructive criminals still merit the label "peaceful."

But at least Capo Peduto has a sharply produced webpage[173] dedicated to the Boss's MBKAP. In fact, in Pittsburgh, the mayor has created a My Brother's Keeper Coordinator position to "evolve and elevate this work." Sounds impressive.

The website exclaims,

> The City of Pittsburgh and Allegheny County embraced [the Boss's] call to action for My Brother's Keeper. In 2015, Mayor Bill Peduto, County Executive Rich Fitzgerald, and community leadership created a cross-sector alliance and made a firm commitment to join the national effort by creating a more equitable and inclusive Pittsburgh.

They've hit all the woke words they need to. They are *such good people*, so much better than we are. If you're interested in learning more, you can become a good person, too, by going to the MBK Pittsburgh–Allegheny County website.[174] Even when conservatives read the plan, they will find some items they can agree with. In fact, much of it. For example, they call for children to read at grade level by the third grade. That's great! But those efforts also work to obfuscate the more radical elements of the organization's agenda.

Jenny Durkan, Seattle, WA

Mayor Durkan is connected to the Boss in more ways than the MBKAP. Her radical values align with his almost perfectly. In fact, before running for Seattle mayor, Durkan served under the Boss as the DOJ's U.S.

Attorney for the District of Washington (State). During that time, she was one of the officials responsible for inflicting a controversial (bogus[175]) federal consent decree on the Seattle Police Department.

Mayor Durkan also made possible and then presided over the infernal CHOP/CHAZ debacle that she predicted could be a "summer of love[176]" 2020. What actually occurred was a summer of assaults, arsons, commercial burglaries, rapes, and the murder of two teens.[177] Durkan also rewarded the short-lived, unsuccessful CHOP/CHAZ "peacemaker," political activist, and self-admitted former pimp Andre Taylor.

As reported at NPA,[178] Durkan appointed Taylor to the position of "Street Czar," where he is to pursue ideas regarding police de-escalation techniques and alternatives to policing. The contract will pay him $150,000 for his efforts.

Taylor brings unique qualifications to the job. As mentioned, he's a former pimp, including using allegedly underaged girls (reportedly, one of whom he got pregnant), for wealthy men in Las Vegas. He also spent time in prison for rape, robbery, and assault. In addition, Taylor has said about police, "Officers are trained to shoot to kill, especially if it's a black man. They have no regard for life."

When asked about the title Street Czar, Taylor said he came up with it himself. He said he was inspired by the Boss who liked to give people the title of "czar" for many office appointments, such as the "Green Jobs Czar." It's staggering the number of things that circle back to the Boss.

A story by the *World Tribune*, published[179] on June 21, 2020, making a Boss connection to Seattle, is too weird not to mention. The headline: "Reports: 'Baby Barack' Lived in Chaz/Chop." The article describes the research some writers were doing to finish the "vetting" that never occurred by the mainstream media before and during the Boss's presidency.

Whether all the claims listed in the article, ostensibly discovered while people sought information about the former president's childhood, are true or not, the claim that the Boss and his mother lived in Seattle appears to be true. Confirmed reports show "Barry" lived with his mother,

Stanley Ann Dunham, and later with his grandmother, Madelyn Lee Payne Dunham, in and near Seattle before moving back to Hawaii.

Erin Sirianni at the website My Mercer Island reports[180] that Obama's mother lived in Mercer Island, a short bridge ride across from Seattle, in south Lake Washington, and graduated from Mercer Island High School. The *World Tribune* journalist Michael Patrick Leahy makes some assertions in his book[181] *What Does Barack Obama Believe?* According to Leahy, rather than Obama's father leaving his mother, she may have "left Barack Obama Sr. in Honolulu and moved to her own apartment in Seattle, Washington" when the Boss was a baby. Leahy reportedly corroborated his claims by obtaining University of Washington records and Dunham's apartment rental records.

The records put Obama and his mother living at an apartment at 516 Thirteenth Avenue East, which is only a few blocks north of CHOP/CHAZ. Either way, the claims that our nation's 44th president once lived in what became known as the CHOP/CHAZ seem to be true. Or, to be accurate, Barack Obama lived somewhat CHOP/CHAZ-adjacent. Still, the Chopistanis' or Chazanians' caustic views about the police and law and order were not far from the future president's sentiments.

These anti-police politicians have earned traditional Americans' disgust. And so have those on this additional list, which still doesn't list all the mayors (and city council members) who've signed the Boss's Foundation's anti-police pledge.

Lindsey P. Horvath, West Hollywood, CA, Mayor

Darrell Steinberg, Sacramento, CA, Mayor

John Cooper, Nashville, TN, Mayor

Tom Barrett, Milwaukee, WI, Mayor (endorsed by the Boss)

Jonathan Busch, Metuchen, NJ, Mayor

Luke Bronin, Hartford, CT, Mayor

Van R. Johnson II, Savannah, GA, Mayor

Joseph A. Curatone, Somerville, MA, Mayor (wrote in support of the Boss's wife)

Michael C. Taylor, Sterling Heights, MI, Mayor (Republican who endorsed Biden)

Marty Walsh, Boston, MA, Mayor

Kim Norton, Rochester, NY, Mayor

Tim Keller, Albuquerque, NM, Mayor

Sam Weaver, Boulder, CO, Mayor

Jon Mitchell, New Bedford, MA, Mayor

Libby Schaff, Oakland, CA, Mayor

Indya Kincannon, Knoxville, TN, Mayor

Anan Abu-Taleb, Oak Park, IL, Mayor

Tom Schwedhelm, Santa Rosa, CA, Mayor

Chapter 11

City Councils—Capos

I n the political crime family hierarchy, city councils are unique because they can act both as soldiers and capos depending on the individuals' political natures. For example, the wacko, socialist Seattle City Council member Kshama Sawant is a good soldier for the Left, pushing for a socialist change. However, she is also a capo who leads her lunatic soldiers in the streets. She led a throng of two hundred radicals to the city hall where she used her key to allow them entry into the building. She also led a mob of protesters to Mayor Jenny Durkan's home. This places her as one radical politician in at least two categories: capo and soldier.

City councils enjoy an advantage over their governor, mayor, and prosecutor colleagues who work solo. Council members can obscure themselves within a collective. But a city council can still do as much damage as a governor, mayor, or district attorney—and some of them, like Sawant, are doing just that.

City councils in Seattle, Portland, San Francisco, and Minneapolis come to mind when considering those cities' headlines about defunding or abolishing the police. These city councils are actively working to the detriment of the public safety they are responsible for ensuring. Despite city charters that mandate they provide sufficient public safety, including police and fire/EMT/medic departments, many have been working feverishly to reimagine, re-envision, defund, and even abolish the police.

Whether or not an individual city council member has signed the Obama Foundation pledge, many implicitly carry out the Boss's anti-cop mission. The Seattle City Council,[182] which wants to defund the police,[183] has an acerbic member mentioned above. Kshama Sawant is a shrill, unreasonable, defiant socialist[184] who literally shrieks for a revolution[185] to achieve a "socialist world." When first elected, she talked about the workers taking over Boeing[186] so instead of airplanes they could build buses and trains.

She has never hidden her animosity toward the city's police officers. She has publicly called two officers "murderers"[187] for the self-defense shooting of a woman who attempted to stab them with scissors. The officers sued Sawant for slander and libel, but Judge Marsha J. Pechman, a Clinton appointee, threw out the case.[188] This is no surprise. The Obama Gang also includes activist judges as a part of its overall plan to remake the criminal justice system.

However, regarding defunding/abolishing the police, specifically, the Minneapolis City Council has led the way. These wankers, to dart into British English for a moment, voted[189] unanimously to abolish their police department. The *New York Post* reported, "The proposal gained popularity among city council members amid widespread protests and riots in the city following the killing of George Floyd by a city police officer last month."

Not surprisingly, a controversy arose when some Minneapolis City Council[190] members—Andrea Jenkins, Phillipe Cunningham, and Alondra Cano—displaying a case of "good for me but not for thee," hired private security for themselves—at taxpayer expense. According to the *Washington Times*, Ian Miles Cheong, managing editor of *Human Events*, tweeted,[191] "The same clowns that voted to disband the Minneapolis police force have hired private security companies to look after them. They can afford to. You can't." Yeah, *they* can afford to because they're using *your* money.

But, in September came a bit of not unexpected schadenfreude out of Minneapolis for conservatives. According to[192] MPR News, members of the Minneapolis City Council (yes, the people who voted to abolish the police), including Council President Lisa Bender, began asking "Where are the police?" in light of increasing crime. There is not a cop in America who did not predict this.

MPR News reported a story about a scheduled city council meeting on "police reform," i.e., "abolishing the police." MPR News begins,

> For much of the two-hour meeting, council members told police Chief Medaria Arradondo that their constituents are seeing and hearing street racing which sometimes results in crashes, brazen daylight carjackings, robberies, assaults and shootings. And they asked Arradondo what the department is doing about it.

Law-abiding taxpayers are correctly asking, "Where are our cops?" What they should ask, though, is why did we elect such idiots to the city council? Ward 6 council member Jamal Osman complained that he was receiving a ton of constituent complaints that the Minneapolis Police Department (MPD) "are nowhere to be seen." That's not surprising, since Arradondo says the department has recently seen one hundred officers walk out the door. The chief says that's double the normal amount by this time in the year.

Osman also alluded to the abolition vote, saying, "That [MPD] is the only public safety option they have at the moment." Isn't this conveying to residents that the MPD is simply a necessary evil until they can install the magical, socialist utopian "violence interrupters?"

Bender enters the realm of the surreal when she further comments on her supposed surprise at the alleged actions of police officers she holds in such contempt. MPR News writes, "Bender, who was among those leading the call to overhaul [yet another euphemism] the department, suggested officers were being defiant. Her constituents say officers on the street have admitted they're purposely not arresting people who are committing crimes." And they asked Arradondo "what the department is doing about it."

For police officers today, it's not about *choosing* not to enforce the law; it's about not *being able* to enforce the law. City council members are now criticizing officers for not enforcing the law, even as they celebrate rioters and looters as "peaceful protesters," and they also support not prosecuting these violent criminals. Do these political leaders have any self-awareness at all?

When faced with a decision to enforce or not enforce a law, officers first have to consider what happens if even a minor incident becomes violent. They'll be told that they failed to de-escalate, accused of using excessive force, and accused of racism. Police oversight, maybe even the DOJ, may investigate them for civil rights violations. And cop-hating prosecutors, of which there are so many, thanks to the Underboss's shenanigans, might even criminally charge and prosecute officers. Where is the upside for a cop to enforce the law?

The Chief of Police (or *Chief of Mayor: chiefs who act in best interest of the mayor rather than the cops*) Arradondo had the nerve to bring up the officers' oath. When was the last time city politicians adhered to their oaths to protect and defend the Constitution, both state and federal? Defending bad behavior by pointing to other bad behavior? Perhaps. Still, a police officer's oath is not unconditional. It is essentially a contract between him or her and the community. The contract implies cops will take on exceptional risks, including their lives, to protect and serve the people. Commensurately, the community takes on a responsibility to support its police officers.

One way to support the cops is to elect officials who will support police officers. It seems cop critics haul out the "oath argument" when talking about police officers' responsibilities to them. But they toss out their oaths to uphold the law when it comes to their responsibility to police officers. Cops are expected to accept all kinds of liabilities with zero commensurate benefits. This is obviously also fine with the Boss.

This is a perfect example of the colossal ignorance of the Minneapolis City Council. Prepare yourself for a so-stupid-it-hurts comment uttered by 4th Ward council member Phillipe Cunningham. MPR News writes,

> "If we have these systems in place we are getting ahead
> of the violence," said Cunningham. "That's why I have

advocated so strongly for the violence interrupters, because if they are interrupting the violence before the guns are being fired, then the MPD doesn't have to respond to that violence."

Would saying, "what an idiot" be mean? Maybe he's personally a nice guy. But is taking away a community's police department and replacing it with fantasy "violence interrupters" being mean? Yes. Yes, it is—and incredibly stupid.

In June 2020, the Boss held a "virtual roundtable," that included City Council Director Phillipe Cunningham. Jackie Renzetti at *Bring Me the News* reported,[193] "Obama praised the actions of the young protesters, stressed the importance of local change and called on mayors to pledge [MBKAP] to reform use-of-force policies." Which "*actions* of the young protesters [soldiers]," Boss? Burning? Looting? Assaulting?

The Boss's presentation was titled "A Conversation with President Obama: Reimagining Policing in Wake of Continued Police Violence" (there's "police violence" again). The panelists included the aforementioned Cunningham, the Boss's wingman the Consigliere, and Rashad Robinson, president of Color of Change. Amazing how the Boss's people and organizations keep popping up everywhere people come together to hate the police.

To understand the tactics used by the Obama Gang to veil their efforts, it's instructive to review how the Boss's administration operated in the White House. CBS News published a story[194] in 2017 illustrating just how far the Boss will go to fight transparency. CBS reported, "The Obama administration in its final year in office spent a record $36.2 million on legal costs defending its refusal to turn over federal records under Freedom of Information Act, according to [the] Associated Press."

CBS continued, "For a second consecutive year, the Obama administration set a record for the times federal employees told citizens, journalists and others that despite searching they couldn't find a single page of files[195] that were requested." Wow! What a coincidence, eh? Weird for the most transparent administration in history.[196] Further, "[the Obama administration] set records for outright denial of access to files, refusing to quickly consider requests described as especially newsworthy, and forcing people to pay for records who had asked the government to waive search and copy fees."

While this does not deal specifically with the Obama Foundation and the MBKAP (then again, it may, depending on what documents people requested), it illustrates an Obamaland penchant for obscuring agendas and the goings-on during Boss's reign. Which obfuscation, it seems, now using the "deep state's" loyal soldiers, is still occurring today.

Chapter 12

Prosecutors—Capos

When talking about prosecutors, district attorneys, circuit attorneys, city attorneys, state's attorney, or whatever terminology a jurisdiction uses for the title of its top prosecutor, several dubious individuals immediately assault the mind. These individuals, supposedly responsible for prosecuting criminals in their jurisdictions, will be familiar to many. This is because many are among a plethora of the Underboss-funded candidates[197] Soros's money helped get elected. And with all the rioting and chaos, they are behaving just as he'd hoped and even planned they would.

City, county, and state authorities, including the Underboss's prosecutors, are arresting, charging, and prosecuting otherwise law-abiding people for anything from surfing[198]—alone—in the ocean, to playing[199] in a park with their kids, not wearing a facecloth[200] at a church service, or daring to exercise[201] their right to self-defense[202] under the Second Amendment.

Simultaneously, these prosecutors are refusing to file charges or to prosecute the rioters' blatant misdemeanor and felony violations of law. Many of these violations involve violence—sometimes extreme violence. But, in what has become an Orwellian-themed America, many prosecutors have spurned our nation's sacred commitment to jurisprudence, equal justice, and the rule of law. Time to explore what these Marxist automatons are doing to collapse the greatest country the world has ever known.

Kim Foxx, Cook County, Chicago, IL

Ms. Foxx is most infamous for her unethical mischief in the Jussie Smollett hoax.[203] She was cleared of any illegal actions,[204] but investigators admonished her for unethical behavior.[205] Well, that should dissuade her from doing this again, right? Don't put any money on it.

Still, aside from the Smollett case, Ms. Foxx has often revealed her anti–law and order, anti-cop bias. For example, she refused to prosecute the rioters who committed massive amounts of property damage and injured Chicago police officers. A Chicago Tribune analysis[206] "found that Foxx ... has dropped in excess of 25,000 felony cases." Think about that: there's a victim on the other side of each of those cases who will never see justice. That number represents all the people not held accountable for their violent and destructive criminal actions.

The property they damaged represents hundreds of victims who lost millions of dollars. Some looters destroyed the only grocery stores in poor neighborhoods, forcing residents, including the elderly, to travel miles to get their food and medicine instead of simply walking down the block. What kind of justice system lets people get away with that kind of crime?

Jon Dougherty in the BizPac Review reported[207] that John Catanzara, the president of the Chicago Fraternal Order of Police, wrote a letter to U.S. Attorney John R. Lausch Jr. calling on him "to file federal charges against scores of people arrested for looting and causing damage during recent riots." Catanzara summed it up when he wrote that Foxx "has instituted a 'presumption of dismissal' for a host of charges." But she's not the only non-prosecuting, anti-cop prosecutor in America to do this—not nearly.

Racheal Rollins, Suffolk County, Boston, MA

To be fair, Racheal Rollins, the Suffolk County District Attorney, whose jurisdiction includes Boston, is one prosecutor who rode into office on a specific public platform promising not to prosecute several crimes. She campaigned on a list of 15 "nonviolent" and "minor" crimes she would decline to prosecute.[208] The crimes are:

1. Trespassing

2. Shoplifting

3. Larceny under $250

4. Disorderly conduct

5. Disturbing the peace

6. Receiving stolen property

7. Minor driving offenses, including driving with a suspended or revoked license

8. Breaking and entering—"where it is into a vacant property or where it is for the purpose of sleeping or seeking refuge from the cold and there is no actual damage to property"

9. Wanton or malicious destruction of property

10. Threats (excluding domestic violence)

11. Minor in possession of alcohol

12. Drug possession

13. Drug possession with intent to distribute

14. Resisting arrest, when it is the only charge

15. Resisting arrest when combined with charges for the preceding offenses

The list could be longer now that she's been in office for a while. The odd thing is, all district attorneys swear an oath upon assuming office that they will enforce the law. When swearing her oath, the opposite seems to have been her intent. In that case, to what did she swear? Well, since she was at least partially funded by the Underboss, was she actually silently swearing allegiance to him, or perhaps to the Boss? After all, according to the *Boston Globe*, the Boss gave Rollins a "shoutout in a speech."[209]

Think about DA Rollins's list of crimes she will not prosecute. Again, as with Foxx, where is the justice for the victims? And how about respect for police officers who've arrested people who resisted arrest and are not prosecuted? Now people know they can resist arrest without consequences. Do you think that will make people more or less likely to obey police orders? If someone resists, and the officer knows the DA will not prosecute the offender, why attempt to enforce the law in the first place? *Bingo!* This entire cabal, this gang, does not want the law enforced—at least, not against criminals. Cops—now, those they will prosecute. They won't rest until they can entirely replace equal justice with leftist-defined social justice.

Many apologists for district attorneys like DA Rollins defend them by saying they are using "prosecutorial discretion." But that's a sham. DAs use prosecutorial discretion when reviewing specific cases of specific people charged for specific crimes to determine if there is enough evidence to get a conviction.

DA Rollins, in a wholesale manner, is abdicating her responsibility to prosecute more than a dozen crimes. She is not reviewing individual cases for sufficient evidence to prosecute. She's telling cops: if you bring me a case with one of these charges, I will not prosecute the offender—*period!* People have heard of jury nullification. Well, this is de facto prosecutor nullification, ignoring a violation of certain people committing certain crimes.

The voters in the commonwealth elect legislators who then pass laws. When these are violated, the district attorney is supposed to prosecute the violators. In these cases, District Attorney Rollins isn't enforcing the law according to equal justice, as constitutionally required. She's enforcing the law according to social justice as informed by her personal leftist political biases. So, it's no surprise the NPA filed a complaint[210] against this DA who puts all Boston area cops in danger.

Chesa Boudin, San Francisco, CA

District Attorney Chesa Boudin's election would turn heads almost anywhere except in San Francisco. This Rhodes scholar, multiple language–speaking, anti-cop politician has a curriculum vitae to make any far-leftist swoon. As written at the NPA in November 2019, "San Franciscans have elected a Yale-educated defense attorney to be the city's lead prosecutor. A man who hasn't prosecuted a single person[211] for a single crime. These city voters are not alone in their lunacy, though."

As appeared in an article [212]on the topic at the NPA website:

> Among Boudin's other anti-bona fides, his parents[213] [Kathy Boudin and David Gilbert] belonged to the infamous Weather Underground. When Boudin was a baby, the court sentenced both parents to long prison terms for their roles in murdering two police officers[214] and a security guard back in the 80s. His mother is out of prison and now teaching at Columbia University. (well, how else would you reward a cop-killer but with a professorship?). His father is still in prison.
>
> Since his parents were doing long stretches in the hoosegow, fellow unapologetic Weather Underground terrorists, and the Boss's friends, Bill Ayers and Bernadine Dorn[215] adopted and raised Boudin. Ayers and Dorn also did prison time after the FBI arrested them following years as fugitives.

Boudin's connection to the Boss is self-contained in who his adopted parents are. It was, as Sean Hannity so often describes them, "the unrepentant terrorists" Ayers and Dorn in whose home[216] Barack began his political career in Illinois.

While a child cannot be held accountable for his parents' evil actions and radical political views, it seems this child had not fallen far from the proverbial tree. Regardless of his adoptive parents' influence as he grew up, he is an adult now and responsible for his actions—and inactions.

One of those actions was to take his formidable education and, according[217] to the *American Thinker*, go to work for the late Venezuelan dictator Hugo Chavez. Boudin served the socialist tyrant as a "trusted propagandist, translator and advisor." While Boudin was running for office, Michelle Malkin referred to Boudin[218] as the "nation's most toxic DA candidate." Today, he has lots of competition for the title. He is among the many prosecutors the Underboss funded who came into office promising *not* to prosecute criminals.

Boudin does not keep his agenda a secret. Gabe Greschler at KQED wrote,[219] "Just two days into his tenure ... Chesa Boudin fired at least seven prosecuting attorneys. Likely, a cadre of prosecutors that dared to *prosecute* criminals. Can't have that. Boudin said the actions were necessary to carry out the progressive policies he campaigned on." Think this was good news for the city's police officers? No.

This once-beautiful city has descended into a morass of junkies, people living on the streets in filth, and crime going unpunished. No one has to look any further than a report that seems to have come from a parody site like the Onion or Babylon Bee. San Francisco actually has a "poop map,"[220] warning people where they might have to hop-scotch past piles of, not dog crap, but human waste.

This is the city where two politicians, one who could be considered an underboss, the other a capo, live. To their everlasting shame, Speaker of the House Nancy Pelosi and Senator Diane Feinstein live in San Francisco. One aspect of their legacies, and of Boudin's, will be the San Francisco Poop Map. Well done, San Francisco voters.

Larry Krasner, Philadelphia, PA

As an introduction to this infamous Underboss-funded DA, this appeared[221] at LifeZette:

> Another toxic waste dump of an incident has occurred in the Philadelphia criminal justice system, languishing under the reckless stewardship of the George Soros-funded[222] District Attorney Larry Krasner.
>
> This time the result of Krasner's perverted, social *in*-justice policies was the needless murder of Philadelphia Police Department (PPD) Corporal and SWAT officer James O'Connor. Murder suspect Hassan Elliot participated in allegedly gunning down[223] the 23-year veteran cop while he and other SWAT officers attempted to serve an arrest warrant.

The U.S. Attorney for the Eastern District of Pennsylvania, William M. McSwain, in a statement about the incident, virtually body-slammed Krasner. "Elliot was on the street for one reason: Because of District Attorney Krasner's pro-violent defendant policies." Krasner gave Elliot a lenient charging and sentencing deal on a firearms violation, apparently giving him the benefit of the doubt (despite there being video evidence showing Elliot holding a gun during the incident). So, the criminal was back out on the street where he took advantage of the opportunity Krasner gave him and allegedly killed a cop.

Krasner, being a good capo, named one of the Boss's former White House officials,[224] Robert Listenbee, his First Assistant DA. For four years, Listenbee was the Boss's Administrator of the Office of Juvenile Justice and Delinquency Prevention. So, a law-and-order prosecutor he ain't. Philadelphia's criminal justice system continues to collapse under the weight of corrupt so-called prosecutors like Krasner.

Dan Satterberg, King County, WA

Seattle talk show host and Rush Limbaugh guest host Todd Herman[225] often refers to this county prosecutor as "Heroin Dan Satterberg." This is because of this prosecutor's penchant for wanting to establish "heroin dens" in Seattle and other King County communities. He euphemistically calls these heroin dens "safe injection sites."[226] When is injecting a deadly drug into your veins ever "safe"?

More recently, as covered by the NPA,[227] Satterberg raised Seattle cops' hackles when he refused to prosecute "CHOP/CHAZ residents" for felonies after they resisted arrest when police were finally allowed to clear the "Durkanistan" established by radicals and condoned by Mayor Jenny Durkan.[228] President Trump often said Durkan acted only because if she didn't, he would have. There doesn't appear to be any direct or significant connection to the Underboss or the Boss. But Satterberg operates his prosecutor's office in a manner that both men would likely approve of enthusiastically.

John Creuzot, Dallas, TX

The first thing that assaults a cop's sensibilities is that this supposed prosecutor hails from the great state of Texas. Texas, especially because of its size, history, and reputation, is to many a last bastion of true American freedom and liberty. Then again, Creuzot was born in New Orleans, so ...

The problem is, progressivism is infecting even red states via their large cities. Liberals fleeing other basket case cities, especially in California, because of the political damage done, turn around and try to do the same thing in their new residences, thus ruining another city and state. They always believe socialism's failures mean they just didn't do it the "right" way and just need to try again.

Creuzot decided in 2019[229] that he would no longer prosecute thefts valued at $750 or less—if they are considered "necessary items." Like, maybe, $749 worth of diapers? Before we decide that, shouldn't we define "necessary"? But Creuzot is not the only woke prosecutor who wants to divine a criminal's motivations for committing a crime. Less surprisingly, this social justice, crystal ball reading also happens in—where else?—California.

Diane Becton, Contra Costa County, CA

DA Diane Becton is going further than her other Underboss-funded DA colleagues, exceeding even Creuzot's wokeness. According[230] to the *New York Post*, Becton "is requiring her prosecutors to consider looters' 'needs' when weighing criminal charges against them." This county sits on the outskirts of San Francisco where her ideological kin, DA Chesa Boudin, holds office. Like Boudin, Becton refuses to prosecute certain crimes against certain people.

Well, that is, unless someone has the nerve to paint over a yellow BLM mural with black paint on black pavement. Only then is Becton interested in being a prosecutor—or should we say persecutor? Becton is pedal-to-the-metal going after these "erasists" for daring to show a similar anti-social opposition to BLM as BLM shows to conservatives and American culture. But rather than a fine for committing graffiti or another form of "property damage," she is charging a couple with a "hate crime."

Aren't both actions expressions of First Amendment rights—or at least only civil disobedience? Admittedly, it is not nice to paint over someone's political pavement mural. But it's also not nice to paint a mural depicting the name, and de facto logo, of a cop-hating violent Marxist organization on a city street, right? But once a city or county allows some people to express political views on the taxpayers' streets, then shouldn't it be open to other people to "peacefully" express their political views in a similar way?

Think about it this way. Aside from speech, the First Amendment also protects people's rights not to speak and recognizes their right to practice, *or not practice*, a religion. Similarly, if a person can express a political view by painting a mural on public property—in this case, on a street where most ordinances prohibit "pavement markings" other than traffic-related ones—then shouldn't a person be allowed either to erase that expression or to consider such erasure simple civil disobedience? Sanction them, sure, but not with a "hate crime" charge.

If one group of Americans is allowed to paint "BLM" on the street, shouldn't another group of Americans be allowed to paint "MAGA" on the street? If not, why not? Oh, right. Freedom of speech is only allowed for speech politicians agree with. In fact, if painting over a BLM mural is a hate crime, then painting a MAGA mural or, God forbid, a "thin blue line" flag would constitute a crime against humanity.

Aside from these non-prosecuting prosecutors, some organizations exist exclusively to put these "prosecutors" in office. Award-winning journalist Lara Logan tweeted about a group that fits into the associate (and possibly soldier) category. The People's DA Coalition wants people to "join us for a conversation on how District Attorneys uphold mass incarceration, and what is needed to create change." The Tweet is about an associated group, Black Futures Lab[231] (BFL). On BFL's website, they introduce their "allies." You may recognize a name or group or two.

Lateefah Simon: Akonadi Foundation

Melissa Harris-Perry: https://politics.wfu.edu/faculty-and-staff/melissa-harris-perry/

Anthony Thigpenn: California Calls

Heather McGhee: Demos

Tracy Sturdivant: The League

Tim Silard: Rosenberg Foundation

Rashad Robinson: Color of Change (*There it is again!*)

The inevitable connections arise once again. Since joining the Rosenberg Foundation, Tim Silard has led statewide and national criminal justice reform as a core grant-making focus. In 2011, Rosenberg joined with other funders to create an affinity group focused on criminal justice reform, Funders for Safety and Justice in California. FSJC includes the Open Society Foundations. (*And there's another one.*)

BFL tweets, "Ongoing state violence against Black people has led to a growing movement demanding radical transformation of the legal system. But, often focused on the role of police, little attention is given to DA's & the power they have to prosecute in ways that harm our communities."

There seem to be plenty of people and groups hating on the cops, so these folks are training their sites on working directly to put non-prosecuting district attorneys in office. This is yet another example of changes to the criminal justice system coming from DC Comics' backward Bizarro World.

Chapter 13

ACLU—Capos

The ACLU—the American Civil Liberties *for Liberals* Union—is a leftist luminary among the Boss's caporegimes. In recent decades, the ACLU, an organization famous for defending even Nazis' constitutional rights, has strayed from its intellectually honest path. For example, the ACLU has adopted an anti-police, pro-rioter stance. How so? The ACLU keeps suing the cops on behalf of rioters.

Law enforcement in a free country is not supposed to be easy. In totalitarian, socialist, and Marxist dictatorships, the police can pick up anyone, anywhere, anytime, for anything—or for nothing. In the United States, cops must follow the U.S. Constitution, specifically the Bill of Rights. That's how it should be, and that's how it is.

However, a once-venerable civil rights organization is attempting to make law enforcement not just hard but impossible. Their ruse is immediately apparent in their dishonesty. They file a lawsuit conflating peaceful protests with violent riots. Then they premise their entire case on the fallacy that police are abusing *protesters* when they are using necessary force against *rioters*.

Bloomberg City Lab reported that in October 2020 the ACLU New York branch joined the Legal Aid Society in a lawsuit against the NYPD.[232] The ACLU tries to cloak itself in the First Amendment, but that raiment no longer fits. If, as they allege, police are using "brutal force" against "peaceful protesters," where's the evidence? Why isn't the left-wing media showing endless video loops of the "abuse"? Because it's not happening. Nearly every second of the video evidence is of rioters using violence against the police, while the politicians (and ACLU) hobble cops trying to restore order.

University of California, Los Angeles (UCLA) School of Law professor Joanna Schwartz contends, "The growing list [of lawsuits] shows that departments are not fixing the issues that land them in court." By "fixing the issues," she means acquiescing to the mob. And the cops cannot stop the ACLU from filing frivolous lawsuits.

The ACLU enters the fray with a predetermined perspective: *it's the cops' fault—always.* In other words, ACAB.[233] ACLU attorney Daniel Lambright says, "We don't think there was a 'bad apple' problem. We think these were part of policies and practices endorsed by the [NYC] mayor and the [NYPD] commissioner."

Aside from bogus claims against cops in court, Prof. Schwartz fires this ballistic missile of conflation: "It is a really distressing sign of our times that police departments are sometimes responding to what has been an unprecedented outcry against police misconduct with more misconduct, and sometimes even more blatant misconduct and excessive force than we've seen in the past." The ACLU constructs a proprietary definition for "misconduct" and then uses the flawed definition to bludgeon the cops.

This fantasy only exists in the imaginations of people like Prof. Schwartz. She is not an objective analyst presenting an unbiased case. She implies that no force is ever necessary even after a demonstration turns into a riot. Her lack of understanding of law enforcement is astounding. There's more proof.

Everyone knows the violence Americans are seeing so frequently is being perpetrated by the ACLU's clients assisted by a complicit media. Otherwise, why would a Bloomberg CityLab article on the subject not contain the word "riot" or a synonym for it even once? This is despite the fact that their client's allegations came from incidents where peaceful protests became violent riots. Check the dates and times of the complaints.

It's no surprise that the Boss has a close relationship with the ACLU. After all, they sing off the same sheet of music—a cop-hating aria. In fact, in 2014, when the Consigliere was still the Boss's AG, he tapped Vanita Gupta to head the DOJ's civil rights unit. This is significant because Gupta was recruited from the ACLU where she served as its top lawyer.

The Hill reported[234] that the Consigliere said, "Vanita has spent her entire career working to ensure that our nation lives up to its promise of equal justice for all." He continued, "Even as she has done trailblazing work as a civil rights lawyer, Vanita is also known as a unifier and consensus builder." A unifier and consensus builder? *Really*?

In 2016, the Boss and Capo Gupta considered the debate about a referendum over transgender men and women's access to public restrooms in North Carolina to be a "civil rights" issue. The DOJ sued to stop South Carolina from passing a law requiring people to use the bathroom assigned to their biological gender at birth.

This is not even a matter of a person going through or having gone through hormone therapy and sex reassignment surgery. The DOJ would only require a biological man or woman to "self-identify" as the opposite sex. Whether this self-identification lasts for a minute, week, month, year, or lifetime, and then maybe revert back, doesn't seem to matter. This makes the issue a problem for cops when reasonable people complain about "men" in a women's restroom and when "men" must be placed in a jail or prison cell with women.

Does the following comment sound like Capo Gupta is "consensus-building"? As David Harsanyi of the *Federalist* put it,[235] "Civil Rights' Division Chief Vanita Gupta says,[236] '[That's sex discrimination, plain and simple….] Transgender men are men.... Transgender women are women.' So sayeth Vanita Gupta, so sayeth we all. Or else. And now 300 million people have to adhere to the Obama administration's relativistic notions about nature and gender." As mentioned earlier, Capo Gupta brought the ACLU's penchant for changing a definition and then attacking opponents with it.

As mentioned earlier, a part of the NPA's mission to assist the nation's law enforcement officers is filing friend of the court (amicus) briefs in certain court cases. In one such case, on July 22, 2020, according to KATU News,[237] the NPA filed a brief [238] in an "ACLU suit against officers 'use of excess force' in Portland riots." James Buchal, attorney for the NPA, said, "I filed that brief in order to provide an additional voice for the police. The lawsuit seeks to block federal officers from 'dispersing, arresting, threatening to arrest, or using physical force against journalists or legal observers.'"

Just watch the news videos of rioters throwing paint on officers' face shields, trying to blind them with industrial lasers, and otherwise assaulting them with clubs and an arsenal of thrown objects. How could anyone believe cops could distinguish between violent and "nonviolent" people during a riot?

The ACLU's Matt Borden argues, "You need to have press there documenting what's happening so the narrative doesn't becoming [sic] something that is skewed." (Now, that is rich).

Buchal fired back, "Journalists don't have special rights when riots have been declared."

Just like combat journalists aren't exempt from bombs and bullets in war, if they choose to stay and cover a battle, they are not exempt from being injured in a riot.

Buchal also said, "The things that go on are just incredible. Many people have been seeking body cameras and things like that for years.... We can show the environment they face ... people are shooting them [cops] with slingshots, people are trying to blind them with paint, people are shooting fireworks at them and somehow they're supposed to distinguish, oh this riot person, he's this ... that's how police get killed."

Journalists and legal observers argue that police used force against them—the journalists and legal observers—at "protests." This is a blatant lie. Police only use force against protesters once they become violent, at which time they have morphed from legal protester to illegal rioter.

In July 2019, Cision PR Newswire reported,[239] "The National Police Association (NPA) opposed the ACLU's attack on law enforcement's ability to investigate street gangs, arguing to Massachusetts in a friend-of-the-court brief, it should uphold the right of the Boston Police Department to maintain a confidential gang database." The ACLU argued it's "unfair to gang members." To paraphrase Dirty Harry, "Well, I'm all broken up about unfairness to gang bangers." What about their future victims, some of whom may be cops? The NPA presented its position:

> The NPA's brief argues that given the link between gang membership and violence, and the growing gang population, it is crucial that law enforcement is able to use every available modern technique and tool available to it. To be able to effectively allocate resources and develop programming to combat gang violence, a critical first step is to accurately estimate the magnitude and nature of a particular gang population. And to effectively prosecute gang-related crimes, which by their very nature are more difficult to prosecute, it is critical to understand the interconnected relationships and complex dynamics between rival gangs. Gang Unit investigators need to familiarize themselves with the dynamics of gangs, including, but not limited to their membership size, territory, local hangouts, rivalries, and types of crimes committed, as well as the identification and personal and criminal backgrounds of individual members.

Intelligence gathering has always been an important part of preventative police work. Crime prevention begins with knowledge, which empowers preparedness. Knowledge of the who, where, and when of criminal activity allow cops to prepare plans to deal with crime and criminals. Cops use human intel, such as officers and detectives talking to people and interrogating suspects. However, as technology improves, just as in any other industry, law enforcement also must exploit it to better serve public safety. Remember, the cops are only interested in information that predicts future criminal actions by documenting past criminal actions. And that is exactly what a gang member database serves as: crime prevention. Something, apparently, the ACLU doesn't care about.

The ACLU, again because the edges are blurred in a mob allegory, serves a member of the caporegime, but it also provides soldiers[240] in the form of lawyers in court and "legal observers" at protests and those that become riots. And this neo-ACLU's behavior, on behalf of violence and against peace, can only be fairly known as the American Civil Liberties for Leftists Union, an umbrella under which it serves the Boss well.

Chapter 14

The Five (Hundred) Families

Families come in all forms and dimensions. There is the nuclear family (which BLM has stated it wants to dissolve[241]). There are single-parent families, gay-parent families, gay single-parent, mixed-race, mixed-religion, and mixed-politics families. And there are families comprising people who, though having no blood relation, are linked by love and loyalty. Then there are the infamous families, so often portrayed in film and on TV: the organized crime families.

The primary cultural incarnation and theatrical presentation of the American organized crime family most often reflects those that came to the United States from Italy in the early to mid-twentieth century. While history has portrayed these organizations to be strict and often brutal, they were affectionate and loyal toward their families and friends. But they also had rigid codes of behavior. This was especially true toward "civilians." They primarily perpetrated violence against "soldiers" and people "in the game." This bestowed upon the mob a "mobster with a heart of gold" mythology that could have viewers rooting for the bad guys. This was true of the massive HBO hit series *The Sopranos*.[242]

Each of these crime families was one among several connected families in control of a geographical area. New York City is infamous for its "Five Families,"[243] who have run organized crime in the city and other parts of the country since 1931. Although the Boss's political empire aligned against law enforcement is not a mirror image of the mob, there are some inescapable similarities. First, for the Obama "gang" Foundation, there are many more "interconnected families" than five. For example, the numbers of people and methods of operation differ to various degrees. In organized crime you have a boss, underboss(es), consigliere, captains (capos), soldiers, and then associates. It's obviously different with political revolutions. But the comparisons are still fun, right?

So, the former president is the "Don" or "Boss" of the "family" or "gang." As the last Democrat to be president as of 2020, it's his natural role. But, whereas being the titular head of the party is usually honorific, because most presidents fade away after their one or two terms in office, not this Boss. He has his hands on the reins of the party (gang), and he's not about to let them go. The Underboss, for these purposes, is George Soros, who should have come up by now but will be appearing frequently from here on out. Soros's place is granted because of his seeming omnipresence where the neosocialist political and financial worlds intersect. Where the Boss is, the Underboss (or at least his support) is never far away.

However, the cloaked and interdependent nature of the organizations is where most similarities occur. And while the mob's goal was to gain financial security and maintain control over a territory, the Boss's territory is the United States of America, and his mission is to "fundamentally transform" it (and eventually the world) into something unrecognizable to traditional Americans who revere their country as founded.

The extreme violence committed by the mob's "soldiers" at the behest of the hierarchy seems (or seemed) less similar to the Boss's anti-America, anti-police gang. However, with their violence increasing in savagery (cops assaulted with baseball bats,[244] set on fire,[245] and shot,[246] and conservative Trump supporters beaten[247] and murdered[248]), the disparities regarding violence are narrowing.

Where they are similar is having a powerful person sitting atop the primary organization's operational structure. Subordinate organizations support the top organization, which is run by people who function as "captains" (capos) for the Boss. Those capos do the Boss's bidding, including issuing, implicitly or explicitly, orders to the soldiers, and they shield him from harm or criminal exposure. He has earned their loyalty—through affection, wealth, and intimidation.

Down the organizational chart, "associates" function outside the primary group(s), but they help to further the Boss's goals. Examples include attorneys who handle financial or other legal aspects of running the gang and, as in this case, attorneys who represent those alleging police brutality or other civil rights violations. Accountants and unethical politicians would also come under the heading of associates.

It's becoming clearer as time passes that this nefarious political crime family works through a system of fibrous affiliations. For example, the Boss and his Obama Foundation provide a framework for implementing an agenda. Through his MBKAP, he intends to "transform" (destroy) traditional America, including law and order, equal justice, and the police. No one can deny this has been his goal since he was the one who promised to "fundamentally transform the"—well, you know it by now.

Using police brutality and racism (and the rest of the ists, isms, and phobias proliferating today) as vehicles, the Boss's political gang recruits capos and soldiers and attracts and cultivates associates who work to achieve the family's goals. The MBKAP functions as the family's loyalty oath—its omerta.[249] And even those who don't literally swear to it pay homage to it figuratively by implicitly carrying out the family's mission: the re-creation of the United States of America as a socialist nation.

So what is the hierarchy? Though even more nebulous, more clandestine, and larger than Tony Soprano and his gang, the subordinate organizations somehow function under the ostensible primary organization. How do they do this? Through vigorous and broad obfuscation. For example, Jennifer Bilek, at the *Federalist*, in 2018 wrote about[250] the Tides Foundation. She was writing about its push to thrust transgenderism into the national focus. And not just transgenderism generally, but the emphasis on allowing biological males to compete in female sports. So, though her story is not related specifically to law enforcement, it demonstrates the interconnected strategies for flushing the American Experiment, including the cops, down the commode.

If adults consider themselves transgender, that's their business and their right. As Americans, they enjoy equal rights, as we all do. But they are not entitled to special rights. And the issue of biological males competing and winning in girls or women's sports, placing in jeopardy biological females' ability to earn college sports scholarships, is a legitimate issue for discussion. It is not settled, as some want everyone to believe.

How does this connect to law enforcement? This issue spills over with the requirement that some in the Boss's sphere of influence are trying to impose on the criminal justice system that would have people incarcerated under the sex "they choose to identify as" rather than their sex at birth. This places biological males who identify as females in lock-up with biological females. Anyone who says they don't see a problem with this is either lying or stupid.

Bilek, about running over girls' and women's rights, wrote, "Concurrent with these rapid changes, I witnessed an overhaul in the English language with new pronouns and a near-tyrannical assault on those who did not use them. Laws mandating new speech[251] were passed. Laws overriding biological sex with the amorphous concept of gender identity are being instituted now. People who speak openly about these changes can find themselves, their families, and their livelihoods threatened." Just ask Martina Navratilova[252] and J. K. Rowling,[253] not exactly right wing, how that works. They've been victims of this mob's intimidation for raising reasonable "truly feminist" concerns.

This is where Bilek's reporting on a radical leftist issue and the Boss's family, to use a leftist term, intersect. Bilek writes, "These funders often go through anonymous funding organizations such as Tides Foundation, founded and operated by [Drummond] Pike. Large corporations, philanthropists, and organizations can send enormous sums of money to the Tides Foundation, specify the direction the funds are to go, and have the funds get to their destinations anonymously. Tides Foundation creates a legal firewall and tax shelter[254] for foundations and funds political campaigns,[255] often using legally dubious tactics."[256] Many individuals and organizations associated with the Boss make use of this financial vehicle.

To illustrate the intentionally amorphous nature of enterprises such as the Tides Foundation, InfluenceWatch writes,[257] "In 1996, the Tides Foundation established the Tides Center,[258] a separate 501(c)(3) nonprofit, to assume its fiscal sponsorship services and form a firewall between its incubation and grantmaking activities." Emphasizing its primary focuses, InfluenceWatch also notes, "Tides' fiscally sponsored groups have been prominent in the anti-war movement, anti-free trade campaigns, gun control, abolition of the death penalty, abortion rights…." Notice all the proper leftist boxes dutifully checked. The Tides Foundation, Tides Center, Tides Nexus,[259] Tides Network,[260] and so on show the Gordian knot that investigators, watchdogs, and researchers must untangle to expose just one thread of this massive shroud of which the Obama Foundation is the apex—well, sort of.

"Sort of" because the obfuscated origins of some of these Tides organizations go back to the 1970s, and maybe even further (back when the baby Boss was living in the CHAZ). Along the way, they have been supporting whatever left-wing, progressive candidates, movements, and organizations whose fleeting star is, at the moment, shining the brightest.

It's important to understand that, unlike traditional mob families who attempt to keep their illegal affairs secret, this new family has turned obfuscation of its financial transactions into an art form. Under the Boss's organization, there are hundreds of subordinates that appear as appendages with no overt link to the Boss they serve. Organizations like the Tides Foundation use Tides as if it were a money-transferring public utility.

Now we come back to him whose name shall not be spoken,[261] the Boss's powerful Underboss, George Soros. If not actively or overtly "advising" the Boss, he works to facilitate and finance his primary work. What has the Underboss been up to, and how does he help move the Boss's anti-police movement forward? A primary way is through the labyrinth of mist-shrouded organizations through which they shuffle donations and then deal them out to other members of the "gang."

Here is a brain-twisting example of the Underboss's three (hundred) card monte game. Allen Alley, a radio host on KXL FM News 101, conducted an interesting experiment[262] at the website Oregon Catalyst. It shines some light on this exploration into the Boss's and Underboss's donation obfuscation dance. Alley says he wondered about the reports regarding donations to BLM being diverted to the Democratic Party through yet another organization, this one called Act Blue.[263]

One problem: Act Blue is not tax deductible, and neither is BLM Global. They needed to find another shell (to mix metaphors) for the game. Enter Thousand Currents. So, donate to BLM through Act Blue, which goes through Thousand Currents, and then back to BLM, and then on to the Tides Foundation, and back to BLM—or so the story goes. Dizzy yet?

Alley was curious about reports that money donated to BLM was, after traveling through the Boss's Silly Straw, winding up at the Democratic Party. He apparently didn't trust all the "debunking" the left-wing media had asserted about this claim. He wanted to find out for himself before making a proper donation.

Alley wrote that he'd been thinking about donating to BLM but wanted to find out a few things first. Like where his money was going. He made a nominal $1.00 donation to BLM so he could see what appeared on his receipt. He was surprised at what he learned.

Alley had to donate through Act Blue, where he found some strange preconditions. He said their disclaimer was unusual for a donation site, "going beyond any sort of 'normal' payment processor disclaimer." He said that he "was forced to register my account and save my information before finalizing my donation." He thought this was "odd in itself but not a big deal."

"Then I read at the bottom: 'Your donation of $1.00 will be forwarded by ActBlue Charities (FIEN 47-3739141), a 501(c)(3) charitable organization, to Thousand Currents (FEIN 77-0071852), a 501(c)(3) organization, *as you requested*'" (emphasis mine). When did Alley "request" that?

Alley explains that Thousand Currents "appears to have little connection to Black Lives Matter (other than through ActBlue)." He notes that

Thousand Currents supports Food Sovereignty, Alternative Economics, and Climate Justice. Alley quips, "All I wanted to do was to support Black Lives Matter, not causes that sound like sound bites from the Democrat Presidential Debates."

Also notable, according[264] to the *Washington Examiner*, is that one of Thousand Currents' board members is a convicted terrorist. Susan Rosenberg, as reported in a *Smithsonian Magazine* article,[265] began her radicalization in high school, hanging out with the Black Panthers and other violent extremists. She is also "suspected of helping [Assata] Shakur escape from prison." This references a convicted cop-killer wanted by the FBI, who they believe escaped to Cuba, where she has been living for decades. She'll come up in a later chapter in further detail, as she is an adored hero of BLM inc.

Note that some organizations primarily provide "soldiers"—boots on the ground—to intimidate and use physical violence on behalf of the Boss and his spiderweb of corrupt allies. Thus, groups such as BLM and Antifa fit simultaneously in two categories: families and soldiers.

Chapter 15

Open Society

Even when researching Open Society[266]—or more appropriately, Closed Society—the organizational obfuscation becomes immediately apparent just in its web address: Open Society Foundations—yes, plural. Nothing within the great socialist cabal is simple. They must envelop their operation within a web of concealment. As another example of leading researchers in the wrong direction, consider the opening headline at OpenSocietyFoundations.org:

THE OPEN SOCIETY FOUNDATIONS WORK TO BUILD VIBRANT AND INCLUSIVE DEMOCRACIES WHOSE GOVERNMENTS ARE ACCOUNTABLE TO THEIR CITIZENS.

Remember: That's citizens not as individuals but as a collective.

This is curious when you consider all the mischief the Underboss has conducted in various democracies around the world. He has interfered with nations' monetary systems, as he did in England. He has mucked with nations' immigration systems, as he did in his home country of Hungary. And, in the United States, he has financed candidates for prosecutors' offices and organizations that don't believe in the rule of law when prosecuting criminals. How democracies operate in true republics, such as in the United States, is the last thing on the Underboss's and his soldiers' minds. They believe in a world controlled by a strong central government. And they claim to be active in "120 countries around the world."

They divide their grant targets into ten categories:

Democratic Practice[267]

Higher Education[268]

Early Childhood and Education[269]

Human Rights Movement and Institutions[270]

Economic Equity and Justice[271]

Information and Digital Rights[272]

Equality and Antidiscrimination[273]

Journalism[274]

Health and Rights[275]

Justice Reform and the Rule of Law[276]

The Open Society website lists its total expenditures at $16.8 billion and its 2020 budget at $1.2 billion, having made over 50,000 grants. This shows an immense reach and influence over politics in the United States. Normally, the society makes grants to organizations it has vetted and chosen. However, it also offers some limited opportunities[277] "through Open Society's network of national and regional funding."

It's not too difficult to find connections between the Boss and Open Society. Many, if not most, if not all of the Underboss/Open Society–backed organizations back the Boss and his mission to crush traditional America by removing the backbone from American policing. Brooke Singman of Fox News wrote an article[278] titled "Obama State Dept Used Taxpayer Dollars to Fund George Soros Group's Political Activities in Albania…." So, again, this cabal is not limited to domestic operations—not nearly. Domestically, this matters because foreign activities allow the organization to further cloud any investigations into its clandestine activities.

Singman writes, "One report, from Feb. 10, 2017 on 'Engagement with the Open Society Foundation for Albania' stated that 'as one of the major assistance providers in Albania, representatives for the Open Society Foundation are frequently asked to participate in technical reviews of applications that we receive for funding.'"

The State Department has denied receiving any funds from or providing any funds to Open Society. However, Judicial Watch (JW) reportedly obtained another memo showing that the "Embassy in Tirana 'sponsored' a survey along with Soros' Open Society Foundation to measure Albanian citizens' 'knowledge, support, and expectations on justice reform.'" JW also states, "Records dated February 2017 show that the State Department used taxpayer funds to co-sponsor a second poll with Open Society Foundation."

Singman concludes the article by informing that JW "is also seeking information regarding Soros' activities in Macedonia, Romania and Colombia." Again, this may not be directly related to anti-police activities in the United States, but it shows the slippery nature of this group's (or these groups') activities generally. It is also believed that what they do overseas is practice for what they want to do in the United States.

Chapter 16

Civil Society 2.0

As with the inappropriately named Open Society, Civil Society 2.0 leads to uncivil societies. CS 2.0 is a government initiative intended to assist nongovernmental organizations (NGOs) and civil society organizations to update and upgrade their usage of new tools and technologies. The U.S. Department of State operated this initiative[279] from 2009 to 2017—essentially, during the Boss's administration.

Its themes include:

- promoting social and economic opportunity;
- ensuring the safety of our citizens;
- strengthening effective institutions of democratic governance;
- and addressing the challenges of energy security and climate change.

Sounds good, right? Innocuous, even. Well, maybe not so much. In exploring the initiative, Glenn Beck, at the Blaze,[280] has done some of the best reporting on this issue. As always, Beck admonishes his viewers, listeners, and readers: "Don't believe me; do your own research."

Civil Society 2.0 was the vehicle the Boss's administration used to muck around in other nations' affairs. One interesting soldier at the Boss's

State Department is Alec Ross, senior advisor on innovation to Secretary of State Hillary Clinton. In 2011, Ross addressed[281] the U.S. Embassy in Ukraine, saying, "Disruptive change. Some might describe this as CHAOS, but ultimately—for those willing to exploit it—the reward is … POWER."

Beck says, "For most of us, no matter which side of the aisle you're on, we all pretty much agree that regime change and stoking chaos is NOT what the American people want. But this is EXACTLY what was going on under the Obama Administration, and it was all being done in YOUR name."

Why is this important? Because the state department's involvement in disrupting political movements overseas appeared to be a dry run for what we are seeing on America's streets today. And, as mentioned previously, unlike other former presidents, the Boss hasn't moved on from Washington, DC. For example, as mentioned earlier, before the 2020 elections, he was busy releasing lists of political endorsements for well over a hundred candidates. He has also "headlined"[282] a "Democrat strategy meeting" at the home of Alex Soros, son of George Soros. Among other Democratic luminaries at the meeting was the Consigliere, Eric Holder.

These activities will exacerbate the civil unrest already occurring, and who will have to deal with the violence and other criminality? The police. As discussed at the beginning of this book, they're looking to unleash an anarcho-communist revolution right here in America.

Chapter 17

Color of Change (PAC)

On September 5, 2020, the *New York Times* published an article written by Pierre-Antoine Louis titled "Color of Change[283] [COC]: Tackling Systemic Racism One Strategy at a Time." The organization assumes "systemic racism" exists in America, and the *Times* barely pretends it's not a partisan political opinion ruse. It doesn't matter that Louis is conflating *systemic* racism with *individual* racism, which will always exist. It fits the narrative.

This is clear not only with depraved acts of individual racism that will always occur but also with the Left's penchant for morphing the criminals who attack police officers and get shot into "victims" of "police violence." Hell, the Marxists are now able to get pro athletes to put criminals' names on their helmets and jerseys. Talk about success. But what is the truth about COC?

The connection to the Boss is in the organization's founding. According to[284] Influence Watch (IW), Color of Change is a community organizing group cofounded by the Boss's short-lived "green jobs czar," Van Jones.[285] James Rucker is Jones's cofounder and a former director of the infamous activist group MoveOn.org. IW reports, "Jones and Rucker formed the group to publicize President George W. Bush's perceived neglect of African-American communities after Hurricane Katrina." "Perceived"? How about *fabricated*? At that time, which doesn't compare with what

President Trump has faced, it was one of the most cynical and racially divisive political attacks ever launched.

The group has attracted financial support from—no surprise—the Underboss, and "moral" support[286] from the Recording Academy[287] (you know, the Grammy folks). It is an artistic association that exists to support and promote recording artists—*leftist* recording artists. Although there was a time when they were fair—well, fairer—they've provided COC with more than moral support. According to *Billboard* in July 2020, "the Recording Academy has made a $1 million donation to the non-profit."

Back in 2014, when the group was relatively unknown, Mark Tapscott, of the *Washington Examiner*, asked,[288] "What's Color of Change hiding about itself?" Tapscott notes that companies such as Coca-Cola and the candy maker Mars, Inc., seemed to kowtow to COC, whom he described then as "the most powerful group in America you've never heard about." But rather than solely soliciting donations from these corporate giants, they demanded the companies cease their support for the conservative American Legislative Exchange Council (ALEC.org).

Other "successes" COC has had with this cancel-culture enterprise were "cancelling" Pat Buchanan, Eric Bolling, Lou Dobbs, and the late Andrew Breitbart. Free speech is not a thing with them, which tells you all you need to know. They also succeeded in "pushing advertisers on Glenn Beck's Fox News Show to withdraw their ads." The action likely had a strong influence on Fox dropping Beck's show.

Fortunately, COC fell far short of silencing Beck, who has become an even more powerful influence. And with the network he founded, TheBlaze.com, he is more insulated from COC-type attacks. Another benefit turned out to be allowing other conservative voices to fill his void on Fox, notably Tucker Carlson and Laura Ingraham.

Citing a favorite charge of the Boss, "voter intimidation of people of color," COC launched an effort to boycott ALEC. Instead, ALEC's executive director, Rob Scheberle, responded to COC's charges of racism. He said, "Over the last 24 hours, ALEC has been inundated with letters of support from elected officials, community leaders, and concerned citizens in response to the intimidation campaign launched by a coalition of extreme liberal activists committed to silencing anyone who disagrees with their agenda." He continued:

> I am thankful for the support and want to take this opportunity to remind people what we are facing:
>
> First, the people now attacking ALEC and its members are the same people who have always pushed for big-government solutions. Our support for free markets and limited government stands in stark contrast to their state-dependent utopia. This is not about one piece of legislation. This is an attempt to silence our organization, and it has been going on for more than a year.
>
> Second, ALEC is one of America's premier ideas laboratories for advocating free-market reforms. We are a target because our opponents believe they have the opportunity to attack an effective, successful organization that promotes free-market, limited government policies that they disagree with.

Although these fascist groups experience some "successes," their efforts to boycott and cancel often result in the opposite occurring. Hobby Lobby,[289] Chick-fil-A,[290] Whole Foods,[291] and, most recently, Goya Foods[292] come to mind. In commenting about the 2009 boycott of Whole Foods, even the *Atlantic* quoted Radley Balko as saying, "Whole Foods is everything leftists talk about when they talk about 'corporate responsibility.'" But then-CEO John Mackey dared to wander off the leftist reservation when he "wrote an op-ed that suggests alternatives to single-payer health care." He began with a harsh smack of reality by quoting a popular notion from former U.K. Prime Minister Margaret Thatcher. "The problem with socialism is that eventually, you run out of other people's money." How dare he state the truth?

COC is another appendage of the Boss's gang, albeit one of the more effective ones because it has learned Saul Alinsky's Rules for Radicals[293] so well and has implemented them so mercilessly against its enemies.

And don't forget about this group's anti-police stances, which match their comrade organizations. On its website, it lists as one of its recent "victories" the resignation of the Rochester Police Department's *black* police chief. How does this advance black lives? It doesn't; it advances acquiring political power.

Chapter 18

Campaign Zero

Yet another of the Boss's family websites that conscripts the image of a black man adopting the "hands up; don't shoot" pose is Campaign Zero.[294] This organization is another among a long list of redundant organizations that serve several similar purposes as other family organizations. Chief among them are to create the illusion of a larger support base than exists and to add to the obfuscation of Obamaland.

The acidic first line reads: "We can live in a world where police don't kill people." Are these people five years old? It's a great notion—fantasy, actually—but as long as criminals try to kill cops or other people, cops will defend themselves and others—with guns. The reality is that some violent people won't leave people alone and don't want to go to jail peacefully. If someone has an incantation that makes even armed, violent felons surrender to cops, out with it, please.

For example, take the unwarranted, manufactured rage[295] by the Boss's capos, associates, and soldiers over an officer shooting a crazed man attacking him with a knife. In Lancaster, Pennsylvania, of all places (Amish country), an officer was alone, investigating a domestic violence disturbance. Suddenly, a suspect armed with a knife burst out a door and charged up the sidewalk at the cop. The officer tactically retreated to put distance between himself and the suspect, then turned. The suspect ran at the cop, knife held high in his right hand, a wild look on his face, forcing the officer to shoot him. The suspect died of his wounds.

And … here they go again. The Boss's soldiers dutifully rioted at such "police violence." No matter where you are on the BLM scale—you support BLM as a slogan, you just don't like the police, or you don't hate the police but just question their judgment sometimes—you think the officer should have done something else. You have no idea what, just something else. Ask yourself what the BLM, Antifa, and other anti-cop activists expected that officer to do—allow the suspect to stab him? Based on their words and actions, BLM and Antifa would probably have preferred that the man kill the cop.

If you think the cop should have done something else instead but nothing reasonable comes to mind, you need to reexamine your criticism. What you're doing is advocating for criminals to severely injure or kill cops if you still believe the cop should have done "something" else. Remember, the officer didn't say one word to the suspect before the enraged man came charging at him with a knife. That magic word, please.

The headline to Heather MacDonald's piece at the *New York Post*[296] tells the story accurately: "Protesters Demand Cops Let Themselves Be Stabbed or Shot." She writes, "If the nation's police officers walked off the job today, it would be hard to blame them for it." She adds, "Sunday's anti-cop riots[297] in Lancaster, Pa.,[298] have made the current de facto rules of engagement clear: Officers may never defend themselves against lethal force if their attacker is a minority. They should accept being shot or stabbed as penance for their alleged racism."

How can this be explained any differently? Again, there is nothing about BLM and its allies' ultimate anti-cop goals that even approaches reasonable. They are all about collapsing the criminal justice system, which is clear in their support even for dangerous, armed criminals who get themselves shot while trying to kill police officers.

Chapter 19

#8cantwait

On #8cantwait.org's home page, the organization, connected directly to the Boss's MBKAP, claims, "Research shows more restrictive use of force policies can reduce killings by police and save lives. Tell your city to adopt all eight of these policies." There is more to this than it seems, especially if you engage your critical thinking before you draw any conclusions. "Reduce police killings" may sound good. But think about what that means. This exclusively refers to the suspects police officers kill, implying the criminals are innocent or that lethal force was not warranted. The FBI statistics tell us that nearly every single person police officers kill is a dangerous, armed criminal, trying to kill officers at the time cops kill them.

So, when "killings by police are reduced," don't they mean that police will kill fewer violent criminals trying to kill them or others? They won't acknowledge that almost all the people police kill are violent felons. And, as pointed out earlier, criminals get a vote in who lives and dies. By extension, if officers are not killing violent felons who attack police, doesn't this imply those felons will kill more police officers?

By now, don't we have to assume it's acceptable to the Left that criminals kill cops? Recall the BLM chant about wanting "dead cops." Recall the dead cops. It brings up the obvious question: in police use-of-force situations, what would BLM, Antifa, or their ilk consider being a violent, armed criminal who cops could shoot? With their comments and behavior following the Lancaster incident, the apparent answer is, there isn't one.

Therefore, BLM, Antifa, and others in the anti-cop factions have turned the real world into Bizarro World,[299] where everything is backward. Violent criminals are the victims, and law enforcement officers are the criminals. Isn't this how the Boss's fundamental transformation of the United States of America would work? It already does in many places.

Civil rights attorney and longtime Democrat-turned-Republican Trump voter Leo Terrell, on Sean Hannity's Fox News show, spoke out against[300] the Boss "using a house of worship—a funeral (for U.S. Rep. John Lewis)—to raise a Democratic campaign speech." Terrell took particular issue with the Boss's false assertions demonizing "federal troops" (including U.S. Marshals, ATF, ICE, and so on).

Terrell said, "What amazes me is that he [the Boss] basically lied on television when he said federal troops were used for peaceful protesters. There's not a peaceful protester who's trying to demolish a federal building." However, this has become a common intentional distortion among members of this neo-socialist, Democratic Party—oh, and their bosom media buddies.

The #8cantwait website lists the status of "Use of Force Policies Enacted in America's 100 Largest Cities Since June." A chart lists the cities and their "Existing Restrictions," "New Restrictions," "Reviewing," and "Not Enacted" anti-police edicts. The specific eight items listed are:

1. Requires De-Escalation. (Cops have always done this.)

2. Duty to Intervene. (Again, cops do this already, when warranted.)

3. Bans Chokeholds and Strangleholds. (Makes lefties feel good.)

4. Requires Warning Before Shooting. (If practicable?)

5. Bans Shooting at Moving Vehicles. (What if the car is moving *at* you?)

6. Exhaust Alternatives Before Shooting. (Again, cops do this now.)

7. Use of Force Continuum. (Like cops have been doing for decades?)

8. Comprehensive Force Reporting. (Takes cops off the streets.)

There is also a list of items with some of the most ironic headings annotated.

Immediate Harm Reduction (reduction for criminals, increase for cops)

- Use of Force Policies (to be determined by untrained civilians)

- Demilitarization (endangering the public and cops)

- DOJ Consent Decrees (forgot the adjective: bogus)

- Police Union Contracts (which cities often break)

Comprehensive Community Safety

- Divest from Police (perhaps the most ironic)

- Invest in Community, Including Housing, Jobs, and Education (why are these mutually exclusive from supporting police?)

- Pay Living Wage (which is related to public safety how?)

- Dramatically Reduce Jail & Prison Populations (releasing criminals promotes public safety?)

- Restorative Justice (socialist blather!)

- **Abolition** (now we're getting to the nugget)

- Fund Community Safety (by abolishing the police?)

- Move Money to Alternatives (wealth transfer from equal justice to social justice)

- End the Carceral State (more socialist blather)

Chapter 20

Civil Rights Corps

A radical organization that was critical of the Boss as president but that now marches in solidarity with the Obama Foundation is Civil Rights Corps[301] (CRC), founded by Alec Karakatsanis. Navigating to civilrightscorps.org, people are met with a donation portal, which contains the requisite victimology and racialist hyperbole. It is another organization not satisfied with attracting supporters but also uses its energy to sap any support for conservative organizations that support law enforcement (a little on the nose, but they even use the word "comrade"). Apparently, even though no empirical evidence supports it, they assert there are "two pandemics—COVID-19 and racism." Do they support locking down the nation for "racism," as they've redefined it, as well as for COVID-19? Probably.

So, what are these folks up to? According to a story in the *Loredo Morning Times*,[302] Harris County court records show that "a Houston man with six felony convictions is out on bond after being charged with murder this summer while on bail for three other felony offenses." The man, 24-year-old Vern Minifee, was out on bail for murder, set at $150,000, for which he posted $50,000 to get out on a burglary charge. But wait … there's more.

The *LMT* also reported, "Menifee had open cases of felon in possession of a firearm, engaging in organized criminal activity and burglary of a building when he was accused in the April 27 fatal shooting and robbery of Guy Anthony Owen Allen." In all, "Menifee has posted a total of $575K in surety bonds."

How in the world is this guy getting bail, and who is putting up the bond? The president of the Harris County Deputies' Organization, David Cuevas, says he believes Harris's repeated bail is a result of a "pending challenge to felony bail." Cuevas added, "Bail reform has done nothing but cause unintended consequences. It's a victory for criminals and it's a loss for law abiding citizens."

Enter the CRCs executive director, Alec Karakatsanis. He sued on behalf of "indigent defendants." Karakatsanis charges that opponents of the lawsuit are using "fear mongering tactics." The victims of those suspects released back into the community to commit more crimes may have a different opinion. Their fear is genuine. In fact, in Menifee's case, he'd already accumulated quite a criminal history that should have affected future bail in the interest of public safety. That is, it should have, but it didn't.

The *LMT* reported that Menifee "had been convicted between 2013 and 2018 of evading arrest, unauthorized use of a vehicle, burglary of a building, aggravated assault of a family member, felon in possession of weapon, and attempted possession of a firearm, all felonies." And CRC is suing to have predators like this, those who have demonstrated they will reoffend, often violently, released back into the community.

It's not that a discussion about bail issues shouldn't occur, but it should only happen as it applies to first-time and certain repeat, but nonviolent, offenders. Where is the care for public safety when authorities release a violent, career felon back into neighborhoods? Still, in this case, we're talking about one man, Vernon Menifee. Again, an ex-con released on bail after already out on bail for other crimes—including for *murder*! Who does that? The Civil Rights Corps does.

It's not that there isn't some merit to Karakatsanis's legal work. He seems concerned with equity in the justice system. However, as with cases like Menifee's, he seems to push the envelope too far. In 2015, though his goals today appear to sync with the Obama Foundation's, he wrote an article critical of the Boss's federal criminal justice system as president.

It's tough to have much sympathy for a person arrested for possession of over 50 grams of cocaine with the intent to distribute (sell). Regardless of where someone stands on the issue of drug legalization or decriminalization, this drug dealer knew that what he was doing was illegal, and he knew the penalties could be severe if he got caught. He got caught.

However, Karakatsanis wrote[303] eloquently in the *New York Times* about a technicality in the case. Without going into the minutia, the defendant had petitioned the court for his release. A federal appellate court ruled that the lower court had wrongly denied the petition. The Boss's DOJ argued that even if the denial was illegal, the convict should serve out his sentence based on the importance of "finality" in criminal cases. *What?*

Much like when the DOJ places a consent decree on a police department even though the evidence used is bogus, they still enforce the decree on the cops. Ultimately, as Karakatsanis also wrote, "the judges rejected the administration's argument as a departure from basic fairness and explained that it simply could not be the law in America that a person had to serve a prison sentence that everyone admitted was illegal."

According to Karakatsanis, the ex-convict "returned home and stayed out of trouble." That's fine, and hopefully that man will redeem himself and live a good, law-abiding, productive life. But we're not talking about that man. This is about a man who refused to go home and stay out of trouble. In fact, Menifee sought trouble while out on bail for other crimes for which he'd already been arrested and bailed out.

If there is any doubt of Karakatsanis's leftist credentials, in an August 2020 article at currentaffairs.org titled[304] "Why 'Crime' Isn't the Question and Police Aren't the Answer," he wrote, "Revolutionary moments like this one are exciting because they explode previous conceptions of what is possible and produce new consciousness." "Revolutionary moments," indeed.

Again, Karakatsanis and his CRC don't appear to have been enamored with federal criminal justice during the Boss's administration. However, as in any organized crime family, not everyone will see eye to eye on every detail. This seems to be the case here, regarding efforts to "reimagine the police." Still, based on the Boss's recent speeches, including at the

2020 Democratic National Convention, he and folks like Karakatsanis are obviously comrades.

Chapter 21

Minnesota Freedom Fund

The Minnesota Freedom Fund (MFF), founded in 2016 by Simon Cecil,[305] sounds like so much fun, right? Minnesota is a beautiful state. Freedom is great. And funds help people. All good stuff. Unless the *fund* pays for the *freedom* of violent rioters to loot and pillage Minnesota, and that is what Cecil apparently created the MFF to do. He wants to free rioters from jail, many with violent criminal histories who will commit more crimes.

Influence Watch describes MFF founder Simon Cecil as "a University of Minnesota student who was studying public policy and business management." Cecil's organization focuses on posting bond for "indigent" arrestees. The MFF also advocates using the CCP virus as an excuse to release prisoners from jail.

After the in-custody death of George Floyd, Legal Insurrection reported[306] the MFF received over $30 million in donations. But only $200,000 had been used to spring rioters from the hoosegow. This, and a reported lack of transparency, has raised questions among the group's critics about how MFF is using the funds. More organizational fog.

And, speaking of funds, up pops our friendly neighborhood socialist philanthropist, the Underboss, again. Breitbart describes MFF's executive director, Tonja Honsey, as a "George Soros acolyte who is also a convicted drug offender." According to Breitbart,[307] Honsey has served time for an arrest at a meth lab bust and also for theft and check forgery. At least no one can say she doesn't have the practical experience to head such a dubious organization.

There is also an odd little dustup by some MFF supporters who assert that Honsey has claimed Native American heritage, Lakota or Ojibwa ancestry, in her efforts to raise funds for MFF. A Facebook page called "Tonja Honsey—Native Rachel Dolezal" makes those allegations and also claims the MFF fired Honsey. The Facebook site[308] alleges that the MFF may have sacked Honsey because she is suing the organization for "reverse racism" because she is white. Ironically, this supposed anti-racism Facebook site makes routine racist comments against white people.

This is yet another example of the Left consuming its own. But at least someone is calling a fake out, even if it is Left of Left. An example of anti-white racist comments at the site is, "That's exactly what we have come to expect from a white person like her, suing an organization that works to bail out the poor and Indigenous, Black [sic], and people of color because she was held accountable for her harm to these same communities. Reverse racism doesn't exist, but racism does. And Tonja Honsey is racist." But *they* are not. Okay.

Well, according to AlphaNewsMn.com,[309] the Open Society Foundation (OSF) named the "racist" Honsey a "George Soros fellow" in 2019. This award comes with it a monetary award of either $94,500 or $127,500, "depending on their level of experience per Open Society Foundation."[310]

Patty McMurray, in an article[311] at the website 100 Percent Fed Up, writes, "MFF has been suspected of harboring Antifa sympathies through its close collaboration with the National Lawyers Guild, a radical leftist organization that has been called Antifa's 'unofficial legal arm.'[312] President Donald Trump's decision to classify Antifa as a domestic terror group could bring federal scrutiny to how MFF is using its money."

Where did MFF get its money? Well, not only from the Underboss. Politicians and celebrities got in on the act, opening their wallets wide to get rioters and looters out of jail. In a website called Bounding into Comics,

Jorge Arenas lists over 40 Hollywood celebrities[313] who have donated to the MFF and BLM. The list includes such political scholars as Steve Carell, Seth Rogan, J.J. Abrams, John Cena, Ryan Reynolds, Chris Evans, Leonardo DiCaprio, and Angelina Jolie.

These folks have obviously fallen for the "cops arrested the *mostly peaceful* protesters" lie. Perhaps they might want to speak with some of the cops that these "mostly peaceful protesters" have pelted, burned, and blinded. Or they could talk to some victims of property damage and looting committed by those they've helped release from jail, who return to commit more destruction and violence. But these celebrities are said to be such good people—much better than people who think different from them.

Even worse, there were some high-profile politicians and/or their staffs who donated to the MFF. CNS News's Craig Bannister reported,[314] "Staff members of Democrat presidential candidate Joe Biden and his running mate, Sen. Kamala Harris (D-Calif.), are supporters of the Minnesota Freedom Fund (MFF), which pays the bail of people arrested in Minneapolis, where riots and looting have devastated local businesses." Also, according[315] to Breitbart, the MFF "received donations from a number of Joe Biden campaign staffers."

This comes as no surprise. Recall that Sen. Harris also told Jacob Blake of Kenosha, an alleged rapist, that she was proud of him. What can anyone do with a statement like that coming from a major party vice presidential candidate? Perhaps California's former top prosecutor should have spoken with Blake's alleged rape victim before praising him.

Bannister notes, from an article[316] in *U.S. News and World Report*, "At least 13 Biden campaign staff members posted on Twitter on Friday and Saturday that they made donations to the Minnesota Freedom Fund." *U.S. News* also reported that Joe Biden's campaign spokesman issued a statement to Reuters that Biden opposes cash bail as a "modern day debtor's prison." *C'mon, man* ... These folks need an American history lesson, badly. Oh, right—they want to destroy America's history.

This is the same banning of cash bail that resulted in New York authorities releasing an MS-13 gang member who was facing federal murder charges. The first paragraph of Rebecca Rosenberg and Bruce Golding's *New York Post* article[317] should make all law-abiding Americans shudder. "[New York] State prison officials put a reputed MS-13 gang member back on the streets—even though the feds wanted him held on a murder charge that carries the death penalty." Normal people don't release people like this back into their communities.

The full range of the gang member's crimes include "racketeering charges that cover six murders, two attempted murders and a kidnapping conspiracy." A spokesman for the Department of Corrections and Community Supervision said, "The agency never received a physical warrant, which it needs to hold Morales-Lopez, so released him to community supervision in accordance with state law."

Is no one responsible? What about the people who passed and implemented these dangerous policies and laws? Gov. Andrew Cuomo supports such laws.[318] Mayor Bill de Blasio supports such laws. Does the buck stop on their desks? Not likely, since they blame President Trump for Cuomo's Covid-19 nursing home catastrophe[319] (which he wrote a book[320] denying) and de Blasio's ruinous NYC lockdowns. So, why would they take blame for this alleged murderer's release?

Which brings the conversation back to the MFF and what kind of creeps are being released in Minneapolis. As reported by[321] Mairead McArdle at *National Review*, the MFF's interim executive director, Greg Lewin, said, "The last time we were down there [jail], the clerk said, 'we hate it when you bail out these sex offenders.'" To which Lewin added this unnerving statement, "I often don't even look at a charge when I bail someone out. I will see it after I pay the bill because it is not the point. The point is the system we are fighting." It's the ol' "ends justify the means"— they don't care who gets hurt, just that they get their way. The victims of those they spring from jail are just necessary collateral damage to advance their ideology.

Chapter 22

Media Matters (for America)

Founded by David Brock, MediaMatters.org (MM) is yet another radical leftist organization that, no surprise, has multiple appendages. According to Influence Watch, the "left-wing group" focuses on media criticism. The group includes Media Matters for America[322] and Media Matters Action Network[323] (there's never just one). Their "donor organizations" are listed as:

1. Bauman Family Foundation (Nonprofit)

2. NEO Philanthropy Action Fund (Nonprofit)

3. NEO Philanthropy (Nonprofit)

4. <u>Sixteen Thirty Fund (1630 Fund) (Nonprofit)</u>

There is also one "vendor," listed as Democracy Corps (Nonprofit).

The organization, ironically, fancies itself a "fact-checker" (isn't that like a burglar considering himself a "security specialist"?). MM criticizes conservative media and calls out "bias and inaccuracies." The problem here is that what it calls "bias and inaccuracies" are often merely points of disagreement. Another issue arises with an organization for which no thinking person could accept its description of itself and its goals as legitimate.

And since we're talking about thinking people, the *American Thinker* published a critical piece in April 2020 slamming "David Brock's loathsome Media Matters," who, apparently, had been "accused of corruption—again." Monica Showalter described[324] Brock as "the freakish little Soros-financed far-left gnome who just can't quit Hillary Clinton, [and] has got his name back into the news again."

MM is also another leftist organization dedicated to advancing "cancel culture." What they call "fact-checking" is what honest people call disagreement. But, to organizations such as MM, disagreements are not allowed. They wish to silence people who disagree with their perspective on, well, everything.

As just one example, MM cancel culture was deployed against a lesser-known conservative online presence, Amber Athey. She wrote[325] in the *Spectator* about anti-Semitic comments made by Rep. Rashida Tlaib (D-MI). So Timothy Johnson, a researcher at MM, pounced. Athey said Johnson smeared her by publicizing "Jewish jokes" that Athey had made on Twitter years ago. This prompted people to call for her "firing and orders that she kill herself." Several bookings she had scheduled were cancelled.

What had she actually done? Long story short: the jokes she'd tweeted that were anti-Semitic were posted when she was seventeen, and they were posted to her *Jewish* boyfriend. She said she and her boyfriend were highlighting "the absurdity of anti-Semitism by googling 'most offensive Jewish jokes' and tweeting the results to each other." Typical teenager stuff. Johnson did not care.

At first, all the negative responses crushed Athey. But then she realized something about outfits like MM. She said that Johnson "didn't care whether or not my tweets revealed hatred for Jewish people." She felt that, if he had cared, he would have contacted her to get the true nature of what had happened before releasing the information. Though she'd deleted those posts a year earlier, she said it appears Johnson kept a screenshot of the posts so he could use them against her at an appropriate time. How creepy is that?

Chapter 23

MoveOn.org

Like Media Matters, MoveOn.org[326] is another of the most infamous leftist, anti-cop, anti-free speech organizations. MoveOn was created to "move on" from the Bill Clinton impeachment disgrace. And, as with so many of these organizations, perhaps even all of them, describing MoveOn begins with noting its appendages—or tentacles. What began as one organization split into two primary organizations for tax purposes. It then further segmented into several subordinate entities. The organization also obscures its operations by having no headquarters, with contributors working from remote locations across the country.

Influence Watch describes MoveOn as jointly operated with MoveOn Political Action,[327] and they are associated with MoveOn Civic Action.[328] Influence Watch points out that MoveOn "describes itself as 'the largest independent, progressive, digitally-connected organizing group in the United States.'"

MoveOn isn't satisfied just going after police departments. It also goes after police unions.[329] Isn't the Left supposed to be all about labor unions? Not if they're comprised of loathsome cops. On a page at its website titled "Police Unions Exposed," MoveOn announced its campaigns to oppose police unions.

In fact, according to MoveOn,[330] "Aurora, Colorado's police force is clearly dangerous." The organization wants Aurora's chief to "follow the lead of the police chief of Minneapolis and refuse to negotiate with police unions over accountability and reform." That's "accountability" and "reform" as the Left describes it. Speaking of which, MoveOn says[331] Lt. Bob Kroll, president of the Minneapolis Police Union, "is violent and a racist." According to MoveOn, "he has to go." MoveOn also supports Minneapolis leftist radicals who demonstrated against Lt. Kroll and his wife *at their home.*

"The head of Buffalo's police union is threatening the city & defending police violence." Oh, the humanity! "Police violence" *again*, eh? Nice touch. Wonder where they came up with that phrase? Oh, according to MoveOn, writing of the Buffalo P.D. union president, "he also has to go." Of course he does. He disagrees with their political views.

Does anyone think any police department or police union in America today would qualify, under the impeccable standards MoveOn must have, for its version of "proper" law enforcement? No.

Chapter 24

Citizen Engagement Laboratory:

The Citizen Engagement Laboratory[332] (CEL) is another 501(c)(3) organizational tree divided into subordinate branches. Influence Watch explains that each branch "operates a distinct role in the umbrella organization" and that the CEL's "primary focus" is "helping clients 'plan, staff, resource, and execute innovative social change projects.'" Aside from its own divisions, CEL further obscures its work with other groups that act "as it's Engagement Consulting Partners":

- America by the Numbers

- Asian Americans Advancing Justice (AAJC)

- CounterPAC

- The Ford Foundation

- The Kapor Center for Social Impact

- Open Society Foundations

- The Years Project (Years of Living Dangerously)

In addition, CEL lists even more groups described as its "Acceleration Services Partners":

- Arts in a Changing America

- Climate Parents (a project of the Sierra Club Foundation)

- Climate Relief Fund (formerly named Forecast the Facts)

- Colibri Center

- CultureStrike

- Demand Progress

- Faces of Fracking

- Faithful America (Christians who reject Amy Coney Barret's nomination—*really?*)

- Latino Startup Alliance

- MPower Change

- Open Summit

- Presente

- Stellar

- Transform Finance

- Ultraviolet

The Capital Research Center describes[333] the CEL as "a well-funded beehive of progressive advocacy that uses foundation money to fight for left-progressive causes. It is also an incubator of nascent left-wing groups that it creates and assists to carry the radical agenda forward." As with Color of Change, the ALEC "is a favorite target" of the CEL, too.

Not surprisingly, Capital Research lists among CEL's funding sources "George Soros's Open Society Foundations," which donated over a million dollars since 2012. Former Democratic presidential candidate, leftist billionaire, and part-time presidential candidate Tom Steyer also donated $100,000 to CEL. The group lists as one of its board members Vanessa Fajans-Turner, who has been "involved in Barack Obama's presidential campaigns."

Chapter 25

Indivisible (and ACORN)

The Indivisible movement minces no words about its feeling for President Trump, whose election, according[334] to Influence Watch, provoked the creation of the organization. "BEAT TRUMP & SAVE DEMOCRACY," greets their homepage. It's followed up with the moderate declaration, "Trump is an abomination. Our democracy is under threat. We're fighting back. People like you are leading local Indivisible groups in every single state. Be part of history—join the Indivisible movement." The projection is astounding, once again claiming others are doing to them what they are doing to others.

Indivisible "was founded by two left-wing activists with congressional experience and ties to the left-of-center economic policy advocacy group Prosperity Now" (formerly the Corporation for Enterprise Development, or CFED[335]). Prosperity Now advocates against "wealth inequality." It's delusional to believe there will be wealth equality under socialism. In every national socialist attempt in history, the middle class becomes poor, and the poor become poorer. Only the leaders—the elites in the movement—will become or remain wealthy.

This also reminds us of another obfuscation tactic: *change the organization's name.* The most infamous of the Boss's community organizing groups was the Association of Community Organizers for Reform Now (ACORN). After getting slapped down for massive voter registration fraud[336] (well, *massive* before the 2020 national elections) and other corruption charges, according to Judicial Watch (JW), the organization, which changed its name and splintered in 2010, is still alive and well. Judicial Watch has reported that "ACORN affiliates from coast-to-coast—including New York and California—have broken away and changed their names in order to dump the group's crooked reputation."

JW, which "has extensively investigated ACORN," notes the organization's "strong ties to Obama." At the link immediately above, JW provides public records detailing the "ACORN scandals." As JW puts it, "A mere name change can't possibly erase the history." In fact, JW expands on the corruption, which is remarkably similar to how so many of these organizations operate:

> The nonprofit's history of fraud and corruption led to a congressional investigation that determined the community group is a criminal enterprise. A lengthy report published by the House Committee on Government Reform reveals that ACORN has repeatedly and deliberately engaged in systematic fraud and that the group hides behind a paper wall of nonprofit corporate protections to conceal a criminal conspiracy by its directors, to launder federal money in order to pursue a partisan political agenda and to manipulate the American electorate.

Wow, that's a little on the nose, isn't it?

Once again, just look at what Indivisible is accusing conservatives of doing, and you'll know precisely what they are up to. They have no interest in democracy—not if it's attached to a republic. They are interested in obtaining and retaining immense, single-party political power. Indivisible's primary mission seems to be community organizing nationally but focusing on the local level. They claim to be active in all 50 states. They even describe activities to build "rural and red state progressive power." Their reported support comes from the Underboss through—where else?—the Tides Foundation.

Chapter 26

Transition Integrity Project

O ne of the most recent groups created by the usual leftist "suspects" is the Transition Integrity Project[337] (TIP). The founders claim the TIP was created to avoid chaos during the next presidential transition if Joe Biden were elected. After digging into its goals, the TIP wants anything but integrity in our next national election.[338] TIP was cofounded by Professor Rosa Brooks[339] (who "suggested [a] military coup against Trump days after [the] inauguration"). The group's other cofounder, Nils Gilman, is even worse. According[340] to the National Pulse, Gilman called "for EXECUTION of [a] former Trump official."

Why death? Because death is the ultimate "cancellation" in "cancel culture," isn't it? Gilman was upset with Michael Anton, a former National Security Official in the Trump administration, because Anton wrote about TIP's "efforts to steal the 2020 election and secure victory for Democratic presidential candidate Joe Biden." A prescient statement and an allegation of theft for which there is a flood of evidence coming to light every day. To paraphrase what Irishman ("It's *my* island") Stephen said to William Wallace in the movie *Brave Heart*, "[They're] not right—*in the head*."

Well, shouldn't both Gilman and Brooks know that some people just don't like it when other people steal elections from their candidate, as they're now finding out? In creating this organization with the most ironic of names, they have engraved in their behavior the adage so often repeated: they do what they accuse others of doing.

It was the epitome of cynicism to choose the name "Transition Integrity Project" to represent the group's ostensible concern with a peaceful transition of power from the current president to a newly elected president. That's because, for TIP, integrity doesn't matter. The mission is a transition to a new president whether or not their candidate wins. Recall that in September 2020, Hillary Clinton advised[341] Joe Biden that he "should not concede under any circumstances." This means even if he loses, right?

Clinton, also warned, ironically, "We have to have our own teams of people to counter the force of intimidation that [our opponents] are going to put outside polling places." After the leftist violence the nation has experienced this year, isn't the Left's warning about right-wing intimidation and violence absurd? More transference and projection. Have you turned on a TV lately? It's clear that 99.9 percent of the violence comes from the Left.

The TIP had the temerity to "wargame" the aftermath of the presidential elections. Judicial Watch published the "Executive Summary[342]" of TIP participants' leftist partisan political playdate. It sounds silly, yes, but they are serious about this mission to eject the current president from the presidency—somehow. Even the title of an article[343] by the *New Republic's* Osita Nwanevu called the war-gaming "ridiculous." The *New Republic's* subtitle reads, "Trump's opponents are so concerned that he might steal the election that they have forgotten to worry that he might simply win it."

Once again, the Left asserts it is worried about Trump "stealing" the election. Interesting, since they've apparently been trying to steal or overturn the last election for the past four years. So far, it hasn't yet been proven in court such a level of civil and/or criminal fraud could happen in a presidential election, but that proof is being uncovered at a rapid pace. The Boss said he didn't believe it could be done. But that doesn't mean they didn't try. When distilled to only having to affect certain counties in a handful of swing states, it doesn't seem as daunting. The Boss seems to believe that if the Democrats can get the presidency back, he'll once again have his hands on the levers of power to reclaim his "legacy" and finish destroying law enforcement.

The incestuous relations continue with the TIP's associations. A story that appeared[344] at the *Republic Post Informer* (TRPI), informs that the TIP's "founder dined with the Underboss and Biden Campaign advisors, [and] offered 'substantive help.'" The connections proliferate from there. TRPI writes, "In a damning blow to the Transition Integrity Project's facade of bipartisanship and neutrality, an unearthed email[345] reveals founder Rosa Brooks's close ties to globalist mega donor George Soros, Hillary Clinton Campaign Chairman John Podesta, and former National Security Adviser to Joe Biden Jake Sullivan."

TRP reports TIP's founders' "deep ties to Biden-linked, Democratic Party heavyweights." TRP links them when Rosa Brooks emailed John "Podesta, President Bill Clinton's Deputy Chief of Staff, Counselor to Barack Obama, and Chairman of Hillary Clinton's 2016 presidential campaign, a message entitled 'Following up on conversation at the Soros dinner.' Another recipient of the email, also mentioned in the text itself, is Jake Sullivan,[346] a former National Security Advisor to Joe Biden and Deputy Chief of Staff to Secretary of State Hillary Clinton."

The Gateway Pundit also published an article,[347] "NO SURPRISE: The Transition 'Integrity' Project Is Working to Remove President Trump from Office No Matter What—Has Connections to China, Soros, Obama and Hunter Biden," showing the TIP's connections to the usual socialist suspects.

Joe Hoft also writes, "The Transition Integrity Project—the antithesis of integrity—is building up an army of Trump and America haters in an effort to remove President Trump from office no matter what. The far left and Never-Trump group has connections to China, Obama, Soros and Hunter Biden, and yet it claims it is full of integrity and is non-biased." Once again, the reporting continues to show the Boss is never far away from those acting to remove President Trump from power. In order to continue his anti–law and order agenda, he must end Trump's presidency.

And, in order to end Trump's presidency, he needs to damage or destroy traditional law enforcement.

The TIP also shows that these ideologues intend to set up a situation that increases the divisions among Americans and the likelihood—or even certainty—of violence regardless of who wins. This is violence that police officers across the nation will have to deal with on the front lines. More people will be injured and killed, including cops. Guess that's just the price the leftist radicals will have to pay, right?

Despite its ill-fitting name, the TIP has no interest in the integrity of this or any presidential transition. Honest elections just impede the maintaining of political power, don't they? Frustrating, right? Otherwise, two things would not have happened: one, the conscription of an army of lawyers,[348] numbering in the hundreds, which President Trump must match. And two, again, Hillary Clinton's warning Biden not to "concede the election under any circumstances." They're trying to convince the public that even if Trump wins in a landslide on election night (which legitimate evidence shows may have actually happened), the uncounted mail-in ballots will turn the tide in favor of Biden. They could only know that if they have a plan to make that happen. And there is an abundance of evidence that this has happened.

Chapter 27

The Revolution Playbook

The Revolution Playbook[349] is one of the insurrectionists' blueprints for cultural revolution. As mentioned previously, Glenn Beck has done some of the best investigative reporting[350] on this subject, depicting what the radicals are doing as "color revolutions."[351] These are the street uprisings in various parts of the world such as Georgia's Rose Revolution, the Orange Revolution in Ukraine, and Kyrgyzstan's Tulip Revolution. The Russians also had one of these, the White Revolution, which failed.

Linda Goudsmit at the *Independent Sentinel* describes[352] the phenomenon: "A color revolution is a known tactical CIA operation that uses a seemingly spontaneous act as the precipitating event to destabilize a country and effect regime change. The color revolution is what is happening in America, and its front-line soldiers are Antifa and Black Lives Matter (BLM)."

More can be found about color revolutions, specifically America's nascent one, by reading "America's Own Color Revolution" at geopolitics. co.[353] Goudsmit says this article explains how "hundreds of thousands of young Americans are being used as a battering ram to not only topple a U.S. President but in the process, the very structures of the U.S. Constitutional order." This revolution obviously includes annihilating traditional law enforcement.

Today, folks like Beck and Goudsmit are concerned about a color revolution in the streets of America. An appropriate selection of color for America's revolution might be red, considering the socialism and even Marxism being violently finagled on America. Beck cites the Boss's ambassador to Russia Michael McFaul's "7 Pillars of a Color Revolution." McFaul says these were the steps necessary to foment revolution in Eastern Europe. Beck believes many of these steps are in place in the United States today for its own color revolution.

1. Semiautocratic regime (not fully autocratic)—provides opportunity to call incumbent leader "fascist"

2. Appearance of unpopular president or incumbent leader

3. United and organized opposition—Antifa, BLM

4. Effective system to convince the public (well before the election) of voter fraud

5. 5Compliant media to push voter fraud narrative

6. Political opposition organization able to mobilize "thousands to millions in the streets"

7. Division among military and *police* [emphasis mine]

It's hard to argue Beck isn't right about many of these factors existing in the United States today. Add to this the many polls showing the candidate with the least overt support (attracting only dozens or fewer people compared to thousands or even millions[354] at rallies) is leading in the polls by huge amounts, and it sets people up to feel the election was stolen if their candidate loses the election.

This happened in 2016 where the candidate ahead in the polls by huge margins, Secretary Hillary Clinton, lost the election. This set up public support for what turned out to be bogus claims about President Trump's supposed connections to the Russian president. And this caused partisans to accuse President Trump of "Russia collusion" and "stealing the election."

There is ample evidence of an attempt to actually steal an elections in 2020, as a massive election fraud seems to have occurred, making the results of the election implausible if not impossible. A staggering statistical analysis [355] comes from University of Southern California Economics Professor Charles J. Cicchetti, Ph.D. Professor Cicchetti calculated VP Biden's odds of winning Pennsylvania, Michigan, Wisconsin, and Georgia independently, as of 3 a.m. on Nov. 4, 2020, was "less one in a quadrillion (that is 1,000 trillions). The professor further said the odds of Biden winning all four states collectively was one in a quadrillion to the 4th power $(1,000,000,000,000,000^4)$.

Texas AG Ken Paxton included Cicchetti's results in a lawsuit Texas filed, "asking the U.S. Supreme Court to block four battle ground states (listed above) from casting 'unlawful and constitutionally tainted votes' in the Electoral College." The ultimate results of this election weighed on America's waited with proverbial bated breath to either celebrate a pro-police Trump victory or lament an anti-cop Biden taking the office.

Back to the color revolutions. For the purposes of this book, concern about step number seven is obvious. While the rank-and-file in the military and law enforcement is cohesive, with strong support for traditional America, there is evidence of division between the upper and lower ranks.

The president has repeatedly pointed this division out. In September 2020, Trump said,[356] "I'm not saying the military is in love with me, the soldiers are. The top people in the Pentagon probably aren't." But, without division among the troops, for instance, one unit against another over support over political candidates, a revolution in the streets is not likely to find ultimate success. Ultimately, any coup would need the support of the military.

It's similar with law enforcement agencies. The divisions in policing are usually found between the rank-and-file officers and the command staff. Similarly, the higher the rank, the more likely the difference in political views. Rank-and-file cops tend to be conservative and libertarian. They support the Constitution, traditional America, and the commitment to law and order and equal justice. Too many police chiefs and, to a lesser degree, sheriffs, align politically with the radical left.

Again, the division between ranks is not as pronounced with sheriff's departments. This is primarily because most sheriffs are elected by the people in their communities. Most county jurisdictions also include more rural areas, where voters tend to be conservative. Many police chiefs, whose departments are in more urban areas, are appointed by mayors. So, while political divisions exist between police chiefs, many of whom are selected by leftist politicians, and their officers, these divisions are not as pronounced between elected sheriffs and their deputies.

Aside from McFaul, another connection to the Boss is his poorly titled "ethics czar," Norm Eisen. Eisen was also the Boss's ambassador to the Czech Republic. Now, why are we talking about an official ostensibly concerned with presidential ethics in a segment on fomenting color revolutions in America? Because, as with so many others in this book, connections between the Boss and those involved in anti-traditional America and anti-cop efforts keep popping up.

At the website Ron Paul Forums: Liberty Forest, there is a piece entitled[357] "Norm Eisen: Central Operative in the 'Color Revolution' in the U.S." The subtitle reads: "Meet Norm Eisen: Legal Hatchet Man and Central Operative in the 'Color Revolution' against President Trump." Weird, eh? Probably just a coincidence, right?

Norm Eisen is also involved in the TIP. Again, imagine that. Eisen's single mission on earth seems to be to get rid of Donald Trump by almost any means, including aiding the Boss in what evidence is increasingly showing was or is a coup attempt. More on this contention can be found at Revolver News.[358]

Eisen has a book out titled *A Case for the American People: The United States v. Donald J. Trump.* He writes about the impeachment process and, likely reluctantly—even *sadly*—about Trump's acquittal. As reported[359] by NPR, "the book reveals that Eisen had drafted 10 articles of impeachment a month before Pelosi's announcement" of the impeachment effort. Why wait for facts or actual evidence of wrongdoing? Don't think President

Trump's support for law enforcement isn't a significant reason the Left wants to remove him from office. They know that they can't accomplish their socialist goals as long as there is a strong, robust American police force, and that's exactly what America needs and the Boss wants to destroy.

Chapter 28

Cops Killing Black Men Myth

Speaking of anti-police myths, it's time to revisit this ubiquitous fairy tale that continues to proliferate even though it has been debunked repeatedly. The talk among anti-cop activists takes a two-track approach: One, that cops routinely hunt and kill black men. Two, that cops prefer to hunt and kill "unarmed" black men. To the former, as mentioned early on, American police officers kill about one thousand criminal suspects per year. Nearly every one of these suspects is violent, armed, and trying to kill the cops who shoot them.

In 2019, of the suspects police shot and killed, 235 were black. Even when carving out the number of *unarmed* black people cops killed, the number is extremely low. Tucker Carlson on his Fox News Channel show cited[360] the *Washington Post's* report that police shot just nine "unarmed" black suspects (officers also shot nineteen "unarmed" white suspects). Even then, two of the nine "unarmed" black suspects tried to run over cops with their cars, another was armed with a taser, and a fourth had a gun (but was a true tragedy).

So, at least four of the nine "unarmed" people shot by police were not unarmed. One suspect shot a taser at an officer before the officer shot and killed him. Two of the "unarmed" suspects tried to rundown officers with vehicles. In the only apparent true tragedy,[361] a woman homeowner had a gun in her hand, inside her house, when the officer shot her.

Here, it appears, while babysitting her nephew, Atatiana Koquice Jefferson noticed something suspicious outside her house. Having a duty to protect herself and her nephew, she rightly armed herself with a handgun and went to the window to see if someone was outside. The officer contends that after finding a door standing open and not seeing or hearing anyone inside, he checked the outside of the house. While checking, he saw a person through a window, holding a gun, and he fired. Reportedly, the officer then went inside the house and gave medical aid while waiting for medics.

Unfortunately, much of the news reporting decries another black person shot by a white police officer, automatically injecting race into an incident where no evidence of racism exists. Reportedly, the officer "opened fire into what looks like a dark room." No one but the officer who shot Jefferson knows what he perceived while shining a flashlight into a dark room or why he fired. His perception is objectively important. To believe that the officer saw that she was black, and that's why he fired, strains credulity. It insults the humanity that the vast majority of police officers possess. It's dangerous, lazy thinking. It's daunting that the people who turn these tragic events into racist incidents do so absent evidence or investigation. Prosecutors charged the officer with murder.

Organizations like the Obama Foundation, other so-called civil rights groups and attorneys,[362] and even pro sports franchises, management, and athletes continue to promote the "genocide" myth. Here's the formula: a police shooting occurs, and the person shot is black and the officer white (although that's no longer a requirement for radicals to riot; cops of any race will do).

Then activists prematurely knee-jerk the situation and scream "police brutality" and "genocide." Later, in almost every instance, information shows that the person the police shot was committing a crime and posed a danger to the officer. But by then, the damage is done. The anti-police headlines have done their job to sway a public who sees only "yet another black person shot by police." Then, the next time a police officer shoots *any* black suspect, regardless of circumstances, the formula begins again. This creates the illusion of cops shooting "innocent" black people at a high rate.

Again, what happened with Jacob Blake in August 2020 illustrates this blueprint. According to initial reports, an "unarmed" Blake was attempting to de-escalate an argument when police shot him. It's only later the public learned Blake had an arrest warrant, assaulted the officers, had a history of alleged domestic violence, gun crimes, and sex offenses—oh, and he was *armed with a knife*. How is that known? Blake admitted it to investigators.[363] Yet, Democratic presidential and vice presidential candidates Joe Biden and Kamala Harris treated Blake like a hero-victim. Why didn't they visit Blake's alleged rape victim, or the two L.A. County sheriff's deputies ambushed and shot in the head? After all, California, not Wisconsin, is Harris's home state.

Back to the formula: On September 2, 2020, police in Washington, DC, shoot an 18-year-old[364] "unarmed" black man. At least, those are the initial reports. Angry crowds gather around a police precinct to make speeches about how cops "keep killing unarmed black men." Then, police release the video of the suspect clearly armed with a handgun when police shot him. But it doesn't matter. To further the myth, cop-haters use incidents in which the suspects were armed and not complying with lawful police orders when officers shot them. The truth is always the real casualty.

So-called civil rights attorney Benjamin Crump, who is representing George Floyd's family (and those of other "victims") in their lawsuits, endorses the lie that American police officers are conducting a black "genocide." He stomps on the grave of every soul who was a victim of true genocide.

Considering all this, it's no surprise to discover an association between Mr. Crump and the Boss. An article from June 3, 2020, at the website the Conservative Tree House, informs:[365] "Tonight at 5:00 p.m., former President Barack Obama will deliver remarks[366] about race and social justice during a virtual town-hall sponsored by his 'my brother's keeper' initiative. Simultaneous to that announcement, George Floyd family attorney, Benjamin Crump, delivers remarks[367] from Minneapolis about healing, race and social justice. To assist the sympathetic narrative Ben Crump introduces George Floyd's son, Quincy Mason."

Simply put, there is zero evidence that police officers are engaged in a "genocide" against black people. Cop-haters spout off as if a majority of the people shot and killed by police officers annually are innocent victims of "police violence." No, 99.9 percent of suspects were trying to severely injure or kill the cops who shot them. Cop-critics seem to believe if the police kill a thousand criminals, then criminals should get to kill a thousand cops. As if it's supposed to be a fair fight.

Look at who the Left tends to choose for their hero-victims. Even George Floyd, whose death disturbed so many Americans regardless of politics, was no hero. Just ask the Texas woman into whose pregnant belly Floyd pressed his pistol and whom one of Floyd's accomplices pistol-whipped. Also consider that Floyd reportedly[368] died of a heart attack and had enough Fentanyl in his system that, in the medical examiner's initial reports, investigators wondered how the man was still alive to even have a confrontation with police.

The point is: Why do the perpetuators of police lies so rarely find a totally innocent person, whom police had actually wrongly shot, to hold up as a hero? Even in Breonna Taylor's situation, evidence allegedly showed her boyfriend, Kenneth Walker, was receiving drug packages in the mail at Taylor's address.[369] And police recovered a dead body[370] from a car rented by Taylor that her boyfriend used. Dead bodies in trunks don't happen every day (well, outside of New Jersey).

Chapter 29

Demilitarization

Another Obama Foundation line of attack is for so-called police "demilitarization." It usually means depriving police departments of "military-style" weapons, equipment, and armored vehicles. Often, these come as donations from U.S. military surplus.

"Military-style" equipment serves as an insurance policy for when an extraordinary crime, accident, or a natural disaster occurs that needs exceptional response capabilities. Recall the North Hollywood bank robbery shootout alluded to earlier. This incident was explored in my book *De-Policing America: A Street-Cop's View of the Anti-Police State*, which recounts: "Remember the North Hollywood, California shootout[371] in 1997? Bank robbers donned body armor and shot at police with automatic weapons. During a nearly forty-five-minute gun battle, the duo had cops outgunned, firing over 1,100 rounds. These guys avoided or absorbed the cops' bullets and kept coming. Talk about fighting zombies. This was a horror movie come to life for responding officers." To reiterate, the LAPD could have used a healthy dose of militarization that day.

The armored vehicle has also proven its worth in civilian and officer rescues not only at crime scenes but, as mentioned earlier, also during natural disasters. And, as also noted in *De-Policing America*, "In 2014, Alton Nolen, a knife-wielding Islamic terrorist, decapitated a woman[372] at the Vaughan Food distribution center in Moore, Oklahoma. Another employee, an armed—*militarized*—off-duty reserved deputy sheriff, retrieved his rifle and shot the terrorist before he could injure or kill anyone else. Good guys with guns stop bad guys with guns."

The opposition to "militarization" seems to be based mostly on feelings and aesthetics. Opponents don't like what cops using surplus military equipment look like. However, it is not the "look" that police are after. It's the effectiveness of the equipment. People who focus on form rather than function are not operating in the real world. They would risk police officers' lives because of an "appearance" they don't like.

Back in the late 1990s and early 2000s, the Seattle Police Department had its officers change their riot helmet cover three times because of the "appearance." The first one was dark blue, then it went to black to match the color of the new "riot" uniforms. Then someone decided that black was too intimidating (for a helmet cover) and changed the helmet cover color once more, this time to a "United Nations" baby blue. What can be said about leaders who, when people are rioting, are more worried about the color of a helmet cover than about the violence?

Chapter 30

Warrior vs. Guardian

Another wedge MBKAP types are driving between communities and cops is the manufactured debate between viewing officers as warriors vs. guardians. They can be both, can't they? But leading this debate pops up one of the Obama Foundation's staunchest supporters, the thoroughly ineffectual Jacob Frey, mayor of Minneapolis. Tracing the rioting back to the beginning, much of the conflagration consuming so many American cities could have been prevented had one man, Mayor Frey, quelled the riots in his city. Instead, he and his city's police-abolishing politburo (city council) encouraged the rioters, looters, and insurgents. They even lost a police precinct, which likely set up Seattle to lose one of their precincts.

The mayor has inserted into this false narrative by his language,[373] regarding banning "warrior training" for the city's cops. This betrays Frey's contempt for police officers. Ignorantly, Frey contends, "Fear-based trainings violate the values at the heart of community policing." Once again, a politician changes the definition of something and then attacks the fraud he created. How convenient is that?

According to Danny Spewak at KARE11, Police Officers Federation of Minneapolis president Lt. Bob Kroll "said Mayor Frey misrepresented the training." Lt. Kroll stated, "I think the mayor needs to take a more in-depth look at what this training is. It's not truly 'fear-based' training. I think it would be beneficial for him to sit in on one of these trainings. It's survival training." Frey didn't. Being fully informed may have forced him to make a good decision for a change.

That cops are both guardians *and* warriors should be obvious. As guardians is how officers approach the job, and as warriors is how cops prepare themselves to survive on the job. When someone is outside a home at 3 a.m., pounding on the door, the locks about to give way, the children upstairs in bed, wouldn't any homeowner want the guardian who shows up to be a warrior?

Chapter 31

Refusing to Prosecute Criminals Who Resist or Hurt Cops

Recently, the legislature in the Commonwealth of Virginia, having made a sharp left turn, is proposing reducing from felonies to misdemeanors[374] some assaults against police officers. Now, without going into too much detail, it seems some politicians care more about the suspects than the officers. When wishing to reduce instances of a bad behavior, should lawmakers increase or decrease the consequences for it? This is not a trick question.

Sadly, Virginia is not the only place this is happening. Up north, in a fellow commonwealth, a Massachusetts district attorney, one of the Boss's capos mentioned earlier, is Rachael Rollins. One of those crimes DA Rollins promised not to prosecute is resisting arrest, which shows tremendous disrespect for cops.

DA Rollins is so anti-police that she has published[375] a list of 136 cops, current and former, whose credibility she believes is "questionable." Of these, fifty-four are Boston police officers and seventy are Massachusetts State troopers. She'd have people believe this "living list," which she says she will add to (she didn't mention *delete from*) when necessary, is an effort toward transparency. However, DA Rollins's commitment not to enforce the law makes any explanation she offers automatically suspect.

Unfortunately, in many jurisdictions across the country, state and municipal prosecutors (Underboss-supported and others who just have an affinity for *Spooky Dude*) have decided that certain people committing certain crimes are immune from prosecution. This has been demonstrated recently with a plethora of prosecutors refusing to charge or dropping charges against people for looting and rioting in America's cities.

Remember the example in Contra Costa County, California, where a DA (Underboss-funded) refuses to charge looters until it is determined whether the looter "needed" the stolen item(s)?

Though some think it's new, this assault against equal justice has been going on for many years. For example, Seattle city attorney Pete Holmes is an Obama Foundation kindred spirit. He's another prosecutor who'd never prosecuted a criminal before being elected to office. (Seattle has shown that competence is not a prerequisite to serving in political office.) He has replaced equal justice with social justice for roughly the last decade.

For example, during the past ten years, this prosecutor has enforced the traffic crime of driving with license suspended in the third degree (DWLS3) by determining whether the defendant "merits punishment"[376] based on social justice criteria. So, if the driver is poor or of the "right" race or ethnicity, the prosecutor will not prosecute. Also, any other citations that were issued related to the stop are often also dismissed. Holmes said this was more a debt collection than a public safety issue. But is that true, or is it just more obfuscation from anti–law and order folks?

Holmes makes this contention because DWLS3 status is normally issued to drivers who fail to pay a traffic tickets. However, regarding public safety, those other associated tickets are often moving violations that officers issue to enhance public safety by discouraging dangerous driving. Also, for a police officer to determine a person's driving status, an officer must have stopped that driver again. Most often these stops involve a moving violation: red light, stop sign, speeding, failing to yield to a pedestrian in a crosswalk, and so on, which are all public-safety related offenses, not debt collection.

Holmes also won't enforce "civility" crimes against "homeless" people. In 2013, Police Chief Jim Pugel sent Holmes a packet containing the cases[377] of twenty-eight chronic street criminals terrorizing downtown Seattle. Holmes declined to prosecute any of them until the police determined if any of them needed social services. How are police officers supposed to deal with an equal justice system when it's been usurped and replaced with a leftist-defined social justice system? And these are just a few out of so many unethical so-called prosecutors.

Chapter 32

Taking Away Mass Demonstration Tools

In the wake of the George Floyd–sparked demonstrations and riots, many political leaders, like Portland Mayor Ted Wheeler, made the monumentally stupid decision to ban their police departments from using less-than-lethal crowd-control tools, such as tear gas, pepper spray, and pepper balls—tools necessary to manage riots. Wheeler even banned the use of "loud warning sounds"[378] (also known as sonic warning tones[379]) to alert people in crowds that the police have declared a riot. Sadly, in Wheeler's case in Portland, the second worst mayor in America is also the police commissioner.

These politicians intentionally place police in harm's way when they take away their tools to protect themselves. But, as with militarization, many political leaders don't like the "optics." Ironically, professionals developed these tools so officers would not be forced to use impact weapons or firearms on rioters.

Left only with batons and guns, police chiefs, such as Seattle's Carmen Best, warned[380] their cities' politicians and public that they would not deploy their officers into situations where they could not protect themselves.

Since city officials had banned less-lethal crowd-control tools, officers would be forced to use batons, which would cause more injuries and place officers in closer proximity to violent rioters. Lethal force was not an option, so city officials rendered the police inert to the point their chief could not morally or ethically deploy them. As mentioned above, Portland officials made similar decisions about police crowd-control tools, which ignited, at the time of this writing, over 140 consecutive days of rioting.

A court issued a temporary injunction banning police from targeting "journalists and legal observers"[381] during riots. Somehow, cops must distinguish, under riot conditions, legitimate "non-combatants" from violent rioters. This is impossible. The Feds are trying to get it thrown out.[382]

NPA prepared and submitted an amicus brief to support Portland police officers accused of "targeting" press and legal observers during riots. There have been many incidents where people wearing "journalist" or "legal observer" markings were participating in the violence or otherwise supporting rioters. Who didn't see that one coming?

Don't forget about late August 2020, when a BLM-supporting, Antifa radical allegedly murdered a Patriot Prayer member, shooting him from close distance on a Portland street. Was this finally enough for Ted Wheeler to finally act to stop the mayhem? No. Then again, a person he agrees with had shot a person he doesn't agree with, so ... no harm (to the leftist) no foul, right?

Aside from crowd-control tools and techniques, politicians have also taken away effective techniques officers rely on for their safety. It's easy to tell when a politician is on a vote-getting mission rather than a true public safety one. They conflate terminologies to confuse the issue—or maybe they're just stupid and don't know the difference.

This is the case with the rabid discussion of "chokeholds" that occurred after the Floyd incident, even though a chokehold wasn't used. Often, the uninformed confuse "chokeholds," neck holds that constrict a person's airway and could cause asphyxiation, with "sleeper holds" (carotid artery compression), which normally result in restricted blood flow and eventually unconsciousness. Many departments banned the technique, absent deadly force circumstances, after a few rare deaths occurred. Regardless, agencies have always allowed chokeholds as lethal force for when an officer's life is at risk—for example, wrestling with a suspect trying to grab an officer's gun.

Regardless, officer safety should not be a political consensus issue. It should be a force science issue, allowing the reasonable, necessary, and most effective techniques that facilitate officer safety.

Chapter 33

No Cash Bail

Another Obama Foundation–supported concept is "no cash bail." [383] Courts impose cash bail to assure a defendant will appear for a future court date. Opponents of cash bail feel this is unfair to poor defendants, so they want to eliminate it. The problem comes with some judges, using only the defendant's "threat posed to public" parameter for release, who are routinely releasing criminal defendants on their own recognizance.

This means many suspects whom police arrest even for serious crimes are often allowed back on the streets without having to put up a cash bond or having their threat to the public given sufficient consideration. For example, in New York City, robbery and shooting suspects have been released who immediately went out and committed more crimes. In one case, the city released a bank robber, and he went right out and robbed another bank.

In another case, an attempted murder suspect was released with no bail. [384] He used his freedom to commit three more shootings. According to John Boch writing at the website the Truth about Guns, as republished at Concealed Nation, "Remember when New York State Democrats said that their new 'no cash bail' law would not apply to violent crimes? Someone in the city's creaking criminal justice system didn't get the memo."

Proponents argue that cash bail discriminates against poor people. This might be a discussion worth having, but is it right to use a community as a criminal "social" justice laboratory? Real people are getting hurt when violent people are let out of jail without the constrictions of bail. This also gives criminals license to commit mayhem, especially the rioters.

Another unconscionable result of the alliance between the anti-cop radicals, anti-cop media, and anti-cop politicians is the normalizing of killing or attempting to kill police officers. As previously mentioned, some lowlife ambushed[385] and shot two L.A. sheriff's deputies. Bystanders were captured on video laughing, and no one rendered any assistance to the severely wounded cops. In Louisville, another vermin shot two more[386] officers during rioting. An Antifa rioter threw Molotov cocktails[387] at Portland cops. And some scum also hurled Molotov cocktails at officers during an attack on the Seattle Police Officers Guild office.

More recently, a black-clad rioter ran up behind a Seattle bike officer and bashed him in the head[388] with a metal baseball bat. Fortunately, police have a suspect in custody for that crime. That person is apparently also a suspect in an arson committed against the Seattle Police Department's besieged East Precinct.

There have been other attacks on police officers. No American can forget the heinous BLM supporter who, in 2016, shot and killed five Dallas police officers[389] who were, ironically, protecting a peaceful BLM demonstration. And, back to this year's violence, there was the radical that walked up behind a Las Vegas officer early in the "Floyd" riots and shot him in the head.[390]

And, though retired and not officially working as a cop, his cop instincts had retired St. Louis Police Department Captain David Dorn risking danger to help a friend protect his store during the riots. A thug looting his friend's shop callously shot Captain Dorn and watched him die on the sidewalk. Then, just as callously, the so-called Black Lives Matter movement cast the killing of the retired cop aside like so much refuse. Captain Dorn's black life didn't seem to matter at all—to BLM.

Each of these events was off the front pages before the ink dried. The media are not interested in violence against the police, only in supposed police violence against the community. Cops as victims of violent criminals just doesn't fit their narrative. They also seem to believe that the violence against the cops is justified retribution. Similar to people who claim looting is a form of "reparation," some warped people see shooting cops as a form of justice.

And what happens while these selfish political agitators are diverting police resources? The people they claim to want to help—the people of color, the poor—are left without police protection. This results in increased victimhood, not decreased. How does this improve people's quality of life? BLM and Antifa can peddle the lie that police prey on their communities, but that doesn't change that the opposite is true.

Chapter 34

Soldiers—Anarcho-Communist Radicals—Professional Sports Athletes and Leagues—Hollywood and Entertainment Media

The obvious source of the gang's "soldiers" who do the "whacking," when necessary, for the Boss are BLM, Antifa, and other affiliated and like-minded radical, anti-cop groups. After all, they conscript many of their members from criminal gangs,[391] criminal illegal aliens, and the violently mentally ill.[392]

The category of "soldiers" can be loosely divided into four corps.

- First there are the actual "soldiers" by definition. These are the ones who carry out the actual organized, targeted violence. They represent two factions: opportunists and organized. The opportunists add to the mayhem and destruction but for personal gain. They may or may not believe in or even care about the "cause." The organized are those directly align with BLM and Antifa. These are true anarcho-Marxist insurrectionists who fight for the overthrow of the U.S. government.

- There are the truly peaceful protesters who aren't violent and don't protect those who become violent.

- Next, there are those who are not violent but who implicitly or explicitly provide cover for the violent rioters and looters.

- The last faction includes people the most removed from the streets. They are the Hollywood stars, professional athletes, and corporate celebrity CEOS who are deployed, often on social media, to influence and encourage other "soldiers" toward leftist activism at all levels.

Regarding the professional athletes, here is an example. The NFL has thrown in fully with the Marxist, anti-police BLM. To express the NFL's devotion, they are allowing players to place decals with the names of "police shooting victims" on their helmets.

This didn't work out too well for at least one Pittsburgh Steelers player. As the website the *Federalist Papers* reported,[393] Maurkice Pouncey had been wearing the name of Antwon Rose Jr. on his helmet before he "realized he'd made a mistake."

A police officer shot and killed the seventeen-year-old Rose during a traffic stop related to a drive-by shooting that had just occurred, and that Rose was suspected of having participated in. The *Pittsburgh Post-Gazette* reported[394] that the victim of the drive-by shooting told police Rose had shot him. Though the defense contests that assertion, investigators allegedly found gunshot residue on Rose's hand and found two guns under the front passenger's seat where Rose had been reportedly sitting.

The *New York Daily News* reported[395] on the controversial shooting. While there are some questions about the officer's actions, Rose was not a good guy. During the traffic stop, Rose ran. The officer said Rose was holding something in his hand, but he didn't know what it was. That's when he fired, hitting Rose three times.

Investigators determined Rose was not armed when he was shot, but police found the two previously mentioned guns in the car he was in, and the officer was investigating a drive-by shooting that had just occurred. Officers can't afford to wait to "be sure" the unknown item a noncompliant suspect won't drop is not a gun.

Pouncey said he would remove Rose's name from his helmet. Further, the NFL star "offered a sincere apology to law enforcement officials for not initially doing more due diligence on the facts surrounding Rose Jr.'s death."

Pouncey's apology included that he was given only scant information about the incident and should have researched it himself. He also pointed out "all the work he's done with the law enforcement community."

Perhaps the NFL should have done some vetting before okaying these "victims of police violence" for display on their players' helmets. Isn't it the NFL that should be apologizing to the real victim's families, to the police officers, and to the players they are bullying into participating in their political pandering program?

What about the NFL players who don't care about doing research or knowing the truth about the criminals whose names they wear on their helmets? The Boss is finding that some of his most loyal soldiers occupy the rarified air of American professional sports. The NBA, NFL, MLB, MLS, WNBA, U.S. Women's Soccer, NASCAR, and others have all decided the future of their leagues depends on their becoming politically partisan.

WNBA legend Sue Bird, after the Seattle Storm won the 2020 WNBA champion, said that men who don't watch women's basketball are bigots.[396] Sorry, Sue. Men aren't watching the NBA either, so that argument doesn't hold up. A few years ago, she also blamed[397] "homophobia," "racism," and "sexism" for men not watching. I sense a theme. She also backhanded her colleagues in women's soccer, calling them "cute little white girls," as opposed to the WNBA with "a lot of Black [sic], gay, and tall women." Identity politics is truly disgusting.

Unfortunately, though initially a refreshing holdout from the Marxist-supporting, criminal supporting, anti-cop pro sports industry, the NHL finally also bent its knee to the mob. Some NHL hockey players even insisted their views were not political but that those who disagreed with them were being political. Nice formula, right there.

Many people will recall the then–St. Louis Rams players who came out on the field sporting "hands up, don't shoot"[398] gestures, hands held over their heads. Did they ever apologize to the cops who protected the team and stadium? Did they say sorry to Officer Darren Wilson after the Consigliere's DOJ investigation found that the incident that sparked "hands up, don't shoot" never happened? If they did, it hasn't been widely disseminated. Rather, pro athletes like LeBron James seem to be doubling and tripling down on promoting anti-police myths. And they've attracted the attention of their glorious leader, the Boss.

Mediaite reported[399] the Boss's praise for athletes speaking out about another anti-cop myth: the Kenosha police officer shooting of an "unarmed" twenty-nine-year-old Jacob Blake, which was discussed earlier. In yet another salvo against America's police officers by the former commander-in-chief, the Boss lauded the "players for protesting their games" by not playing. He expressed his delight that the Milwaukee Bucks declined to play a playoff game.

This knocked over a row of dominoes that eventually included all the NBA and WNBA games for that night. Many people will likely hold on to their bias against the officer because he shot the suspect seven times. However, the suspect continued to resist. That he is still alive attests to the fact the initial rounds did not stop him—and he had a knife.

Anyone who has problems with the number of shots fired should take a look at this ABC news video[400] of a police shooting in Athens, Georgia, in 2019. Reportedly, the officer had shot the knife-wielding suspect *seven times*, after which the suspect got to his feet and attacked that officer until another officer shot him again, multiple times. It's not like on TV, folks.

Remarkably, along with his praise of the pro sports leagues, the Boss included a video of L.A. Clippers head coach Doc Rivers. In the clip, Coach Rivers condemns "the Republican Party for focusing on 'law and order' and stoking fear during unrest." Fear of what, arrest? How does any reasonable person argue against "law and order"? Ah, the answer is in the question: *reasonable*.

Coach Rivers's video in mind, the Boss said, "I commend the players on the Bucks for standing up for what they believe in, coaches like Doc Rivers, and the NBA and WNBA for setting an example. It's going to take all our institutions to stand up for our values." *Our* values? When he speaks of "our values," considering the extended members of his radical activist family, "our values" means socialist values. For traditional Americans, socialist values are not "our values."

Some may wonder how the Boss, an obviously intelligent former college professor and ostensible constitutional scholar, can argue against law and order. However, accumulating evidence points to a conspiracy to obstruct a presidential campaign and then take down a pro–law and order president.

And the conspiracists appear to be using the law enforcement and intelligence apparatus of the federal government. So, it's not hard to imagine such people would do almost anything to bring down the legal system. After all, with Republicans still in control, the DOJ could still hold the Boss, the Underboss, the "family," and associates accountable for any illegal capers in which they may have been involved.

Also included in Doc Rivers's comments is a repeated fabrication that, sadly, Coach Rivers probably truly believes. "All you hear is Donald Trump and all of them talking about fear," Rivers said of the GOP National Convention. "We're the ones getting killed. We're the ones getting shot. We're the ones that we're denied to live in certain communities. We've been hung. We've been shot. And all you do is keep hearing about fear."

Perpetuating a myth, Doc Rivers claimed, "We're the ones getting killed." By "we" it's assumed he means black people, especially males. It gets so disheartening to continue to argue that FBI statistics and scholarly studies do not corroborate this view. As stated previously, police officers kill only around one thousand suspects per year, out of which about four hundred are black, out of a nation of some 330 million people. That's 0.0003 percent of the population killed by cops. For black people killed, the number is 0.0001 percent. And, to reiterate, nearly every single one of those people were armed and trying to kill the cops who shot them.

For the last few years, there has been a demoralizing onslaught of pro athletes endorsing the agenda of violent socialist, fascists, and Marxist radicals. Drew Brees, one of the most popular and respected men in any professional sport, has apparently succumbed to the racialist mob's intimidation. Reportedly, Brees, a quarterback for the New Orleans Saints, and his teammates sported the name of "Jacob Blake" on their helmets[401] during practices, honoring him as a "victim" of "police violence."

Georgi Boorman of the *Federalist* asks the question many informed people are asking: "Why is Drew Brees wearing the name of an alleged rapist on his helmet?" Brees and his teammates have access to all the online, print, and TV information everyone else has. They can do the research, too. Is it possible every single member of the Saints believed Jacob Blake was a victim? Is it possible no one knew he had an arrest warrant for allegedly raping his girlfriend and trying to steal her car, was armed with a knife, fought with officers, was tased, and disobeyed lawful police orders for him to comply? Did no one tell Brees that Blake's criminal history includes alleged car theft, firearms offenses, domestic violence, and sexual assault?

Or are there some players or coaches who know these facts, but the "cancel culture" has become so intimidating that they don't dare speak out? It would be sad if it has come to that. But sadder still is the fact that a former U.S. president, the Boss, is actively praising players and coaches who leap to the conclusion that criminals are always good and that "all cops are bastards."

Regardless, the front offices, the coaches, and players, and the NFL leadership form a powerful reserve of soldiers available to the Obama Foundation and others with similar agendas. Many people, especially impressionable youth, revere these athletes. It's likely kids attribute to them the authority of knowledge, awareness, and opinion that they simply do not deserve.

It remains to be seen what the financial impact will be on professional sports. With the NBA wearing Communist Chinese Government shackles, they may be less financially affected, considering that nation's potential billion-person audience. For the other leagues, the initial news isn't promising.

Never have so many fans expressed emotions ranging from disappointment to outrage at what they view as their sports leagues, teams, and heroes betraying them. Even fans who agree with the anti-cop radicals' views don't want politics in their sports. Do a press conference before the game. Do a podcast after the game. But while the game is going on, you are at work, and your job is to entertain an audience. If your audience is no longer entertained for whatever reason, they will stop buying your team's gear, going to games, or even watching games on TV.

The anti-cop antics of the pig sock–wearing Colin Kaepernick, that anti-American, disgusting piece of … um, gentleman (for the sake of decorum), should have taught the NFL a lesson. But NFL Commissioner Roger Goeddel, who plays both puppet (of social justice warriors) and puppet master (of the NFL), doesn't seem to care. Is he actually letting it all happen *again*? Under his watch, are players coercing other players into swearing allegiance to a new NFL monoculture dedicated to perpetuating lies about police officers and the nation? Regardless, it looks like the Boss will have this corps of sycophantic soldiers he can call up when he needs them.

Still, it should be mentioned that some athletes oppose their misguided colleagues' support for this anti-police movement. Herschel Walker, NFL star, Heisman Trophy winner, and perhaps the greatest college football player in history, gave a powerful speech[402] at the Republican National Convention in August 2020. The most potent part of his speech was when he challenged anyone who says that, after being friends with President Trump for nearly forty years, he would associate with a racist.

Several weeks later, in a Twitter video posted[403] at Parler by Dan Bongino, Walker is shown lambasting pro sports leagues and athletes who express support for BLM, a Marxist movement. The heading to Walker's video reads, "I have finally WOKE UP … I am shaking you America! As Maya [Angelou] said, 'when someone tells you who they are, believe them.' #doyourhomework @FoxNews @CNN @espn @AJC @POTUS @ MSNBC @HouseDemocrats @GOP @dallasnews"

In the video, Walker says,

> First, I want to apologize to the American people because I was blind but now, I can see. I was deaf but now I can hear. The other day I was listening to one of the founders of Black Lives Matter, and I heard her say

that they are "trained Marxists." And I've heard that statement so many times.

But then yesterday, I finally heard it. And I saw it with my own eyes. And I'm challenging every owner in the NFL, every owner of major league sports, every owner of stadiums, every commissioner, every leader in Washington, every church. I'm challenging every professional player: Is this who you're support-ing? Because a trained Marxist tells you that they're anti-government; they're anti-American; they're anti-Christian; they're anti-everything.

They're saying it with their own mouths. They're not afraid to tell you that. I think whoever is for that, need to come out and tell the American people exactly who it is they're standing for because I see all these signs, I see all these logos, I see all these commercials, I see all of this stuff. And it's okay, 'cause we're in America. You can support who you want and do what you want, but I need you to know, and the American people need to know, that when you talk about supporting BLM, are you supporting the group that said that they are trained Marxists? Because they're making a lot of money, and I'd like to know.

Another former star NFL football player, and Republican Utah's 4th District U.S. representative in Utah's 4th District, Burgess Owens, is as bold, brash, and convicted as Herschel Walker in his defense of tradi-tional America. Also noting BLM is a Marxist organization, Owens spoke with[404] Martha McCallum on her Fox News program, *The Story*. Reacting to a question, McCallum posed a question of his own about Ariel Atkins, a Chicago BLM organizer who, in a video, "condoned looting as 'repara-tions.'" According to a summary of the interview by Scott Morefield at the *Daily Caller*, Owens said,

We have one vision that says we the people are empowered by education and we will give that power to the people and the other side is they want to empower themselves by stealing our education, stealing our history. Which should not be a surprise, and for those who can go to Google, you'll find out that BLM Inc. is nothing but a Marxist organization.

Morefield noted: "'They hate God, they hate the family unit, the nuclear family, and they hate capitalism, so of course they are going to feel this way,' said Owens before referencing[405] the 'mayhem and death' happening in major U.S. cities along with 'black business owners going out of business and black people being killed in the streets of Chicago.'" Owens continued:

Our country needs to stand up, and the black community needs to have people that understand our history and do not feel sorry for us but give us an opportunity to go out there and live our life, liberty and pursuit of happiness like everybody else.

Owens spoke passionately about what Americans need to do to combat this radical opposition that wants to topple the greatest nation in history. "We need to fight for our country against these Marxists and these bullies and cowards that are destroying everything they touch. We can't stand by and let this happen."

He's right, and as long as the bullies continue to influence some of America's politicians, the police will still have to risk injury and death battling domestic terrorists in the streets of their cities because their political leaders hobble them and refuse to allow them to retake their cities for the good people who live there.

As an example of the bullying, Owens cites BLM supporters slamming[406] Utah Jazz coach Quin Snyder, a white man, for donating "$500 2x" to Owens's campaign. Andy Larsen[407] of the *Salt Lake Tribune* made this innocuous gesture a story when Larsen tweeted about the donation, highlighting Owens's anti-BLM comments. Reporter Lucas Hann reportedly tweeted, "Thank you for writing this, Andy, in a local climate that is clearly hostile toward efforts to name white supremacy and hold its perpetrators accountable." So, a white man donating to a black candidate is "white supremacy"? As Archie Bunker of the 1970s sitcom *All in the Family* would say, "Aw, geez!"[408]

While BLM and Antifa certainly qualify as "soldiers," their leaders also qualify as "capos," and their organizations as crime "families" or criminal "gangs." This being the case, it seems appropriate to dedicate to these two entities their own chapters.

Chapter 35

Black Lives Matter (Global Network Foundation)

Before discussing Black Lives Matter (BLM), a note: in fairness—but don't ever expect fairness to be reciprocated by these groups—the intent is to provide readers as often as possible with links to an organization's own website. A video[409] posted by the Heritage Foundation at YouTube includes cofounder Patrisse Kahn-Cullors discussing BLM's ideology and saying, "Myself and Alicia [Garza] in particular are trained organizers. We are trained Marxists." The third founding member is Opal Tometi.[410] Judging by Tometi's TED Talks biography, TED also believes BLM's radical Marxist views are, as their motto says, "Ideas worth spreading."[411]

This is not an anti-racism organization; it is an anti-police, anti-Capitalism, anti-liberty, pro-Marxist outfit. People are familiar with the ubiquitous reporting of BLM activists in New York City chanting, "What do we want? Dead Cops. When do we want them? Now!" Sadly, they have been getting their wish. In 2019 there were 148 officers killed in the line of duty. In 2020, there were 328. Along with Antifa, BLM includes the most vehemently anti-police factions known in America today. Juxtapose this with no apparent concern for the black lives massacred in Chicago and other big cities, and it's clear anti-racism is not the goal—socialism/communism is.

In an article[412] at the *Washington Times*, Cal Thomas warns about the goals of BLM. "Black lives matter because like all lives, everyone is endowed with unalienable rights. But the BLM[413] movement might be more harmful than helpful to African-Americans. BLM's foundational principles and goals seem closer to those of China and the former Soviet Union. If more people understood that, they might wake up and realize that the United States, as Ronald Reagan used to say, is 'only one generation from losing it all.'"

Before digging deeper into BLM, we should clear up some confusion regarding the perceived "difference" between the sentiment "black lives matter" and the Marxist organization "Black Lives Matter." Is there truly a difference between the sentiment and the organization other than people trying to justify their support for what is, in fact, a communist, anti-police organization?

First, that "black lives matter" is so obvious it is an insult to a person's intelligence and humanity even to have to say it and certainly for BLM to pressure or force people to say it. It's like saying "the sky is blue." It's obvious. And, while some attempt to assert a total disconnect between the organization and the sentiment, it is the BLM organization who originated the cynical BLM sentiment as the ubiquitous motto it's become.

BLM's founders are the people who conscripted the motto "black lives matter" for the name of their Marxist organization. In reality, associating a universally accepted sentiment with the name of a violent communist group was an act of hyper-diabolical genius. Now, in actuality, it is impossible to post a sign reading "Black Lives Matter" or to chant "black lives matter" without implicitly, explicitly, or even ignorantly supporting the BLM organization.

In July, after the BLM violence was well underway, the *Washington Examiner's* Jerry Dunleavy examined[414] the question "Who is Black Lives Matter?" Concurring with the observation made in the above paragraphs, Dunleavy refers to "the organization with the innocuous-sounding name, Black Lives Matter." *Innocuous sounding*, yes; innocuous in reality, no.

Dunleavy writes of BLM's unapologetic and revolutionary goal of "upending American society," which, incidentally, includes their opposition to the traditional family structure: the nuclear family. It seems they prefer Hillary Clinton's "it takes a village" approach. BLM is not trying to make America *better*; BLM is trying to make America *different—worse*. In 2013, BLM celebrated their fourth anniversary. On their page celebrating[415] the anniversary, there are images of people, including the cofounders, marching with the requisite mythological gesture, "hands up, don't shoot."

In the page's "Guiding Principles" section, BLM writes, "We disrupt the Western-prescribed nuclear family structure requirement by supporting each other as extended families and 'villages' that collectively care for one another, especially our children, to the degree that mothers, parents, and children are comfortable."

Some things pop out immediately: "Disrupt … the … nuclear family" and "collectively care for." Also, notice they leave out fathers, referencing "mothers, parents, and children." "Parents" could imply a mother and father, but with this bunch, it's not likely.

Does this mean they are anti–nuclear family because they are anti-male? Apparently so, as they do speak out often and negatively about a "patriarchy." The website Breitbart provides a video[416] featuring a BLM activist saying, "there is 'one common enemy: the white man' and therefore 'we need to get rid of them.'"

Marxists, no longer able to cajole the American worker for support, now employ identity politics as a replacement recruiting tactic. This way, by exploiting historical wrongs that no longer exist, they can continue to foster myths about traditional American society and then manufacture and sell "victimhood" to weak-minded people to attract followers.

The Examiner article also cited a report from 2017 where BLM "describes its founders… as 'three radical Black organizers.' The women espouse Marxism and openly push radical identity politics."

As if America's police officers needed another reason to loathe BLM, not only do they advocate killing cops, their leaders hold up as a role model and icon a convicted cop killer. As alluded to previously, Joanne Deborah

Chesimard (aka Assata Shakur) was convicted of murdering New Jersey state trooper Werner Foerster.[417] The FBI placed her on the list of "Most Wanted Terrorists," the first female ever to be included.

According to the FBI, "In 1977, Chesimard was found guilty of first-degree murder, assault and battery of a police officer, assault with a dangerous weapon, assault with intent to kill, illegal possession of a weapon, and armed robbery. She was sentenced to life in prison. On November 2, 1979, Chesimard escaped from prison and lived underground before being located in Cuba in 1984. She is thought to currently still be living in Cuba."

The FBI also reports Chesimard was a member of the Black Liberation Army, and at the time of her arrest for murder, she "was wanted for her involvement in several felonies, including bank robbery." Reportedly, along with her comrades, during a traffic stop Chesimard shot at two troopers, wounding one. The FBI says, "The other [trooper] was shot and killed execution-style at point-blank range." One terrorist was killed and the other was captured and is in prison.

BLM's founders and supporters revere not only this Marxist cop-killer but also Chesimard's communist dictator benefactor, Fidel Castro. The website Townhall reported a statement[418] from BLM about Chesimard and Castro. "We are particularly grateful to Fidel for holding Mama Assata Shakur, who continues to inspire us…. As Fidel ascends to the realm of the ancestors, we summon his guidance, strength, and power as we recommit ourselves to the struggle for universal freedom, Fidel Vive!" BLM also wrote, about the Marxist dictator, "We are feeling many things as we awaken to a world without Fidel Castro. There is an overwhelming sense of loss." The FBI is currently offering a one-million-dollar reward to anyone who can provide information that directly leads to Chesimard's capture.

Digressing a bit, we must stop to wonder how BLM became the organization that pro athletes, pro sports leagues, corporations (large, medium, and small), Wall Street banks, academia, Hollywood, Silicon Valley, and the Democratic Party have embraced.

The Marxist founders of BLM say the creation of the organization was in response to the acquittal of George Zimmerman, described by the

New York Times[419] as a twenty-eight-year-old "white Hispanic"[420] accused in the killing of Treyvon Martin. While Zimmerman is no hero, a jury found that, regardless of what occurred prior to the physical altercation, Martin was seriously injuring Zimmerman, reportedly pounding his head into a concrete sidewalk,[421] when Zimmerman shot Martin in self-defense. The ubiquitous photo picturing an innocent youth did not represent Martin on that fateful day. This misrepresentation is something cops get used to. Defense attorneys and the media do it all the time.

BLM cofounder Cullors also reveres fellow Marxist and the 1980 and 1984 vice presidential nominee for the Communist Party USA (CPUSA), Angela Davis.[422] The *Examiner* reports that Davis, a big fan of the 1917 Russian Revolution, won "the Soviet Union's Lenin Peace Prize." Davis, like Chesimard, was also affiliated with the Black Panthers. She was among the terrorists who allegedly took over a courtroom[423] in California in 1970 and killed four people, including the judge, using guns whose registrations reportedly traced back to Davis.

The Marxist Davis has endorsed[424] Democratic candidate Joe Biden for president of the United States for the 2020 election. She was particularly honest when explaining her support when she told *Russia Today*, "I don't see this election as being about choosing a candidate who will be able to lead us in the right direction. It will be about choosing a candidate who can be most effectively pressured into allowing more space for the evolving anti-racist movement." Get that? They specifically do not want a strong, independent leader. "Anti-racist," right? No, anti-liberty. In other words, they want more "space" for rioters and looters to assault and kill police officers without consequences.

Davis also said, "Biden is far more likely to take mass demands seriously. The election will ask us not so much to vote for the best candidate, but to vote for or against ourselves. And to vote for ourselves [Marxists] I think means that we will have to campaign for and vote for Biden." Well, with the Tony Bobulinski revelations[425] spilling the proverbial beans on Biden's alleged international crime spree, he'll fit right in with those folks. In fact, now the NPA may have to do another book on the Vice Boss's "crime family."

As alluded to earlier, a Thousand Currents board member, and another one of the BLM founders' heroes, is Susan Rosenberg. Rosenberg is listed as the vice chair[426] of the Thousand Current's Board of Directors. The *Examiner* reports Rosenberg has been involved in many serious terroristic crimes in the '60s and '70s, including bombings and being "tied to a 1981 Brinks armored car robbery in which a guard and two police officers were killed." Sensing a connecting thread yet? These people truly hate cops.

It's no surprise that BLM was one of the first of the radical entities to sponsor a petition[427] to defund the police. When considering BLM's legitimacy within mainstream politics, only a few things need to be considered: BLM has called for killing cops (recall the suspect claiming BLM membership who allegedly murdered five Dallas cops), and BLM has declared its reverence for suspected and convicted cop-killers and for a communist dictator who provided sanctuary to one of those cop-killers.

Jack Cashill wrote an article for World Net Daily about the Boss's influence with BLM titled "The Day Barack Obama Launched Black Lives Matter."[428] Cashill cites things the Boss has said that Cashill asserts incited the creation of BLM. As discussed previously, BLM initially formed to oppose the acquittal of George Zimmerman for killing Trayvon Martin. Though Obama knew the truth about what happened, the self-defense aspect, that did not stop him from saying, "My main message is to the parents of Trayvon: If I had a son, he would look like Trayvon."

Cashill writes, "In projecting Trayvon as a 'son,' Obama strongly suggested that all black children were equally vulnerable to the predations of white men. Four weeks after the shooting, Obama had no excuse for not knowing the facts of the case. This would prove to be the most destructive moment of his presidency." One that, apparently, rather than making amends for, he's using to intensify his efforts to racially divide this nation.

Ironically, though the Boss threw the full weight of the federal criminal justice system at Zimmerman, Ben Shapiro, writing in Breitbart[429] in 2013, pointed out that Zimmerman was reportedly a Democrat, voted for the Boss, and solicited his family members to vote for the Boss too. Hardly the "white (*Hispanic*) supremacist" the media were trying to conjure.

Probably one of the most insidious behaviors BLM is responsible for is its tactic of descending on peaceful diners who are simply pursuing their happiness, attempting to eat a meal with friends and family. Straying well beyond all borders of civil behavior, BLM supporters have entered restaurants or invaded sidewalk cafes to harass, intimidate, and sometimes even physically assault customers.

A simple DuckDuckGo search brings up[430] a glut of examples of these crimes from across the nation, including in Pittsburgh, PA, Washington, DC, Dallas, TX, Los Angeles, CA, Seattle, WA, Portland, OR; Palm Beach, FL, Baton Rouge, LA, and Denver, CO. Stories abound of BLM goons trespassing onto restaurant property and chiding customers to say "black lives matter" or to stand up and raise their fists (signaling black power) into the air.

In one internet search, the first story[431] that popped up, from the *New York Post*, contains a disgusting image. The image is of a little boy, perhaps eight or nine years old, standing straight, right arm raised, fist in the air. The radical indoctrination continues.

It's normally inappropriate to use Nazi or Hitler references. But sometimes the comparison is so glaring it becomes not only appropriate but necessary to explore, so history is not repeated. Looking at that poor child, intimidated by radical adults to adopt its preferred political gesture and motto, it is difficult not to envision a member of the Hitler Youth,[432] arm also aloft, in World War II Germany. Never has Phillipe K. Dick's alternative history novel *The Man in the High Castle*[433] resonated so ominously.

The White Rose Movement website, where the linked photo resides on the internet, is eerily prescient of today's Antifa/BLM-occupied American cities. The site notes this para-political strategy quote[434] from Adolf Hitler: "Demoralize the enemy from within by surprise, terror, sabotage, assassination. This is the war of the future." These are all being done, right now, in the United States.

And a person's age, young and old, is no barrier to BLM's antisocial behavior. The link above to the Pittsburgh incident shows CBS KDKA 2 News video footage of "protesters" descending on restaurant customers, simply sitting outside trying to enjoy their meals. One particularly uncouth young woman struts to the table where an elderly couple sits. Without hesitation, she grabs a glass off the couple's table and insolently drinks down the beverage. "Reparations," some are calling it.

In DC, where the above-mentioned child was pictured raising his fist to BLM, the website Legal Insurrection headlined,[435] "DC Mob Harasses White Diners, Demanding They Raise Fists in Solidarity." Apparently, the woman at the other end of their fascistic wrath, their faces within inches of her face, demanded she raise her fist and recite "black lives matter." She refused.

She later admitted she is (was?) a BLM supporter but drew the line at being forced to make the gesture. The *Sun* reported,[436] "The brave diner who refused to be forced into raising a fist by a mob has revealed she is a Black Lives Matter supporter herself—but that 'it didn't feel right' to join them that night.'"

The sad thing is, while this brave soul did not bow to the fascists, many other patrons did. So, for those people who say Americans could never fall for what 1930s Germans did, this regrettably disproves that notion. In the right (or wrong) circumstances, there is a percentage of people—cowards—who will go along with tyranny—for whatever reason.

There's a disturbing though enlightening book called *Ordinary Men: Reserve Police Battalion 101 and the Final Solution in Poland*.[437] In it, Christopher R. Browning explores how ordinary German police officers—surprisingly, more as a result of peer pressure than orders from superiors—wound up carrying out some dreadful acts, even shooting and killing innocent women and children.

But ordinary people don't begin by killing other people. They begin by reporting their neighbors for political (anti-Nazi) "misbehavior" and use psychological intimidation to coerce "proper" behavior—such as being forced to *stand, raise a fist into the air, and recite "black lives matter"?* In Germany, such political intimidation eventually led to property damage, looting, assault, and, eventually, murder. Other ordinary Germans who tried to warn people where this behavior was leading were told they were overreacting and to shut up. More recently, do you think some Venezuelans[438] also tried to warn their neighbors about the socialist tyranny approaching? Quite likely they did, and they were told to shut up too. Who is now telling ordinary Americans who are warning people about socialism to shut up? The usual leftist suspects.

Eventually the intimidation transitions to physical violence. To this point, BLM and Antifa are intimidating and assaulting Trump supporters who dare to wear MAGA hats and display other campaign gear. Sean Hannity, on his Fox News Channel program, reported[439] about two "ordinary women," BLM supporters, attending the Democratic National Convention. They stole a MAGA hat off a Trump supporter's young son's head. When the man the boy had borrowed the hat from tried to retrieve it, one of the women allegedly (the incident was captured on video by the boy's mom) punched the man.

Another President Trump supporter, wearing a MAGA hat at a New Jersey grocery store, was assaulted by "an unidentified male from Franklin Township." The victim suffered minor injuries. It should be mentioned that the Trump supporter was an eighty-one-year-old man. Fox also reported that a woman allegedly assaulted a MAGA-hat-wearing twenty-three-year-old at a Cape Cod restaurant. Reportedly, the woman was detained by Immigration and Customs Enforcement (ICE). And in September 2020, a shoe store fired an employee who allegedly cursed a "14-year-old customer wearing the signature cap [MAGA] at a store in Kansas." This is chaos. This is insanity. But this is also exactly what the Boss's anti–traditional America, anti–law enforcement forces need to succeed politically. Shockingly, many political leaders are encouraging this behavior.

On a similar note, people getting into people's faces, even committing assaults, and those reporting their neighbors for not following their states' CCP virus mandates are examples of people who behave like some people behaved in the former Soviet Union or in China today. A woman in California allegedly pepper-sprayed[440] a man and woman who weren't wearing masks. The couple was sitting at a picnic table eating their lunch— or had been trying to. Not surprisingly, the Right tends to see wearing masks as an individual decision, while the Left tends to support government mandates. And, as usual, cops have to deal with these unnecessary calls.

Forbes reported[441] several incidents of harassment or violence resulting from "mask shaming." One example involved a Florida man who allegedly pointed a gun at a person and said, "I'll kill you," while telling him to wear a mask. While the similarities between the violent BLM and Antifa, the "Karen"[442] mask-Nazis, and historical Marxists and fascists may be uncomfortable, they are too dangerous to ignore. History is a great teacher. And who supports these strict state edicts that set people against people and people against the police? The Boss's folks.

And BLM has not stopped calling for killing police. On October 27, 2020, during a protest of a man shot by police after he came at them with a knife, BLM activists raised this lovely chant.[443] "No justice, no peace. Shoot back at the police"—"back" alluding to the myth that cops are shooting innocent people.

Chapter 36

Antifa (Revolutionary Abolitionist Movement)

J ournalist Andy Ngo has been severely beaten[444] by Antifa criminals several times while attempting to bring Americans Antifa's brutal story. Ngo posted a video on Twitter, which the Daily Wire picked up,[445] of BLM radicals surrounding a pickup truck. The thugs were preventing the male driver and a passenger from leaving, intimidating them into giving the black power salute and shouting at them to say "black lives matter." The fascist tactic worked. Obviously fearing for their lives, the driver and passenger gave the salute and repeated, "black lives matter."

Their appeasement didn't matter. Ngo tweeted, "The truck was smashed up later." People have to understand there is no appeasing terrorists. Acquiescence only conveys weakness, which they will exploit. That's why even people who put BLM signs in their yards and shout to the Antifa black bloc[446] rioters "I'm on your side" get rocks thrown through their windows or pummeled too.

This is no criticism of the men in the truck. None of us knows how we will react to such a circumstance in a given moment. They were obviously outnumbered by the violent, armed thugs. However, authorities should fully investigate this crime and put these violent political predators in prison where they belong.

In August 2020, Acting Homeland Security secretary Chad Wolf gave a "harsh evaluation" of Antifa. An article[447] in the *Federalist* states, "[Wolf] declares 'the left-wing group absolutely meets the standards worthy of condemnation as a 'domestic terrorist group.'" He cited how the group's amorphous nature creates difficulties for investigators and prosecutors in doing their jobs. That sounds familiar, doesn't it?

Wolf went on to condemn city leaders where Antifa proliferates and commits its crimes. He said, "Fault lies with those local leaders and those local law enforcement of not doing their job. This country is about rule of law." But is it? Leaders such as Mayors de Blasio, Wheeler, and Durkan seem to believe criticizing the police and protecting criminals is their "rule of law."

Wolf concluded, "We need the police to step up any time we have criminal riots and looting occur. Law enforcement needs to step in, restore that rule of law so that private citizens don't have to do this or that, you don't have counterprotests that become violent. That only happens in the absence of rule of law." Secretary Wolf needs to remember that cops want to quell these riots, but their leaders won't let them. This must be reaffirmed and often.

With its supposedly nebulous organization or non-organization, Antifa, as a group, can be difficult to nail down. That doesn't mean law enforcement won't keep trying. Though there is an Antifa website at www. revolutionaryabolition.org, probably the best way to describe Antifa is to observe not how their critics describe them but how their own behavior defines them. Antifa describes itself as "anti-fascist." Yet their behavior is the epitome of fascistic behavior.

Apparently, Antifa has "evolved" into the Revolutionary Abolitionist Movement[448] (RAM). A YouTube video[449] about the group, made by somebody called Wild Smile, begins, "Antifa has had a facelift.... This group of activists seeks to undermine police activity, immigration policy, and even train revolutionaries to carry out their agenda." Is there really anything else anyone needs to hear to determine this group is truly a terrorist organization?

Notice the video doesn't say "fight against police brutality." No, they wish to *undermine police activity*, which means *anything* the police do, right? And the manner in which they intend to do it is, according to the creator of the video, by "train[ing] revolutionaries to carry out their [Antifa's] agenda," which is direct action, including extreme violence. As mentioned earlier, an Antifa soldier pulled out his gun and murdered a police-supporting counterprotester on a Portland street. It does not get more violent than that.

Greeting people at the Antifa website are these declarations, "RAM & New Afrikan Black Panther Party Rally: Demand Amnesty for All Arrested During the Uprising." And they do mean "all" when they also write, "Whether felony or misdemeanor, property destruction or civil disobedience, we reject the divisions externally imposed upon the movement by the State and insist that all charges be immediately dropped."

Steve Doocy, cohost of *Fox and Friends*, asked Fox Nation host Lara Logan to describe Antifa's[450] amorphous (dis)organization. Logan said,

> It [Antifa] is scattered, and that's by design. Because it's a massive network that spreads, you know, all across the U.S. and across the world. Actually, it's a global movement. That's not my words, that's their words, right? And, of course, legal experts, all these people want you to believe that you can't designate them, why? Because it brings with it significant authority. So, for example, all those people contributing bail money now to members of Antifa and other anarchist groups. If they're terrorist organizations, then they are contributing to terrorist groups, and that's illegal. Money will dry up. Certainly, sources of funding will dry up.

Logan goes on to explain why they move across state lines to commit crimes. She told Doocy that as things stand, the authorities can't get them. But "you can if they're designated as terrorists." She said critics of the terrorist designation are "contributing to the propaganda," which Logan says is in "overdrive." She says the *New York Times* is contributing to the problem by dismissing "what you're seeing in front of your eyes" as a "conspiracy theory."

Logan calls the charge of conspiracy theory a term of "information warfare … meant to shut down … conversation … silence … and intimidate" in an effort "to get us to self-censor." She says no one "wants to be accused of being crazy right-wing conspiracy theorists."

"Copaganda" is how Logan describes Antifa's ploy to use police concessions to enhance their messaging—for example, showing cops who are taking a knee with the BLM and Antifa radicals. Logan called this "the grossest, most blatant attempt at copaganda I've ever seen. Anyone hugging or kneeling with them is a fool or is doing counterinsurgency." Logan says all people have to do is ask people in intel or law enforcement. "They use the tactic they accuse you of." Again, this is very common with all leftist radicals.

Logan encourages people not to take her word about Antifa. She says to take a look at original sources like their own website at revolutionaryabolition.org. She asks, "What do they want to do here?"

Logan then lists the radical litany of the goals these anarcho-communists (or is it communo-anarchists?) display on their website. After mentioning the cops, military, and other government authorities that need to be disbanded, in item number 10, the anarchists actually betray that they will have a "system of government" of sorts. "Militant networks will defend our revolutionary communities. Liberation begins where America dies." *Liberation begins where America dies.* This is at the core of their ideology.

Finally, as of September 2020, there had been some movement in the investigation of Antifa fascists' violence. Following Andy Ngo's reporting via the Daily Wire,[451] Catherine Herridge of CBS News reported on a former high-ranking person at the Department of Homeland Security (DHS) whose email was leaked. The email "stated that the department had 'overwhelming intelligence' that the extremist violence in Portland was 'organized' by individuals with an ideology categorized as 'Violent Antifa Anarchist Inspired (VAAI).'"

Daily Wire pointed out a tweet from Herridge in which she identified the official whose letter was leaked as former DHS Acting Under
Secretary for Intelligence and Analysis Brian Murphy. Murphy identified
an evolution of Antifa violence, stating that "the violence in Portland had
reached a level that officials could no longer state that the violence was
'opportunistic' but that it was 'organized.'"

Murphy went on: "A core set of threat actors are organized, show
up night after night, share common TTPs [tactics, techniques and proce-
dures] and drawing [sic] on like-minded individuals to their cause."

As an excellent example of Antifa's organization and tactics, during a
video presentation[452] provided to Portland Mayor Ted Wheeler by Portland
Police Bureau Deputy Police Chief Chris Davis, the deputy police chief
presented a PDF of Antifa's "organizational operations chart." The PDF
identified the following as protest roles:

- Shield Soldier: frontliners who use wood boards, swim boards, or
  signs to form a first line of defense.

- Peaceful Protester: protesters who don't want to fight, but join
  hand in hand with frontliners, sometimes using their phones to
  film police aggression.

- Frontliner: protesters who use umbrellas to guard against projectiles and cameras, while keeping hand free for when help is
  needed.

- Range Soldier: protesters who throw bottles, umbrellas, and trash
  to stop police from advancing.

- Flag Bearer: uses signs or a phone to signal to protesters when
  police are advancing or attacking.

- Fire Mage: protesters who come prepared to set fire to barricades
  and throw flammable projectiles.

- Fire Squads: protesters who use water and traffic cones to suppress and extinguish tear gas cannisters.

- Light Mage: protesters who use laser pointers to obstruct surveillance cameras, drones, and police visors [may be typo for vision].

- Medic: protest supporters who are able to treat injuries or have materials to treat tear gas exposure.

- Copwatch: protest supporters who use phones to record violent police and document police tactics and weaponry [to defeat at future actions].

- Barricader: protesters who build barricades out of found objects at strategic positions to block oncoming police and traffic that trails the protests.

- Online Comms: online protesters who use social media apps like Signal and Telegram to report on police strategies and provide protesters with real-time strategic updates.

- Designers: protest supporters who make inspiring graphics, helpful infographics, or banners for protests.

And the people are not happy. A DHM Research poll[453] showed that, as of September 3, 2020, "66% of Oregonians disapproved of the [Portland] protests" (riots). And 60 percent believe either the level of police use of force should be increased (42%) or the current level is fine (18%). The news was worse for the cop-hating, law and order–corrupting Oregon Governor Kate Brown. The Daily Wire (link above) also reported "only 10% of respondents approved of [Brown's] response to the protests." But even she beat Portland's disastrous Mayor Ted Wheeler, the second worst mayor in America. The pathetic Wheeler garnered only "8% of respondents … [who] approved of [Wheeler's] response."

All of this is occurring as city and state leaders have hobbled their cops. They have banned crowd-control tactics, equipment, and technologies, such as facial recognition, that could assist with arresting and prosecuting violent rioters, looters, and arsonists. In fact, Portland went as far as to prevent even "private entities in places of public accommodation" in Portland from using facial recognition technology.

City government is saturated with a hatred of the police and a love of the violent anarcho-communists. The link to the "new rule" indicated above would have been provided here. However, it seems the city has taken the page down. No surprise there. But the real question is why are state and city leaders working so hard to protect those who are harming their once-beautiful city?

As mentioned previously, there have been reports of Antifa recruiting "soldiers"[454] from violent criminal and mentally ill populations. Some of this has been verified after suspected members are arrested and their criminal histories exposed. Rutgers and Network Contagion Research Institute (ncri.io) published a detailed and thorough public report [455] titled "Network-Enabled Anarchy: How Militant Anarcho-Socialist Networks Use Social Media to Instigate Widespread Violence against Political Opponents and Law Enforcement."

There is too much to cover here in this amazing report, authored by well-qualified academics and high-ranking law enforcement experts. However, the nugget that proves Antifa is an organization and not simply an "idea," as if that's not obvious by now, is contained in the first paragraph of the Introduction and Overview. It lists the "Three tactics characteristic of extremist online communities have allowed them to become influential in recent years: 1) they use memes as propaganda, 2) they employ sophisticated communication networks for both planning and recruiting, making use of both fringe and private, online forums, and 3) they organize militias, and inspire lone wolf actors for violent action."

According to Quarter Master News [456] (QMN), Antifa, a radical group President Trump and Attorney General Barr have declared a terrorist organization, is apparently training soldiers in the Middle East. (At the same time, they designated the KKK[457] one too—but shouldn't that have happened, like, a century ago?) QMN writes, "A reciprocal relationship [with Antifa] has formed with the YPG and PKK terrorist groups, that are now returning to European countries, Canada, Australia, and the U.S."

This relationship allows Antifa to share information, training, and strategies between "freedom fighters" around the world. QMN says this also "highlights this global underworld of armed thugs across the globe." This demonstrates Antifa is indeed an organized group no matter how many people want to pretend it is only a "myth," as Rep. Jerry Nadler has said, or just an "idea," as then-former Vice President Joe Biden said during his first presidential debate with President Trump.

The connections between both Antifa and BLM and Middle East terrorists are deeper than most Americans imagine. This is mostly because the American mainstream media will not investigate or cover these connections. They remain belligerently incurious "journalists." Christine Douglass-Williams, at Jihad Watch, wrote an article[458] titled "Islamic Republic of Iran Stands with Antifa and BLM, Calls American Law Enforcement 'Vicious Dogs.'" And Israel National News (INN) reported[459] on a connection between BLM and Palestinian activists during the Ferguson riots.

Pro-Palestinian activist Anna Baltzer works for Boycott, Divestment, and Sanctions[460] (BDS), a movement promoting sanctions against Israel. Lee Kaplan of Israel National News, in an article titled "Hamas and Black Lives Matter: A Marriage Made in Hell," wrote that Baltzer "urged her followers to descend on Ferguson, Missouri." She put out an email blast, according to Kaplan, "for action 'From Ferguson to Palestine,' bringing the BDS movement and Palestinian groups, both domestic and abroad, to ally with U.S. black 'liberation' groups and radicals, and tying the goals of Hamas to domestic complaints by American blacks over alleged unfair treatment by US law enforcement." *Ebony* magazine also covered such a trip[461] (from an anti-Israeli viewpoint). Did you catch the mention of the "goals of Hamas" and "unfair treatment by US law enforcement"?

How's that for an anti-American, anti-police radical salad? These groups are becoming increasingly interconnected. Kaplan of Israel National News also wrote, "A 'delegation'[462] of Arab Palestinians from Gaza and the Palestinian Authority, college-age Arab activists, arrived in Missouri to plot strategy and tactics with Baltzer's ISM [International Solidarity Movement] group and similar groups in the USA shortly after Michael Brown was killed. Jeff Pickert, alias Max Suchan,[463] another member of the ISM, was arrested by Ferguson police during the riots that ensued for inciting black crowds to riot and attack the police."

As for which side the Boss and his allies align with, just think about his Secretary of State, John Kerry. In 2016, Kerry said emphatically, "There will be no separate peace between Israel and the Arab world [without the Palestinians]. I want to make that very clear with all of you." Oops! President Trump has been shepherding what are known as the "Abraham Accords,"[464] signed by Israel, the UAE, Bahrain, and then Sudan.[465] Compare that to when the Boss attempted to humiliate Israeli Prime Minister Bibi Netanyahu by making him wait while the president had his meal.

As for Hollywood, as touched on in chapter 7, these self-unaware narcissists can always be counted on to do the wrong thing, as long as *they feel* it's the right thing. As previously discussed, one of the latest trends with the anti-cop crowd is springing violent criminals from jail, which allows them to reoffend. Among the previously mentioned 40 Hollywood celebrities are some popular names, such as Jennifer Aniston, Natalie Portman, and Chris Evans. Do they truly care about their legacies? History will judge them harshly for not researching this issue or for researching and donating to get violent criminals released from jail anyway.

To pay into a fund that allows rapists and murderers to go free is objectively unconscionable to normal people, but that's what the bunch of them have done and are doing. This is not hyperbole. They're not just getting ordinary rioters out of jail, which is bad enough; they are getting people charged with serious felonies out.

The NFL's Maurkice Pouncey responded correctly after he learned he was supporting a bad guy by removing the man's name from his helmet. The Hollywood woke crowd seems less inclined to make a similar, honorable gesture. As Greg Lewin of the Minnesota Freedom Fund (MFF) said earlier, he doesn't even look at the charges before he bails suspects out until he sees the paperwork later. These athletes and celebrities don't see the charges either before or after a suspect is released. They just *feel* so good about themselves.

The *Federalist* nailed it with the title for Tristan Justice's article,[466] "Celebrities Bail Out Rioters in Virtueless Virtue Signaling." How does bailing out of jail criminals who are destroying our cities qualify as virtuous?

It doesn't. When these folks look back on this, years from now, when the disinfectant of time clarifies the realities of what happened, will they have the decency to feel shame? Will they have the integrity to apologize?

Justice asks, "Will the same people donating to free protestors to commit more acts of violence then also offer to help pay for repairs to the institutions they helped destroy?" Don't bet on it. And, once again, the police do not arrest *protesters*; they arrest rioters, arsonists, and looters.

The MFF, which was covered in chapter 21, is the bail fund set up in Minneapolis to free rioters and other violent criminals who many Hollywood stars apparently believe are freedom fighters. This despite the fact that they are destroying people's property—right on TV, and many of the properties are black-owned businesses or stores with black employees (*black lives matter*, right?). The Daily Caller reported[467] that several Hollywood celebrities helped the MFF bail out Jaleel Stallings, with bail set at $75,000. Stallings allegedly shot at SWAT officers during one of the riots in May.

If that wasn't bad enough, they also helped get Darnika Floyd released on $100,000 bail. Floyd "has been accused of stabbing a friend to death." Moving up (or down) the bail ladder, these Hollywood stars sent a virtual file in a cake, helping the MFF pay a $350,000 bond to release Christopher Boswell. Boswell, a twice-convicted rapist, had been "charged with kidnapping, assault, and sexual assault in two different cases."

But do these anti-cop, "defund the police" activists truly believe what they say? For example, Alyssa Milano, one of the wokest of the woke, is one Hollywood star who prompts that question. A good soldier, Milano reacted[468] to the Breonna Taylor court decision not to indict officers for murder with an abundance of critical thinking—just kidding. That didn't happen. Did she react by reading the original documents in the investigation, which are available online? [469] Not likely. No, instead she, of course, came out against the involved police officers. She tweeted, "Sleeping while black shouldn't get you killed." How sad it must be to live with those toxic thoughts constantly poisoning her mind. She's also used the hashtag[470] "#ProtectPeopleNotPolice. What a *charming*[471] woman.

Still, does this virtue signaling virtuoso truly believe what she says? Maybe not. Let's use leftist activist and actor Alyssa Milano as an example of Hollywood anti-cop wokeness. In September 2020, Milano was at her home and became terrified at possible criminal behavior near her home. WOR 710 reported[472] that Alyssa Milano called the police. Yes, again, the *defund the police advocate* called the cops. Must have been horrible for her. Especially after watching the video[473] of the response at the *Daily Mail*, which shows nine police cars, including the car recording the dashcam video, responding to her home.

The *Daily Mail* also spoke with[474] one of Milano's neighbors who said, after noticing a helicopter in the area, that "something was going on." The neighbor added, "Then we saw all the police cars parked in front of Alyssa's home. They had their guns at the ready and seemed very serious." Nine patrol cars and a police helicopter. Must have been traumatic, for sure.

In a statement, Milano said she and her husband saw a man dressed in black walking in the woods near her property with a gun. Saying that was a rare sight in their neighborhood, according to the *Daily Mail*, "she called the police." WOR reported that several police officers showed up to the call. They conducted a three-hour search. Deputies eventually located the culprit—a young man shooting at squirrels with an air gun.

WOR reported that "Milano thanked the deputies' response ... and clarified her position on policing." Actually, what she did was to parse her praise for the cops. She said, "The responding officers were amazing and made my family and I feel safe and secure as we 'sheltered in place' until we knew exactly what was happening." She added, "These are exactly the type of situations that police officers are trained for and should be responding to, and we will always support police having the resources they need for appropriate policing actions." Meaning, the cops should respond to what *she* feels is an appropriate police call, like when *she* needs them. What, exactly, is her law enforcement expertise to make such a statement?

Then Milano reverted to her default ignorant mode by saying, "We'd love to see equally trained non-police professionals respond to addiction and mental health crises and non-violent events so that these brave officers can do the jobs they are so good at handling, as they demonstrated this weekend." Again, law and order according to Alyssa et al.

Just one question, Ms. Milano. How does anyone know those "addiction and mental health crises" won't be violent until after the call? Police officers frequently respond to addiction, mental health crises, and "nonviolent events" that become violent in the time it takes to say "nonviolent."

To reiterate the statement from the head of the MFF, Greg Lewin, to whom the Hollywood elite are sending their money, "I often don't even look at a charge when I bail someone out. I will see it after I pay the bill because it is not the point. The point is the system we are fighting." What a guy, eh? Wonder how the next victims of those released will feel? Maybe those Hollywood "heroes" should ask them—well, if the victims are still alive.

Hey, Hollywood celebrities, why not try this? Create a Google Alert for the names of the criminals you bailed out. That way you can be notified when they reoffend. Then you'll know exactly what avoidable horrors the suspect you paid to have released perpetrated on those innocent victims.

Organizations such as The Bail Project[475] (TBP) and the Minnesota Freedom Foundation (MFF) obviously affect the police by putting dangerous criminals back on the streets. As one example, the MFF, to which (Boss-endorsed) Senator Kamala Harris and several of (Boss-endorsed) Vice President Joe Biden's staff donated, released a suspect that allegedly shot at police. And TBP got a man out who was in jail for allegedly beating his wife. As he'd promised to do when he got out, he went back home and beat his wife to death.

Twice, the head of TBP, Michael E. Novogratz, was supposed to appear on *Tucker Carlson Tonight* on the Fox News Channel to explain the "good work" TBP does. Twice, he bailed[476] out of the interview. This was also the organization that reportedly supplied the rioters in Louisville, Kentucky, with a U-Haul truck[477] full of propaganda, including a sign that read "Defund the Police," as well as protective gear and items that Antifa routinely uses as weapons against the police—items paid for with donations from some of America's wealthiest people: Bill Gates, Jack Dorsey, and other millionaires and billionaires.

Chapter 37

Government Education—
Critical Race Theory

Perhaps most ominous for the future of our nation are the efforts of the Boss's Obama Foundation and its comrade fellow social justice organizations to dominate the curricula of America's education system. It's a system that has become increasingly anti-American, anti-liberty, anti-capitalist, and anti-police, and increasingly pro-socialist,[478] pro-Marxist, and pro-revolutionary. These organizations are simultaneously moving Officer Friendly out of schools as they move Karl Marx into schools.

Parents, with their heads already on swivels for their school district's incessant academic subterfuge, now have to contend with the flawed history and propaganda of the 1619 Project.[479] First published in the *New York Times*, the premise is that American History began not in 1776 but when the first slaves arrived in the English colony of Virginia. It also is the year before the Pilgrims landed in Massachusetts, which many on the Left view as the beginning of Native American "genocide." Though many tribes were treated horribly by many U.S. government authorities, this partisan distortion of American history is being criticized in some odd places.

Rich Lowry, at *National Review*, reported,[480] "Then the World Socialist Web Site—of all things—begin publishing interviews with eminent historians slamming the project." Lowry lists three prominent professors from Princeton, CUNY, and Oxford who criticized the project: James McPherson, James Oakes, and Richard Carwardine, respectively.

According to Lowry, "The *Times* published an extraordinary letter from [the three professors] as well as Sean Wilentz of Princeton and Victoria Bynum of Texas State University, demanding 'prominent corrections of all the errors and distortions presented in the 1619 Project.'"

Still, 1619 Project author Nikole Hannah-Jones defends this garbage. But when considering the baseline—the alternate founding year for the United States from which she starts her bastardization of American history—it's no surprise. As reported[481] by Jordan Davidson in the *Federalist*, Hannah-Jones pronounced "Christopher Columbus as 'no different' than Nazi leader Adolf Hitler." Another *Federalist* writer has her stating[482] that "the white race is the biggest murderer, rapist, pillager, and thief of the modern world." There's some objective history, eh? Don't like Columbus? Fine. But saying there is no difference between Chris and Adolf is absurd.

Even Hannah-Jones finally backed away from the premise of her "history" project. Accuracy in Media reported,[483] "Now, however, Jones is backing away from the central premise of her entire project." Apparently, the professors' letter, exposing her flawed history, triggered her reconsideration. They challenged her central premise that the "Founding Fathers wanted separation from Britain in order to ensure slavery would continue. 'This is not true,' they wrote. 'If supportable, the allegation would be astounding—yet every statement offered by the project to validate it is false.'"

Shamefully, the piece of excrement won for Hannah-Jones a Pulitzer Prize (an organization with a penchant for rewarding journalists who lie[484] and for ignoring journalists who tell the truth: Russia Collusion Hoax). Tying the 1619 Project into the current conflagration in the streets, the Accuracy in Media staff wrote, "Jones won the Pulitzer Prize for commentary, became a celebrity journalist and was established at the forefront of the intellectual vanguard that fuels the current Black Lives Matter protests." So, add anti-police to her anti-American history.

Despite learning about the debunking of the 1619 Project authors' "scholarship," the Pulitzer Center defends its decision to award the prize to Hannah-Jones, saying the 1619 Project "challenges us to reframe U.S. history by marking the year when the first enslaved Africans arrived on Virginia soil as our nation's foundational date." Okay, but *it's not* "our nation's foundational date." July 4th, 1776, is. Prior to that date, the United States of America did not exist. The nation's children are under siege by social justice, anti-police warriors led by capos like Hannah-Jones.

According to Robby Soave at Reason, this curriculum is being taught[485] in school districts in Chicago, Buffalo, Washington, DC, New York City, and many others. In the *Frederick News-Post*, Hannah Farrow writes that the 1619 Project is "now taught in more than 4,500 schools nationwide." They are teaching sanctioned lying about history, a negative view of the police, and the promotion of socialism in America in taxpayer funded, public school classrooms. At the same time, public schools are kicking cops out of schools and teaching kids that police officers are racist murderers.

Hannah-Jones is no fan of the cops. John Sexton at HotAir.com has a poignant take[486] on her perspective. Hannah-Jones draws a parallel between the violence in the streets today and the violence during the 1950s and 1960s, fighting for black civil rights. Sexton writes, "Even if you accept her premise that it was the violent reaction that brought change, that still only works because it presents a clear contrast. It's not just two sides battling, it's one side being unfairly brutalized by violent goons and monsters.[487] People have sympathy for victims of violence, not perpetrators."

It's a hard reality for law enforcement officers today that it was the police who perpetrated much of the violence during the Civil Rights Movement against Martin Luther King Jr.'s truly peaceful demonstrators. Today, it's clearly the insurgents who are committing the violence against communities and against law enforcement officers who are trying to do a job made impossible by politicians supporting this Marxist/anarchist revolution.

Fortunately, for four years, Americans had a president who was not afraid to take on the propaganda that fueled the violence being taught by leftists in government, even in public schools. Federal, state, and local governments have been on a mission to indoctrinate government workers (including law enforcement) using blatantly leftist propaganda.

The thing is, if the roles were reversed, the Left would melt down with outrage. Just think about what the Left would do if a conservative mayor attempted to, for example, force employees or students to attend firearms safety classes taught by the National Rifle Association. Their heads would explode even if there were no "propaganda" and it was solely a class specifically focused on the safe handling of firearms.

Christopher Rufo, a director at the Discovery Institute, has been investigating and reporting[488] on government-sponsored critical race theory (CRT) indoctrination of government workers and students. Speaking with Fox News's Tucker Carlson on his TV program, Rufo said, "It's absolutely astonishing how critical race theory has pervaded every institution in the federal government. What I have discovered is that critical race theory has become, in essence, the default ideology of the federal bureaucracy and is now being weaponized against the American people." Rufo referred to the mandated classes as "cult indoctrination," and warned against the "danger and destruction it can wreak." Rufo also broke a story of the King County, Washington, government forcing its employees to attend racial justice indoctrination[489] and is now instituting racial segregation at work. The premise: black people are uncomfortable working around white people—according to the idiots in charge.

In their book *Cynical Theories*,[490] Helen Pluckrose and James Lindsay address CRT in a section titled "The Blurring of the Boundaries." They write that "critical race Theory [sic] encompasses many identity categories simultaneously and tries to be inclusive of 'different ways of knowing.' This results in a messy mixing of the evidenced with the experiential, in which a personal interpretation of lived experience (often informed—or misinformed—by Theory) is elevated to the status of evidence (usually of Theory)."[491] This theoretical blurring acts similarly to how the entities that promote CRT and provide funding, such as the Obama Foundation and the various nebulous Underboss organizations, operate.

President Trump apparently agreed. He took strong actions against this forced, partisan political indoctrination at the federal level. In September 2020, PJ Media reported,[492] "President Donald Trump ordered that federal agencies cease leading any training sessions that push 'critical race theory,' 'white privilege,' or any other 'propaganda effort teaching that either the United States or any race is inherently racist or evil.' On Sunday, he announced that the Department of Education (DOE) is investigating schools that teach the *New York Times*'s '1619 Project' and warned that any school doing so 'will not be funded.'" Biden will likely restore the program.

Many jurisdictions have forced America's law enforcement officers to undergo this unethical, immoral, political CRT brainwashing. But even those cops who've been CRT indoctrinated are still not woke enough for anti-police factions in the nation's public schools. In fact, for many leftist teachers and administrators, as mentioned earlier, the cops are no longer welcome in their schools. But Marxist indoctrinators and inquisitors seems quite welcome. So, is there a direct Boss link to CRT? Of course there is.

According[493] to an article by Ben Shapiro at Western Revival, the Boss has a "close relationship with Derrick Bell, the father of Critical Race Theory (CRT)." Shapiro asks, "Why is it [CRT] so dangerous? And what role does it play in Obama's thinking?" Likely a significant role. At Breitbart, Joel B. Pollak wrote[494] that a story published only after Bell's death in March 2011 showed "a young Barack Obama speaking at a protest at Harvard Law School in favor of Professor Derrick Bell, who had clashed with the university over the issue of faculty diversity."

About the Harvard story mentioned above, Lachlan Markay, writing in the Daily Signal, provides a Breitbart link[495] to a piece written by Ben Shapiro showing what appears to be a video still image of Obama and Bell embracing during what is believed to be the previously mentioned demonstration at Harvard. In 2012, Lachlan Markay also reported,[496] "Visitor logs show that Derrick A. Bell visited the White House twice since President Obama took office."

Markay writes, "Obama tells the crowd to 'Open your hearts and open your minds to the words of professor Derrick Bell.'" Open your hearts and minds to the words of a critical race theorist who believes America is inherently racist and always will be. Not surprisingly, Prof. Bell also held a negative attitude toward police. At the Harvard Law Review Blog, Alexis Hoag recently wrote about Bell's likely view of the current turmoil in the streets, if he were still alive:

> Nothing about this moment—COVID-19's dispropor-
> tionate[497] impact[498] on Black people, Trump's explicit
> anti-Black racism,[499] or the mass demonstrations fol-
> lowing lethal police use of force against[500] Black peo-
> ple—would have surprised Professor Derrick Bell.
> These fault lines are not new; rather, these events
> merely expose longstanding structural damage to the
> nation's foundation.

Once again, a biased leftist dutifully checks all the applicable anti-police boxes.

Acknowledging that "Bell was the founder of the doctrine of Critical Race Theory," Pollack also wrote, "Critical Race Theory holds that the United States is racist by design, because its Constitution and all of its other institutions emerged in a context where slavery was legal. According to theory, the very institution of private property in the U.S. is corrupt because it was enshrined in a system that saw black people as chattels." Slipping into a discussion about race, the American notion of private property as being corrupt rather than essential to liberty obviously puts CRT into the Marxist category.

Those signing on to the Boss's MBKAP are also responsible for changes in policies that are indoctrinating students against police officers and removing cops—as school resource officers—from schools. School districts across the nation have adopted an anti-police agenda, which calls for bans on police officers in schools. This often includes responding to violent incidents, which leads to tragedies such as the mass shooting[501] in Parkland, Florida.

The Los Angeles School District is going even further, using the CCP virus as an excuse to ban cops from classrooms. That district's teacher's union is demanding many non–CCP virus items[502] before they will return to the classroom. Along with demands for federal bailouts for failed state and local governments, Medicare for all, a wealth tax, and banning cops from schools, they are also calling to "defund police."

And pay attention to the familiar language. "*Police violence* [emphasis mine] is a leading cause of death and trauma for Black people and is a serious public health and moral issue. *We must shift the astronomical amount of money devoted to policing, to education and other essential needs such as housing and public health.*"

Wait, have we heard "police violence" before? At the Boss's MBKA webpage at Obama.org, a tweet from the MBK Alliance reads, "This summer, we invited U.S. cities to sign a pledge committing to combating police violence and systemic racism within law enforcement." Yes, "police violence" once again, and its rogue sibling, "systemic racism."

Many school districts have adopted similar policies. The Edmonds School District, in Washington State, has voted to remove[503] its school resource officers. This was despite parental objections, which were reportedly ignored. What was concerning was the adherence to a preferred narrative[504] when implementing the policy. School board president Deborah Kilgore said, "It was critical that the board heard and continue to hear from our students on this and other issues." Kilgore told the *Daily Herald*, "It is unacceptable that students are hurting and feel unsafe in our schools."

Hurting and unsafe? Because police officers are on campus? Did Kilgore and other board members speak to any students who did not express these fears, or to any who expressed fears of schools without officers? Who knows? Apparently, they only cared to speak with "students of color" who were apparently hiding under their desks because they were afraid a big, bad police officer might come to the school. That's if they really spoke with any students at all or just embellished the story to fit the narrative. White liberals have a penchant for telling black people how they feel about stuff.

Edmonds Police Chief Jim Lawless said, "I am disappointed that this process was not more deliberative and inclusive of all parties involved—the district, students, faculty, staff, and yes, the police department." He also mentioned that Kilgore's view of the issue did not reflect the relationships established between Edmonds police officers and Edmonds-Woodway High School students. Lawless added, "I am quite disappointed that she [Kilgore] would paint your police department's efforts with such a broad brush."

Some parents said they contacted the board members who failed to respond to their questions and concerns. One grandparent, who'd raised children in the district and now has grandchildren in district schools, emailed each member of the board twice, once before and once after the vote. He said he only received one reply, and it was an auto-response informing him the board member was retiring at the end of the week.

This shows how some school administrators deal with implementing these policies. If a parent disagrees with the school's preferred political perspective and refuses to perpetuate that narrative, the school is not interested in the parent's opinion. If someone has a different opinion, they are not just wrong, they are racist and therefore evil. These school administrators and school boards tolerate no diversity of thought.

Would you want to be one of those school district board members across the country who've voted to get rid of school resource officers if, God forbid, a mass shooter arrived on campus? How in the world can you believe children are in more danger rather than less when a cop is present? Only when you delude yourself into believing anti-police myths. The anecdotal evidence and comments by the police chief indicate that most students like their resource officers. Funny how that suddenly changes after the adults buy into a national racial justice mythology and adopt radical stances. And the problems don't stop with kicking cops out of schools.

To show just how insidious this radical infection of the public school system is, even if you keep track of your child's curricula, as best you can trust your school board, there may be ways radicals get around parents' scrutiny. An obviously anti-police company called Scholastic: Classroom

Magazines[505] may have a way to avoid school course subject disclosure. Billed as "free magazines for classrooms," the company's website displays the happy images of children on the various magazine covers. What could possibly be wrong with that? A lot, it seems.

It doesn't take long, perusing the site, to realize many of these magazine topics (Racial Justice, Climate Change, and Immigration) could have been written by BLM or Antifa. For example, for grades 3 through 6 (there is also a selection for grades 7 to 12), this is the first, ostensibly objective and nonpolitical, paragraph: "The long history of unjust treatment of Black people in America has become a major focus of this election. Two current crises—police killings of Black Americans and the coronavirus pandemic—have highlighted just how widespread the problem is."

Scholastic continues its "unbiased" thesis: "Individuals and civil rights groups have since joined together in demanding an end to the long history of bias and brutality against Black people by law enforcement." Just imagine being a police officer and thinking about your child or grandchild having to read that garbage. Coming home and asking why mommy, daddy, grandma, or grandpa are racist killers. Or what about the black students? They're being taught cops hate them and want to kill them—specifically. That is straight-up child abuse.

The radical "wolf in sheep's clothing" Scholastic company also adopted the previously discussed, anti–English language, counterconvention of capitalizing *Black* while using lower case for *white*, regarding race. But it's okay; the Associated Press (AP) has endorsed[506] this latest racist, Orwellian twist of the language. What kind of lesson does this teach kids? A racist one.

Nowhere in this Scholastics screed on so-called racial justice does the word "riot" appear. They use only "civil rights demonstrations" and "public gatherings." The word "violence" also does not appear in the 3–6 grade group. It does in the 7–12 grade group, but only as it applies to "violence against Black Americans by the police [which] grew to a historic level." No bias there, eh?

Let's just conclude with a passage that encapsulates this entire segment. Imagine your child is reading this quote from the 7–12 group: "Amid widespread fury over the killing of other Black Americans at the hands of police, the videos [of the George Floyd incident] sparked outrage and protests worldwide in support of the Black Lives Matter movement. (The movement seeks to stop the violence inflicted on Black communities by law enforcement and others, as well as to end white supremacy.)"

Really? Is that truly their goal? Forgive people who are confused by BLM's total disregard for all of the black lives taken in places like Chicago. BLM seems much more geared toward inflicting Marxism on America than truly adopting the creed that all black lives matter. Babies continue to be killed in Chicago with not a peep from BLM. Yet they want to defund or abolish the police.

Is money in a bank safer without a police officer protecting it? Is the jewelry less at risk with a cop protecting the store? Is the president safer with or without his Secret Service detail? The obvious answer is: the money, jewelry, and the president are safer with cops. Why should this equation be any different when protecting America's true national treasure: our children?

Whether it's government indoctrinating Americans, young and old, in anti-American, anti-police mythology such as Critical Race Theory or removing cops from schools, the battle lines have been clearly drawn. Americans who wish to retain their traditions, culture, liberty—and police—must be ever vigilant against the onslaught of those who want to change our nation to something unrecognizable as American. Let people know how you feel. Support your local police, back the blue, and contact your school board members. Do it until they get the message: you won't let traditional America go without a fight.

To close this topic, the Epoch Times has a series of articles[507] examining education in the United States. The title of Part 18 reads, "Schools Using Fake 'History' to Kill America" (recall Antifa's battle cry: "Liberation begins where America dies"). Alex Newman writes about government-educated Americans. He points to their hopeless ignorance "of their own nation's history." He asserts this is by design. He decries Americans' knowledge of civics, world history, and specifically the history of communism. Newman stresses this was not an accident.

He points to "the ongoing corruption of history," including the discredited 1619 Project. Summing up why "history is being rewritten," he says it's "hardly a mystery." To explain it he conscripts George Orwell's classic novel *1984*. The ruling party's motto in the book explains the strategy. "Who controls the past controls the future. Who controls the present past." Newman explains how Mao, in China, was particularly adept at imposing this strategy on his people.

An ironically named organization, Advocates for Youth (AFY), does not advocate for youth—unless they mean advocating for indoctrinating youth with anti-police, pro-Marxist propaganda. Then it's appropriately named. With YouTube video seminars and materials such as the Youth Activist Toolkit,[508] this group teaches young people from fourteen to twenty-four years old how to become activists (or radicals).

They teach kids things such as that the police don't keep us safe. The police know how to abuse power and authority. And when dealing with the police, you just need to "survive the encounter." They say cops don't know anything more than the average person about the U.S. Constitution. This is another lie among a gigantic trash heap of lies.

Law Enforcement Officers learn constitutional law in police academies across America. Cops need to work within the Constitution and apply it on a daily basis. For instance, the Washington State Criminal Justice Training Commission, a police academy, provides officers with a monthly Law Enforcement Digest[509] (LED). The publication contains briefs of federal and state constitutional decisions that affect how cops do their work.

Though the AFY has several videos covering many topics, for these purposes, let's stick to one video they produce,[510] available on YouTube. It's entitled "How to Get Police Out of Your School." So nice, eh? The brief summary accompanying the video reads, "We know that a police presence in our schools is not only unnecessary, but harmful and dangerous to students. In this training, learn how to work with school officials to get cops out of schools and invest in resources that protect and support students." It is these people who are dangerous to students. What kind of person teaches a kid that the police are dangerous? Sociopaths? Deluded people? Doing this to impressionable children is unconscionable.

Jennifer Heine-Withee of SW Washington Parents' Rights in Education told Todd Herman of KTTH 770 Radio that the AFY also indoctrinates youth to believe that if you're white, you're racist, and there's nothing you can do about it. They teach kids they live on "stolen" land, without any historical context. And they're putting kids in danger by telling them to resist and to bully cops.

Heine-Withee said she's learned that on a private teacher's Facebook page, some teachers have asked for "advocacy resources for pre-K and up." Another teacher posted a BLM event and said it would be "good for our kids to go to." These taxpayer-funded folks are teaching kids to hate cops by inundating them with lies. Again, what do the children of cops trapped in these classes think?

Today, not only are government schools teaching kids how bad their country is generally, they're teaching students that cops are intentionally targeting and hunting black people, killing them in the streets. That lie doesn't belong in any American classroom.

Chapter 38

Associates—Social Media, Tech, Wall Street Banks

Apple, Microsoft, Amazon, Alaska Airlines, Bayer, Burger King, AT&T, ESPN, Uber, Subway, 23 and me, The Academy (Awards), Adidas, Airbnb, American Airlines, American Express, Ancestry, Armani, Atlantic Records, AXE, Barnes & Noble, Ben & Jerry (*long time cop-haters*), Billboard, BMW, BP, Booking.com, Burt's Bees, Cadillac, Call of Duty, Capitol Records, Cartoon Network, Chick-fil-A (*What?*), Chipotle, Cisco, Coca Cola, Conde Nast, Converse, CVS, DHL Express, DirectTV, Disney, Doritos, DoorDash, Duolingo, Dropbox, Eaton, Etsy, FedEx, Fender, FILA, Fitbit, Foot Locker, Fox (*What?*), Game Spot, Gibson, GoDaddy, GoFundMe, GoPro, Gorilla Glue, Grammarly, Habitat for Humanity, HBO, Hershey's, Home Depot, Honda, HP, Hulu, Humana, IBM, IKEA, IMAX, Intel, Lego, Levi's, Lexus, LinkedIn, L'Oreal Pairs, Logitech, Lowe's, Louis Vuitton, Lyft, Madden NFL 20, Marvel Entertainment, Mastercard, Mattel, McAfee, McDonalds, Merck, Mercedes Benz, Met Life, Metropolitan Opera, Mozilla, Napster, NASCAR, Netflix, New Balance, New York Life, NFL, NHL, Nickelodeon, Nike, Nintendo, Nordstrom, North Face, Old Spice, Paramount, Peloton, Pepsi, Pfizer, Playstation, Pokemon, Popeye's Chicken, Pop-Tarts, Pornhub, Porsche, Pringles, Procter & Gamble, PUMA, Qualcomm, Quicken Loans, Reddit, Red Lobster, Reebok, Reese's, Rice Krispies, Scholastic, Sesame Street, Showtime, Sephora, Sony, Spotify,

STARZ, Starbuck's, Star Wars, Sysco, Taco Bell, Target, Ticketmaster, TikTok, Timberland, TMobile, Tumblr, Twitch, Ugg, Ulta Beauty, Under Armor, United Health Group, Vanguard, Vans, Verizon, VERSACE, Vevo, VioacomCBS, Virgin Records, Warner Brothers, Wendy's, Xbox, Yamaha Music USA, Yelp, Zara, Zoom.

Wall Street Banks: Barclays Bank, Bank of America, Citigroup, Goldman Sachs, Wells Fargo.

The above-listed corporations were harvested from a list of 269 companies cited by the website Conservative US as financially "supporting BLM and Antifa Riots."[511] The website emphasizes the nebulous nature of not only the organizations under the direct control of the Boss and Underboss, but also those who serve the larger goals as soldiers and associates and whose CEOs serve as capos.

In trying to discern from where the radical groups get their financial support, they write, "Antifa is not a single organization, and therefore, financial details, if any exist, are murky." The "mainstream" companies listed have shown, in one way or another, either moral or financial support for the groups participating in the riots under the umbrella of BLM and Antifa.

One of the most effective associates for the Boss's anti-cop crime family are social media platforms. They are supposed to be simple platforms, nonpartisan "utilities" similar to a telephone company. This is why these social media giants receive special congressional protections from being sued. They are not liable in the way that publishers are, who edit and "fact-check" (censor) content like print, audio, and visual media. But we know that Facebook, Twitter, YouTube, and Google do censor their content and throttle, defund, suspend, and even de-platform conservative individuals and organizations.

It doesn't matter who you call or what you say; the phone companies simply allow people to speak, text, or otherwise communicate to each other on their platform. They don't block a call if a conservative calls the president or uses the phone to order two dozen MAGA hats for his liberal buddies. But Facebook, Twitter, Google, and YouTube will "throttle"[512] how much traffic certain sites can get, and they censor content based on political intent. Recently, scientists with views of the CCP virus that stray from the chosen narrative have been censored. Incredibly, in October 2020, Facebook and Twitter censored a legitimate news story published by the oldest continually operating newspaper in America: the *New York Post*, founded by Alexander Hamilton in 1801. In January 2021, Twitter permanently removed President Trump's account.

They do this even though they receive a specific exemption from Congress through which they cannot be held liable for content on their sites. Once a social media entity editorializes, throttles websites, or censors content, it is violating the rules Congress set up for its exemption. It is behaving more like a publisher than a platform. One of Facebook cofounder Mark Zuckerberg's staunchest critics is Chris Hughes, Facebook's other cofounder.

According to Adam Candeub at the American Conservative, Hughes says that Zuckerberg[513] used to say that "Facebook was just a 'social utility,' a neutral platform for people to communicate what they wished." That is obviously no longer what he believes. And he's becoming increasingly bold about his change of heart. Now, he believes Facebook is entitled to the First Amendment protections he denies his Facebook users—especially conservative users. Hughes now describes Zuckerberg's view as being a "self-appointed arbiter of acceptable public discourse." Hughes believes Facebook should be broken up and says that "the government must hold Mark accountable." Once again, who do people like Zuckerberg and Jack Dorsey (CEO of Twitter) think they are?

The relevant law that protects big tech is 47 U.S. Code § 230.[514] This law was not enacted to ennoble a few select tech giants, shielding them from liabilities other media corporations must observe while engaging in censoring content and silencing political views it does not like. Think about how audacious, self-unaware, and hypocritical it is to be engaged in violating users' free speech rights by claiming their own rights to free speech.

Included in the censoring of "conservative" people and sites is law enforcement–related content. In fact, GoFundMe is in on the act to defund police (officers). *Law Enforcement Today* (LET) reported,[515] "GoFundMe shuts down page for cop's legal expenses, allows ANTIFA to raise funds for criminals." The facts of this action by GoFundMe perfectly illustrate the bias against police inundating America today. Online payment platforms are also complicit, with companies such as PayPal suspending the accounts of law enforcement–related companies based on erroneous, non-vetted complaints.

First, what happened with GoFundMe? LET tells the story about Sgt. Ryan O'Neill, the South Bend Police Department (SBPD) officer GoUnFundMe defunded. Sgt. O'Neill responded to a report of a possible car prowler, located the suspect, and ordered the suspect out of the car. The suspect allegedly had a hunting knife and a woman's purse. Reportedly, the suspect refused to listen to Sgt. O'Neill's orders and advanced on the officer aggressively, knife in hand.

Sgt. O'Neill fired twice and struck the suspect once. The suspect threw the knife at the sergeant, striking him in the arm. The injury was reported as minor. When other units arrived, with the suspect gravely wounded, they decided to "load and go" (some agencies call it "scoop and run") to get the suspect to the hospital rather than wait for an ambulance. This is a judgment call. LET notes the SBPD discussed this procedure with their SWAT unit, which includes a surgeon, who endorsed the procedure. The suspect later succumbed to his wounds at the hospital and died.

According to LET, then–Democratic presidential nominee candidate (and would-be Obama clone) Pete Buttigieg, mayor of South Bend, pandered to the family and critics, "dragging the officer and whole department through the mud." Buttigieg proclaimed that the city and department (which he ran) was plagued by "systematic racism." He also debased himself by using this tragic incident to raise funds for his campaign.

What's worse is who GoFundMe submitted to when it decided to shut down the police fundraiser. LET reported that after the SBPD FOP police union Lodge 36 created the account, *a complaint from Antifa*, accusing Sgt. O'Neill of a "hate crime," was all that was necessary to close the page. So, the cop-loathing Antifa makes a complaint, and GoFundMe just shuts it down. Hey, GoFundMe! Some cops don't like being stabbed by car prowlers. They're funny that way.

The SBPD FOP concurs. "Shockingly, GoFundMe told us that they cancelled the campaign because it was in support of a hate crime. This is fundamentally wrong, and I'm shocked that a company would accuse a police officer of a hate crime simply for defending himself from an armed attacker."

GoFundMe apparently wasn't interested in waiting for an investigation and responded flaccidly to the FOP's inquiries about closing their account. Readers can decide whether GoFundMe is blatantly biased against law enforcement and if their answer has any integrity. The company's "Community Management Team" sent an initial response and then reinforced its decision with an additional, equally limp, missive:

> Unfortunately, our Terms & Conditions, along with strictly enforced policies from the payments industry, prohibit GoFundMe from allow [sic] you to continue raising money on our site.

And then (emphasis mine):

> Campaigns deemed by GoFundMe, in its sole discretion, to be in support of, or for the legal defense of *alleged crimes* associated with hate, violence, harassment, bullying, discrimination, terrorism or intolerance of any kind relating to race, ethnicity, national origin, religious affiliation, sexual orientation, sex, gender or gender identity, or serious disabilities or diseases. We have removed your account.

Sgt. O'Neill had not been charged with an "alleged" crime—hate or otherwise. So, what's GoFundMe's true basis for its decision? Again, the reader can decide. One hang-up critics seem to have is that Sgt. O'Neill's body camera was not activated during the incident. These days, people tend to automatically ascribe a sinister motive whenever a cop's camera did not record an incident.

One of the most common reasons for an officer's camera not being activated is because, being human, the officer simply forgot. People who work in various industries forget to do things they're supposed to do all the time. Critics will argue that in most occupations, forgetting is not a matter of life or death. True, but in most 911 calls, it isn't a matter of life or death either. The problem arises when an officer forgets to activate a camera in what turns out to be a significant event.

Another common reason for forgetting is officers unexpectedly having to bail out of their vehicles to deal with an aggressive suspect before having time to switch on the camera. It happens.

This brings up the point that police officers no longer receive the benefit of the doubt their oath are supposed to warrant unless proof exists to show otherwise. Rather, cops today are treated as if they are guilty until they prove themselves innocent. There are even DUI cases these days where judges are granting defense attorneys' motions for dismissal because the officers' field sobriety tests, for whatever reason, weren't recorded or occurred off camera.

To conclude, again from the book *De-Policing America*:

> This is a dangerous trend. If an officer's word is no longer valued, then not only does the officer's professional reputation suffer but also crime victims pay a price. Let's say an officer witnesses a suspect commit a crime against a victim, but it's not captured on video. Would the [cop] critics deem that crime not to have taken place? There are examples all across the nation of defendants acquitted because the benefit of the doubt is going to those with long criminal records over good cops. De-policing.

Chapter 39

Fighting Back/Call to Action

What to do and how to do it? Back in the '90s, when Rudy Giuliani was the U.S. Attorney for the Southern District of New York, how did he handle the violent Mafia crime families?[516] He didn't appease them. He didn't endorse them. He prosecuted them. A fellow American of Italian ancestry took them down. Today, this may not be an option with the Boss's gang for two reasons: One, many of these political leaders involved either directly, like the Boss, or peripherally, like the Clintons, have so far proven virtually untouchable by the American criminal justice system.

Two, the neo-socialist forces that have taken over a major political party have created a shell game where instead of three shells and one pea, they have hundreds of shells with dozens of peas for each. As we saw earlier, the Underboss's Open Society alone rains financial support down on a cadre of over two hundred subordinate political, media, educational, and various activist organizations. And the Obama Foundation is actively recruiting[517] soldiers to the cause.

"If you're looking to take action—or looking to educate yourselves on these issues—we've gathered some resources from the @ObamaFoundation that can help at Obama.org/anguish and action."[518]

For example, cultural influencers like Glenn Beck repeatedly admonish their listeners and viewers to do independent research to verify the information the Blaze provides. However, the Boss refers potential soldiers, specifically and exclusively, to his own organization. Diversity of thought is not tolerated.

It's important to understand that this "movement," primarily led at the street level by BLM and Antifa, is not organic, the result of a popular uprising. Past movements such as civil rights, anti–Vietnam War, and even women's suffrage, to name three prominent movements over the twentieth century, were organic and popular causes. They may have garnered political sponsorship and a more sophisticated organization later, but their inception was grassroots. The Civil Rights Movement as directed by MLK, aside from being authentic, was also peaceful. Today, the BLM Marxist leadership expresses open disdain[519] for MLK's nonviolence.

The current BLM/Antifa insurrection is not grassroots. There is nothing organic about it. It's organized and well-funded. In the above examples of historical wrongs, those movements involved mostly peaceful protesters who were opposing true oppression.

The Civil Rights Movement was real, and systemic racism against black people existed. Mishandled by politicians, though valiantly fought by the American military, the Vietnam War split a nation—it was real. And women did not have the right to vote, out of which sprang the suffrage movement of the early twentieth century. But those wrongs have been corrected by an ever-evolving American people. This is evinced by people around the world continuing to stream to America's shores.

Today, there are groups of people, including at the Obama Foundation, who, while loosely aligned, are secretly, effectively organized, and funded by a leftist billionaire through a shell game of nebulous organizations.

It is known they are well-funded and organized, as recent evidence exists of unknown sources delivering and staging the weapons the terrorists used to wage riots: rocks, bricks, frozen water bottles, accelerants, protective clothing, industrial lasers, high-grade fireworks, and so on. Someone also provided travel resources to deploy terrorists to other cities.

This happened after violence in Kenosha, Wisconsin, erupted over another false report that police had killed an "unarmed" black man.

Authorities soon revealed the "unarmed" man was armed with a knife, but by then it was too late. Damage done; another fuse lit.

Brendan Matthews, the Kenosha Professional Police Association's lawyer, said,[520] "The purely fictional depiction of events coming from those without direct knowledge of what actually occurred is incredibly harmful, and provides no benefit to anyone whatsoever, other than to perpetuate a misleading narrative."

A citizen called in a 911 report of suspicious behavior among a group of people associated with vehicles with out-of-state plates. The people were also violating Kenosha's curfew, put in place because of the rioting. Kenosha police officers assisted by U.S. Marshals surveilled the group of suspected radicals and observed them filling many containers with gasoline.

Incidentally, the *New York Post* reported on the outstanding arrest warrant[521] the court had issued for Jacob Blake, the latest criminal hero-victim of Kenosha's "mostly peaceful protesters." The judge had issued the warrant "for violating a restraining order stemming from an alleged sexual assault." Well, if that doesn't qualify him as a hero-victim worth destroying lives and businesses over, what does?

And to make sure maximum damage occurred at the newest riot, reportedly, an unknown source transported these alleged rioters from Seattle (and likely Portland) to Kenosha in a black bus, a food van (Riot Kitchen), and a car. Who paid for their travel? Who paid for their supplies? These are questions that likely will not be answered for many months. But investigators must unravel the conspiracy to prevent future violence.

The *New York Post* reported,[522] "Activists from Seattle group 'Riot Kitchen' were arrested in Kenosha, Wisconsin, after they filled up multiple gas cans, prompting law enforcement officials in unmarked cars to take them into custody, according to police and video footage." Riot Kitchen is a violence-promoting group staffed with members of Antifa. While a part of their mission is to provide free food for rioters, they went to Kenosha, as Monica Showalter wrote[523] in American Thinker, with "some unusual cuisine on its menu."

Reportedly, police arrested nine individuals and recovered drugs, illegal fireworks, body armor, gas masks, and helmets. If you're wondering about the U.S. Marshals' presence, note that transporting incendiary devices, especially across state lines, is a federal offense.[524]

Riot Kitchen launched a GoFundMe effort[525] to raise funds to buy a food truck and get it licensed. They initially aimed for $40,000 but upped the goal to $52,000 and have raised over $50,000 at his writing. Keep in mind that GoFundMe has cancelled fundraising pages[526] for falsely accused (by Antifa) police officers but allows violent radicals to raise money.

This is the Antifa appendage's appeal to the mush-for-brains crowd:

> Hey everyone!! We're RIOT KITCHEN, and we are a no charge kitchen serving protestors, activists, movements and those in need in Seattle WA.
>
> We were founded by Maehem, a queer black woman who started out by wanting to help feed the protestors at The George Floyd protests in Seattle, WA.
>
> During CHOP we built a full functioning kitchen in Cal Anderson, with a experienced kitchen staff and a array [sic] of vegan, gluten free, vegetarian and other dishes.
>
> These include:
>
> Vegan and meat kebabs, a plethora of hot and cold sandwiches, vegan sloppy joes, vegan chili Mac, vegetarian chili Mac, vegan and meat breakfast sandwiches, vegan/vegetarian/meat burritos and much more!
>
> We want to continue RIOT KITCHEN on and into the future to keep serving our community!
>
> To do that, we need a food truck and licensing. We need about $40,000 to make this happen!

214

> This fundraiser is run by direct supporters of Maehem and her work, namely Maehem's right hand "Grandpa" and Jennifer Scheurle.
>
> Please support us in enabling this wonderful project and its caring people to enrich Seattle's community now and in the future.

Fighting this insurrection includes making sure potential donors know about groups such as Antifa's Riot Kitchen and the violence they promote and facilitate. Unfortunately, some America-hating radicals have no qualms about putting their names to donations that go to support violence. Giving the benefit of the doubt, perhaps those donors truly thought Riot Kitchen's mission was only to feed actual "peaceful protesters," despite "riot" being in their name. Think any donors will want their contributions back after they find out their money went to sending domestic terrorists to burn down poor little Kenosha, Wisconsin?

One effective way to fight back is to put pressure on political leaders to uncover the connections between groups like the Obama Foundation and Underboss-funded organizations such as Open Society. Again, these consistent mass protests are not organic. Think about it. How can Portland continue to see well-supplied, organized rioters showing up every single day for over four months without financial support from somewhere? Rioting is expensive.

Aside from the Obama Foundation's and Open Society's support for anti-cop groups, many American corporations, such as those listed in the previous chapter, have gotten caught up in the anti-police tidal wave. People can find another list of the companies donating to BLM or BLM-supporting groups at Forbes.com.[527] These well-known companies, such as Home Depot, Apple, and Intel, are donating millions of dollars to avowed "trained Marxists."[528] These corporations' management made the conscious decision to subsidize groups that support the most toxic form of government history has known. And they're doing it based on a provable lie about law enforcement officers.

Another way is to fight back financially. Donate to individuals and groups dedicated to exposing and sending to prison violent members of these Marxist, anarcho-communist, domestic terrorist groups. We've listed many anti-police, anti-American individuals and groups to this point. It's time to list a few individuals and groups dedicated to fighting this violent insurgency led by organizations such as Black Lives Matter, Inc., and Antifa, and expose the people and companies that support them.

The first group, of course, are American law enforcement. Where cops are allowed to fight this insurgency, it is suppressed. After state and city government surrendered a police precinct in Seattle, Washington, violent activists established the now-infamous CHAZ/CHOP "autonomous" zone. But, after months of occupation, when allowed to retake the precinct, Seattle's finest did it in short order. This result is true wherever political leaders allow federal, state, or local law enforcement (sometimes augmented by the National Guard) to do what they are so excellent at doing: restoring public order and peace.

The first individual who comes to mind, mentioned previously, is journalist Andy Ngo.[529] This intrepid freelance reporter, who happens to be a "person of color" and gay, is known for his epic dustups with Antifa. On one occasion, Antifa brutes beat Ngo so badly that he was hospitalized, suffering a brain bleed. He has risked his life and safety to expose some of the most violent domestic terrorists operating on America's, especially Portland's, streets today. If not for Ngo, we would not know nearly as much as we do about these violent thugs.

Another excellent reporter covering this politico-media manufactured tumult is Julio Rosas, senior reporter [530] for Townhall. His reporting, primarily seen on Fox News, has shown Americans what some politicians and the mainstream media have been trying so hard not to let them see: the daily violence wrought by these anti-police radicals. Rosa seems to pop up exactly where he is needed, providing video images of the rioters plying their toxic trade from New York City, Washington, DC, and Louisville; to St. Louis, Chicago, and Kenosha; to Seattle, Portland, and Los Angeles.

Independent journalist Taylor Hansen managed to infiltrate Antifa[531] in Portland one evening. After someone recognized him, Antifa members put out the word to their fellow terrorists. The domestic terrorists found and gave Hansen a beating. A photo accompanying the story shows huge swelling on Hanson's right cheek as well as a bloodied mouth. This is occurring in a major American city where mayors—in this case, Ted Wheeler, the second worst mayor in the United States—allow Antifa to continue assaulting Portland's residents and cops even as they disallow the police from doing their jobs.

Even popular comedian and conservative activist Steven Crowder, who has a show on the Blaze and at his Louder with Crowder website, infiltrated Antifa[532] and, in 2017, captured some revealing video. During his remarkable two-week undercover operation, Crowder got video exposing Antifa's tactics, communications, and weapons.

"Did you bring your gun?" a woman leader asked at an Antifa meeting. "I have … a regular rifle and an assault weapon, and a sawed-off style shotgun," the man responded. The leader replied by saying that she had a handgun and "two AKs coming." Crowder said the media was thoroughly uninterested in this video evidence. As Red Ice TV asks, "Why did it take two late night hosts—comedians—to find this out?" Why, indeed?

Aside from the few intrepid reporters who continue to do honest reporting, perhaps one of the most effective battle strategies against the insurgency is being conducted by the Department of Justice and its able former attorney general, William Barr. With the Underboss-funded prosecutors across the nation dismissing or failing to charge[533] crimes against rioters and looters, the federal government has stepped up its efforts to prosecute these offenders on federal charges.[534] As mentioned early in the book, in support of this effort, the U.S. Marshals Service had federally deputized[535] Oregon state troopers, Multnomah County sheriff's deputies, and Portland police officers. Recall the humorous miscalculation when Mayor Wheeler approved the deputization thinking the move could be used against right-wing counterdemonstrators. Sadly for the inept mayor, there was no violence, and the officers and remained federally deputized until the end of 2020.

The Epoch Times reported[536] on September 21, 2020, that the DOJ has designated three cities, New York, Portland, and Seattle, "as jurisdictions permitting anarchy, violence, destruction of property." The DOJ accused the three cities of failing "to undertake measures to counteract criminal activities." Former Attorney General Barr reportedly approved the list.

In a statement, Barr said, "When state and local leaders impede their own law enforcement officers and agencies from doing their jobs, it endangers innocent citizens who deserve to be protected, including those who are trying to peacefully assemble and protest." Barr may be referring [537] to the Antifa member who, as reported earlier, allegedly shot and killed a member of Patriot Prayer who was attending a pro-Trump counterprotest in Portland.

Barr said he's not interested in wasting federal tax dollars on cities that refuse to protect their citizens. He hopes this strategy will help the incompetent mayors and city councils in these cities to "reverse course and become serious about performing the basic function of government and start protecting their own citizens."

Think about the weight of this comment—that a top federal law enforcement official has to use financial leverage to prompt city officials to do what they are legally and ethically obligated to do instead of aligning themselves with their ideological comrades in the socialist, anarcho-communist movement. Simply stated, Barr is attempting to restore peace to these cities, fulfilling the government's promise made to society in the social contract.[538]

Astonishingly, especially in America, we have devolved to a situation where the DOJ must evaluate whether cities have allowed anarchy. In more detail, as described in the Epoch Times: "Criteria for evaluating whether cities have permitted anarchy and destruction include seeing whether jurisdictions *forbid police officers from intervening to restore order*, whether jurisdictions slash funding to police departments, and whether jurisdictions refuse offers of assistance from the federal government" (emphasis mine). Astonishingly, political officials have been putting their constituents at risk by consciously withholding police protection in some American cities.

Crime in the shameful three cities that Barr specifically names is soaring. All three anti-cop mayors—the worst being Bill "Comrade" de Blasio, the runner-up, Ted "Whining" Wheeler, and finishing a close third, Jenny "Summer of Love" Durkan, all among the Boss's capos—have vehemently refused federal offers of assistance to quell their cities' chaos. Actually, for the feds to "assist" these cities, they'd have to be doing something in the first place, and they haven't been. In fact, de Blasio, Wheeler, and Durkan have all blamed President Trump's federal cops for exacerbating the violence. Another of the Boss's capos (perhaps even another underboss), Speaker Nancy Pelosi even called CPB agents "stormtroopers."[539] A ludicrous charge, considering the violence had been occurring for months *before* any federal forces arrived and has continued for months *after* they've left.

Now is a good time for a much-needed moment of levity. In response to this sane move by AG Barr, President Trump's opponents have come up with a hilarious talking point. Some are now attacking the president, accusing him of "defunding the police" by withholding federal funds from cities who are, well, defunding the police. The cliché "you can't make this stuff up" truly applies here.

The three mayors will probably respond, as they have in the past, with deflection and projection. They never accept responsibility or guilt for any destruction or violence that they allow. Infamously, Mayor Durkan callously failed to contact the father of the teen who was shot and killed in the lawless CHAZ/CHOP zone (aka Durkanistan).

Somehow, this is supposedly all the fault of President Trump (who did call that father), the conservatives, and Republicans. How does that work? To reiterate, only when activists invaded Durkan's front lawn did the Summer of Love maven have police remove them. Soon after the short-lived JAZ (Jenny's [front yard] Autonomous Zone) ended, so did the CHAZ/CHOP occupation.

Another way to fight is to continue to pressure a compliant mainstream media to put stories in their proper contexts and perspectives, and to stop reporting untruths. One of these untruths is that "right-wing, white supremacist" groups are the ones responsible for the destruction and violence. This is so ridiculous it begs a thesaurus to create a string of new adjectives for the word "ridiculous." After all, this idiocy deserves a new lexicon, doesn't it?

Finally, the most potent way to fight this onslaught against American law enforcement is to become ever aware of what the Obama Gang is up to. He obviously did not give up his mission to fundamentally change the United States of America. This is on display when reviewing the goals of his My Brother's Keeper Alliance Pledge—or omerta—that his capos sign on to, after which they draw up their soldiers' marching orders and send them into the streets to fight our nation's law enforcement officers.

The Boss made an illuminating comment this summer, during the height of the anti-cop rioting, that sheds light on his thought process about the anti-police violence in the streets. Reportedly, early in June, the Boss warned his capos and soldiers against participating in the violence, thinking it was working against Biden. "Never let a crisis go to waste," said one of the Boss's capos.

However, later in June, after Don Obama believed the rioting was hurting Trump in the polls, National Review reported,[540] "Former President Barack Obama told aides this month that the nationwide protests following the death of George Floyd are 'a tailor-made moment' to help his former vice president Joe Biden defeat Donald Trump in November." People may think something like that, but who says it out loud?

In conclusion, I think it's fair to say, number one, that any of us would be pretty angry (at attacks on cops); number two, that the leader of the Obama Gang *acted stupidly* (in providing moral and financial support to people who hate the police); and number three, that there is a long history of Don Obama and his gang working to destroying law enforcement in America. It's long past time to stop them, isn't it?

Notes

1 Emma Colton, "Two lawyers hit with federal charges for throwing Molotov cocktail at NYPD car" (May 31, 2020) at Washington Examiner https://www.washingtonexaminer.com/news/two-lawyers-hit-with-federal-charges-for-throwing-molotov-cocktail-at-nypd-car (accessed October 22, 2020).

2 Libby Emmons, "EXPOSED: BLM quietly scrubs anti-American, Marxist language from its website" (September 20, 2029) at the Post Millennial https://thepostmillennial.com/exposed-blm-quietly-scrubs-anti-american-marxist-language-from-its-website (accessed September 29, 2020).

3 Ronald Reagan, "Address to British Parliament" (June 8, 1982) at The History Place: Great Speeches Collection http://www.historyplace.com/speeches/reagan-parliament.htm (accessed September 18, 2020).

4 Stacey Lennox, "Flashback: Democrat leaders have encouraged political violence, beginning with Barack Obama" (August 29, 2020) at PJ Media https://pjmedia.com/news-and-politics/stacey-lennox/2020/08/29/flashback-democrat-leaders-encouraging-violence-beginning-with-barack-obama-n863918 (accessed October 26, 2020).

5 Evie Fordham, "What is Patriot Prayer, the pro-Trump group whose member was killed in Portland?" (August 31, 2020) at Fox News https://www.foxnews.com/politics/patriot-prayer-joey-bishop-portland-killed?ocid=uxbndlbing (Accessed September 18, 2020).

6 Topher Gauk-Roger, Aaron J. Danielson, "Portland shooting victim wasn't an agitator or radical, friend says" (September 1, 2020) at CNN https://www.msn.com/en-us/news/us/aaron-j-danielson-portland-shooting-victim-wasnt-an-agitator-or-radical-friend-says/ar-BB18AMZg (accessed October 23, 2020).

7 Dom Calicchio, "Suspect in Portland fatal shooting killed as federal task force moved in" (September 4, 2020) at Fox News https://www.foxnews.com/us/suspect-in-portland-fatal-shooting-has-been-killed-reports (accessed September 18, 2020).

8 "Mafia's Law of Omerta" (2020) at Weebly.com https://the-mafia.weebly.com/omerta.html (accessed October 13, 2020).

9 Chandler Gill, "Earnest: White House Still Won't Light Up in Blue to Honor Fallen Police" (July 18, 2016) at Washington Free Beacon

https://freebeacon.com/politics/white-house-still-wont-light-blue-police/ (accessed September 22, 2020).

10 Lauren Lantry, "Commemorating the SCOTUS gay marriage decision 5 years later" (June 26, 2020) at ABC News https://abcnews.go.com/Politics/commemorating-scotus-gay-marriage-decision-years/story?id=71473138 (accessed September 22, 2020).

11 "Trump orders blue lighting on White House to honor fallen police officers" (May 16, 2019) at Fox News https://www.foxnews.com/us/trump-orders-blue-lighting-on-white-house-to-honor-fallen-police-officers (accessed September 22, 2020).

12 Josh Gerstein, "Eric Holder: I'm still the president's wingman" (April 4, 2013) at Politico https://www.politico.com/blogs/politico44/2013/04/eric-holder-im-still-the-presidents-wingman-160861 (accessed September 22, 2020).

13 Erick Trickery, "The Obama-Era Police Reform Biden Can't Wait to Restart" (June 29, 2020) at Politico https://www.politico.com/news/magazine/2020/06/29/obama-police-reform-341685 (accessed October 23, 2020).

14 Steve Pomper, "De-Policing America: A Street Cop's View of the Anti-Police State" (Post Hill Press, 2018)

15 Matt Margolis, "Barack Obama's Partisan Eulogy for John Lewis Reminded Many of the Paul Wellstone Funeral" (July 30, 2020) at PJ Media https://pjmedia.com/news-and-politics/matt-margolis/2020/07/30/barack-obamas-partisan-eulogy-for-john-lewis-reminded-many-of-the-paul-wellstone-funeral-n733195 (accessed September 22, 2020).

16 Victor Davis Hanson, "When Funerals Become Politics" (September 6, 2018) at Townhall https://townhall.com/columnists/victordavishanson/2018/09/06/when-funerals-become-politics-n2516094 (accessed September 22, 2020).

17 Jerry Eldred, "Loony Jerry Nadler Calls ANTIFA a Myth Despite Two Hispanic Marines Attacked Them" (July 29, 2020) at YouTube https://www.youtube.com/watch?v=3WvbdaL3GJ4 (accessed September 23, 2020).

18 Washington Examiner, "Keith Ellison resigns from DNC post amid sexual assault claims" (November 9, 2018) at Fox News https://www.foxnews.com/politics/keith-ellison-resigns-from-dnc-post-amid-sexual-assault-claims (accessed October 23, 2020).

19 Haley Kennignton, "Minnesota Attorney General Keith Ellison

Tries to Explain away Photo of Him Holding Antifa Handbook, Makes Excuses for Son's Public Support for the Terrorist Organization" (June 6, 2020) at Loomerred https://loomered.com/2020/06/06/minnesota-attorney-general-keith-ellison-tries-to-explain-away-photo-of-him-holding-antifa-handbook-makes-excuses-for-sons-public-support-for-the-terrorist-organization/ (accessed October 23, 2020).

20 Lee Brown, "BLM mob beats white man unconscious after making him crash truck: video" (August 17, 2020) at New York Post https://nypost.com/2020/08/17/blm-mob-beat-white-man-unconscious-after-making-him-crash-truck/ (accessed September 23, 2020).

21 Emma Colton, "Man who was beaten by mob in Portland was reportedly helping transgender woman before the attack" (August 18, 2020) at Washington Examiner https://www.washingtonexaminer.com/news/man-who-was-beaten-by-mob-in-portland-was-reportedly-helping-transgender-woman-before-the-attack (accessed September 23, 2020).

22 Victoria Taft, "[GRAPHIC VIDEO] Portland Rioters Threaten Man They Kicked In the Head—'Do Not Protest against Black Lives'" (May 31, 2020) at PJ Media https://pjmedia.com/news-and-politics/victoria-taft/2020/05/31/graphic-video-portland-rioters-threaten-man-they-kicked-in-the-head-do-not-protest-against-black-lives-n472094 (September 23, 2020).

23 MBK Alliance, "We Are Our Brothers' Keepers" (2014) at MBK Alliance https://www.obama.org/mbka/ (accessed September 29, 2020).

24 BET Staff, "Obama Demands Every American Mayor Review Use of Force Policies" (June 3, 2020) at BET https://www.bet.com/news/national/2020/06/03/president-barack-obama-virtual-town-hall-george-floyd-killing.html (accessed September 29, 2020).

25 Culp for Governor, "Loren Culp for Governor: Leading Washington's Comeback" (2020) at Culp for Governor https://culpforgovernor.com/ (accessed October 23, 2020).

26 Caleb Parke, "Detroit police chief defends 'necessary' force when protesters aren't peaceful" (September 7, 2020) at Fox News https://www.foxnews.com/us/detroit-police-chief-peaceful-protesters-force (accessed October 23, 2020).

27 Cam Edwards, "Virginia Sheriff Takes First Steps to Deputize Thousands of Armed Citizens" (July 22, 2020) at Bearing Arms https://bearingarms.com/cam-e/2020/07/22/sheriff-deputize-armed-citizens/ (accessed October 23, 2020).

28 Marisa Herman, "Washington Sheriff Won't Enforce Stay-at-Home Order" (April 22, 2020) at Newsmax https://www.newsmax.com/us/washington-sheriff-stay-at-home-virus/2020/04/22/id/964153/ (accessed October 23, 2020).

29 The 191st General Court of The Commonwealth of Massachusetts, Mass. General Laws Section 53 (2020) at malegislature.gov https://malegislature.gov/Laws/GeneralLaws/PartIV/TitleI/Chapter272/Section53 (accessed October 23, 2020).

30 Fox News, "'Disgraceful': Cops Angry after Obama Slams Arrest of Black Scholar" (July 24, 2009) at Fox News https://www.foxnews.com/story/disgraceful-cops-angry-after-obama-slams-arrest-of-black-scholar (accessed October 23, 2020).

31 ABC News, "Obama on Gates' Arrest: The Police Acted Stupidly" (July 23, 2009) at YouTube https://www.youtube.com/watch?v=LcANl-pO8_70 (accessed October 23, 2020).

32 Stu Cvrk, "Lest We Forget Who Jump-Started Racial Divisions in the US" (August 19, 2020) at UncoverDC https://uncoverdc.com/2020/08/19/lest-we-forget-who-jump-started-racial-divisions-in-the-us/ (accessed October 23, 2020).

33 Tracy Jan, "No charge, but Gates case seethes" (July 22, 2009) at boston.com http://archive.boston.com/news/local/massachusetts/articles/2009/07/22/no_charge_but_gates_case_seethes/ (accessed October 23, 2020).

34 Dianny, "Flashback: The Beer Summit" (July 12, 2016) at Patriot Retort https://patriotretort.com/flashback-beer-summit/ (accessed October 23, 2020).

35 Zennie62, "Obama Beer Summit Janes Crowley Press Conference" (July 31, 2009) at YouTube https://www.youtube.com/watch?v=X-wywZNPf8S8 (accessed October 23, 2020).

36 James Crowley, "Henry Louis Gates, Jr. Police Report" (July 16, 2020) at the smoking gun http://www.thesmokinggun.com/file/henry-louis-gates-jr-police-report (accessed October 23, 2020).

37 Lisa Miller, "Henry Louis Gates Jr. on Race, New PBS Series" (April 10, 2011) at Newsweek https://www.newsweek.com/henry-louis-gates-jr-race-new-pbs-series-66567 (accessed October 9, 2020).

38 Associated Press, "Review of Harvard Professor Arrest Finds Incident Was Avoidable" (June 30, 2010) at Fox News https://www.foxnews.com/politics/review-of-harvard-professor-arrest-finds-incident-was-avoi-

dable (accessed October 23, 2020).

39 Queenie Wong, "10 Things You Didn't Know about Henry Louis Gates Jr." (July 24, 2009) at U.S. News & World Report https://www.us-news.com/news/national/articles/2009/07/24/10-things-you-didnt-know-about-henry-louis-gates-jr (accessed October 23, 2020).

40 Kevin Lindemann, "African American Communist: W.E.B. Du Bois (1868-1963)" (February 28, 2009) at Communist Party USA https://www.cpusa.org/party_info/african-american-communist-w-e-b-du-bois-1868-1963/ (accessed October 23, 2020).

41 Gus Hall, "Application for Membership in the Communist Party by W.E.B. Du Bois" (February 28, 2009) at Communist Party USA, https://www.cpusa.org/party_info/application-to-join-the-cpusa-by-w-e-b-du-bois-1961/ (accessed October 23, 2020).

42 Dartunorro Clark and Caroline Vakil, "Obama calls for police reforms, tells protesters to 'make people in power uncomfortable'" (June 3, 2020) at NBC News https://www.nbcnews.com/politics/politics-news/obama-calls-police-reforms-tells-protesters-make-people-power-uncom-fortable-n1224161 (accessed October 23, 2020).

43 NBC News, "After George Floyd" (2020) at NBC News https://www.nbcnews.com/george-floyd-death (accessed October 23, 2020).

44 Jeffrey Dorfman, "Sorry Bernie Bros but Nordic Countries Are Not Socialist" (July 8, 2018) at Forbes https://www.forbes.com/sites/jeffreydorfman/2018/07/08/sorry-bernie-bros-but-nordic-coun-tries-are-not-socialist/#7abb49af74ad (accessed October 23, 2020).

45 Ian Schwartz, "Black Lives Matter Leader: 'We Will Burn Down This System' If Country Doesn't Give Us What We Want" (June 25, 2020) at Real Clear Politics https://www.realclearpolitics.com/vid-eo/2020/06/25/black_lives_matter_leader_we_will_burn_down_this_sys-tem_if_country_doesnt_give_us_what_we_want.html (accessed October 23, 2020).

46 Patriot Prayer, "Patriot Prayer" (2020) at gibsonforfreedom.com https://gibsonforfreedom.com/ (accessed October 23, 2020).

47 Evie Fordham, "What is Patriot Prayer, the pro-Trump group whose member was killed in Portland?" (August 31, 2020) at Fox News https://www.foxnews.com/politics/patriot-prayer-joey-bishop-port-land-killed (accessed October 23, 2020).

48 Miranda Devine, "BLM 'activists' celebrated as Trump sup-porter was killed" (August 30, 2020) at New York Post https://ny-

post.com/2020/08/30/blm-activists-celebrated-as-trump-support-er-killed-devine/ (accessed October 23, 2020).

49 Aaron Feis, "Patriot Prayer 'supporter' Aaron 'Jay' Danielson identified as Portland shooting victim" (August 30, 2020) at New York Post https://nypost.com/2020/08/30/patriot-prayer-supporter-identi-fied-as-portland-shooting-victim/ (accessed October 23, 2020).

50 Bill Federer, "Hitler's Brownshirts used Antifa tactics to over-throw Germany's Republic; D-Day" (June 6, 2020) at American Minute https://newsmaven.io/americanminute/american-history/hitler-s-brown-shirts-used-antifa-tactics-to-overthrow-germany-s-republic-d-day-B-YhR8qHLUO7VMEa8x7ceQ (accessed October 23, 2020).

51 Maxine Bernstein, Noelle Crombie, Shane Dixon Kavanaugh, and Fedor Zarkhin, et. al. "Portland protests bring out hundreds to Proud Boys, opposing demonstrations Saturday" (September 26, 2020) at Ore-gonLive (The Oregonian) https://www.oregonlive.com/portland/2020/09/portland-protests-bring-proud-boys-counter-demonstrators-satur-day-live-updates.html (accessed October 23, 2020).

52 Ibid., "Update" (September 29, 2020) (accessed October 23, 2020).

53 Proud Boys, "The Proud Boys vehemently denounce hate groups, much the same way @realDonaldTrump has done" (October 1, 2020) at Twitter https://twitter.com/i/status/1311643918912684032 (accessed October 23, 2020).

54 Maxine Bernstein, "Some Portland police officers to be deputized as federal officers for Saturday's Proud Boy rally, counter-protests" (Sep-tember 26, 2020) at OregonLive (The Oregonian) https://www.oregonlive.com/portland/2020/09/some-portland-police-officers-to-be-deputized-as-federal-officers-for-saturdays-proud-boy-rally-counter-protests.html (accessed October 23, 2020)

55 Noelle Crombie, "Far-right rally and counter-protests in Portland end without violence Saturday, as Proud Boy rally smaller, shorter than expected" (September 27, 2020) at OregonLive (The Oregonian) https://www.oregonlive.com/portland/2020/09/far-right-rallies-and-counter-protests-in-portland-ended-without-violence-saturday-as-the-daytime-gatherings-were-smaller-shorter-than-expected.html (accessed October 23, 2020).

56 Rush Limbaugh, "The Proud Boys Have a Black Leader" (October 1, 2020) at the Rush Limbaugh Show https://www.rushlimbaugh.com/

daily/2020/10/01/the-proud-boys-have-a-black-leader/ (accessed October 23, 2020).

57 NBC 5 Chicago, "Shot 7 times in Front of His Children: Lt. Governor of Wis. Says Police Shooting Not an Accident" (August 24, 2020) at NBC Chicago https://www.nbcchicago.com/news/local/kenosha-jacob-blake-wisconsin-lieutenant-governor-mandela-barnes/2327451/ (accessed October 23, 2020).

58 John Bowden, "Lawyer says Kenosha officer who shot Jacob Blake thought he was trying to kidnap child" (September 28, 2020) at The Hill https://thehill.com/blogs/blog-briefing-room/news/518560-lawyer-says-kenosha-officer-who-shot-jacob-blake-thought-he-was (accessed October 23, 2020).

59 Greg Reynolds, "Breaking: Jacob Blake's Criminal History and Arrest Warrant Finally Revealed after Police Shooting in Kenosha" (August 25, 2020) at 24 News https://us24news.com/blog/2020/08/25/breaking-jacob-blakes-criminal-history-and-arrest-warrant-finally-revealed-after-police-shooting-in-kenosha/ (accessed October 23, 2020).

60 Brittany Bernstien, "Kamala Harris Told Jacob Blake She Was 'Proud' of Him, Lawyer Says" (September 8, 2020) at Yahoo News https://news.yahoo.com/kamala-harris-told-jacob-blake-130728218.html (accessed October 23, 2020).

61 Steve Pomper, "Defund the Police Is Not Enough as Radicals Target Police Foundations" (September 23, 2020) at National Police Association, https://nationalpolice.org/defund-the-police-is-not-enough-as-radicals-target-police-foundations/ (accessed October 6, 2020).

62 Seattle Police Foundation, https://www.seattlepolicefoundation.org/ (accessed October 23, 2020).

63 Seattle Police Foundation, "We've Got Your Six" (2020) at Seattle Police Foundation https://www.seattlepolicefoundation.org/support-us (accessed October 23, 2020).

64 Steven Nelson, "Federal officers in Portland suffered 113 eye injuries from lasers, DHS official says" (August 4, 2020) at New York Post https://nypost.com/2020/08/04/federal-officers-in-portland-suffered-113-eye-injuries-from-lasers-dhs/ (accessed October 6, 2020).

65 Zachary Warmbrodt, "New racial justice target: Defund the police foundations" (September 18, 2020) at Politico https://www.politico.com/news/2020/09/18/new-racial-justice-target-defund-police-foundations-417423 (accessed October 23, 2020).

66 ACLU, "Demand Justice Now" (2020) at ACLU.org https://www.aclu.org/news/by/scott-roberts/ (accessed October 23, 2020).

67 Seattle PI, "Wells Fargo Bank Robbery" (June 21, 2000) at Seattle PI https://www.seattlepi.com/news/slideshow/Wells-Fargo-Bank-Robbery-6678.php (accessed October 23, 2020).

68 Kitsap Sun, "Seattle: Cop shot, suspect killed in robbery attempt" (June 23, 2000) at Kitsap Sun https://products.kitsapsun.com/archive/2000/06-23/0026_seattle__cop_shot__suspect_killed.html (accessed October 23, 2020).

69 Nick Gillespie, "81 Percent of Black Americans Want the Same Level, or More, of Police Presence: Gallup" (August 6, 2020) at Reason https://reason.com/2020/08/06/81-percent-of-black-americans-want-the-same-level-or-more-of-police-presence-gallup/ (accessed October 23, 2020).

70 Heather MacDonald, *The War on Cops: How the New Attack on Law and Order Makes Everyone Less Safe* (Encounter Books, 2017).

71 Ronald Reagan, "Shining City upon a Hill" (January 11, 1989) at YouTube https://www.youtube.com/watch?v=c32G868tor0 (accessed October 23, 2020).

72 CNN, "Transcript: Barack Obama's DNC Speech" (August 20, 2020) at CNN https://www.cnn.com/2020/08/19/politics/barack-obama-speech-transcript/index.html (accessed October 23, 2020).

73 Rev, "Barack Obama Eulogy Speech Transcript at John Lewis Funeral July 30" (July 30, 2020) at Rev https://www.rev.com/blog/transcripts/barack-obama-eulogy-transcript-at-john-lewis-funeral-july-30 (accessed October 23, 2020).

74 David Barton, *Setting the Record Straight: American History in Black & White* (WallBuilder Press, 2004).

75 Heather Higgins, "Barack Obama's Poor Understanding of the Constitution" (November 3, 2008) at U.S. News & World Report https://www.usnews.com/opinion/articles/2008/11/03/barack-obamas-poor-understanding-of-the-constitution (accessed October 23, 2020).

76 Danielle Allen, *Our Declaration: A Reading of the Declaration of Independence in Defense of Equality* (Liveright, 2015).

77 Daniel Greenfield, "Kamala Harris Blames American Racism for Failed Campaign" (November 4, 2019) at Frontpage Magazine https://www.frontpagemag.com/fpm/2019/11/kamala-harris-blames-ameri-

can-racism-failed-daniel-greenfield/ (accessed October 23, 2020).

78 *The Dan Bongino Show* (2020) at Bongino.com https://bongino.com/ (accessed October 23, 2020).

79 Grateful American, "CNN Claims Kenosha Protests Are 'Fiery but Mostly Peaceful' as City Burns behind Reporter" (August 26, 2020) at YouTube https://www.youtube.com/watch?v=klVhCkhOTRQ (accessed October 23, 2020).

80 TheDC Shorts, "MSNBC Reporter Says Riots Not Unruly As Flames Engulf Building Behind Him" (May 30, 2020) at YouTube https://www.youtube.com/watch?v=tyILjGn96gw (accessed October 23, 2020).

81 FOPLodge27, "Less than 48 hours ..." (August 6, 2020) at Twitter https://twitter.com/FopLodge27/status/1291467255386189826 (accessed October 23, 2020).

82 Delaware County, Lodge 27, PA Fraternal Order of Police (2020) at fop27.org http://www.fop27.org/ (accessed October 23, 2020).

83 "Barney Fife: Finding the Way Back to Mayberry" (2020) at BarneyFife.com http://www.barneyfife.com/ (accessed October 23, 2020).

84 Peter Robinson. "Ruins of the Great Society" (interview with Amity Shlaes), *Hoover Digest*, Summer 2020, 150.

85 Lara Logan, "'Lara Logan Has No Agenda: The Socialist Invasion' on Fox Nation" (September 9, 2020) at Fox News https://video.foxnews.com/v/6189114462001#sp=show-clips (accessed October 23, 2020).

86 Zachariah Hughes, "Upper Darby announces policing reforms and policy review" (July 15, 2020) at WHYY PBS NPR https://whyy.org/articles/upper-darby-announces-policing-reforms-and-policy-review/ (accessed October 23, 2020).

87 "Reimagine Policing" (2020) at Obama.org https://www.obama.org/mayor-pledge/ (accessed October 23, 2020).

88 "Number of people shot to death by police in the United States from 2017 to 2020" (2020) at Statistia.com https://www.statista.com/statistics/585152/people-shot-to-death-by-us-police-by-race/ (accessed October 23, 2020).

89 Jeffrey James Higgins, "Higgins: Enough of the lying—just look at the data. There's no epidemic of racist police officers killing black Americans" (June 26, 2020) at Law Enforcement Today https://www.lawenforcementtoday.com/systematic-racism-in-policing-its-time-to-stop-the-lying/ (accessed October 23, 2020).

90 "Benjamin Disraeli" (2020) at GoodReads https://www.goodreads.com/quotes/tag/statistics (accessed October 23, 2020).

91 "Upper Darby Police Department" (2020) at UDPD.org https://udpd.org/ (accessed October 23, 2020).

92 "Creating a New Era of Public Safety" (2020) at the Leadership Conference Education Fund https://civilrights.org/edfund/creating-a-new-era-of-public-safety/ (accessed October 23, 2020).

93 Jonathan Capehart, "Hands up, don't shoot" was built on a lie" (March 16, 2020) at The Washington Post https://www.washingtonpost.com/blogs/post-partisan/wp/2015/03/16/lesson-learned-from-the-shooting-of-michael-brown/ (accessed December 9, 2020)

94 "DOJ clears Darren Wilson in Michael Brown killing" (March 4, 2015) at CBS News https://www.cbsnews.com/news/darren-wilson-cleared-in-michael-brown-ferguson-killing-by-justice-department/ (accessed October 23, 2020).

95 Alana Wise, "Latest Probe Ends in No Charges for Former Ferguson Officer Who Killed Michael Brown" (July 30, 2020) at NPR https://www.npr.org/2020/07/30/897475866/latest-probe-ends-in-no-charges-for-former-ferguson-officer-who-killed-michael-b (accessed October 23, 2020).

96 Sean Philip Cotter, "Progressive critics continue to slam Mass. Bail Fund" (August 11, 2020) at Boston Herald https://www.bostonherald.com/2020/08/11/rollins-defends-allowing-bail-for-mcclinton-slams-mass-bail-fund-again/ (accessed October 23, 2020).

97 Bill Rankin, "GBI opens probe of Fulton DA Paul Howard over use of nonprofit funds" (May 5, 2020) at Atlanta Journal Constitution https://www.ajc.com/news/local/gbi-opens-probe-fulton-paul-howard-over-use-nonprofit-funds/cgSq6UgzmHbCfGNJcxMJ6O/ (accessed October 23, 2020).

98 Beth Bauman, "Former Gangster Drops a Truth Bomb about Rayshard Brooks' Death" (June 15, 2020) at Townhall https://townhall.com/tipsheet/bethbaumann/2020/06/15/former-gangster-drops-a-truth-bomb-about-rayshard-brooks-death-n2570711 (accessed October 23, 2020).

99 "Paul Howard ousted after serving more than 2 decades as Fulton County DA" (August 12, 2020) at Fox 5 Atlanta https://www.fox5atlanta.com/news/paul-howard-ousted-after-serving-more-than-2-decades-as-fulton-county-da (accessed October 23, 2020).

100 Marina Medvin, "Hope for Atlanta Officer Rolfe after DA Loses Re-Election" (August 13, 2020) at Townhall https://townhall.com/columnists/marinamedvin/2020/08/13/hope-for-atlanta-officer-rolfe-after-da-loses-reelection-n2574302 (accessed November 28, 2020).

101 Marina Medvin, "Hope for Atlanta Officer Rolfe after DA Loses Re-Election" (August 13, 2020) at Townhall https://townhall.com/columnists/marinamedvin/2020/08/13/hope-for-atlanta-officer-rolfe-after-da-loses-reelection-n2574302 (accessed October 23, 2020).

102 Daniel John Sobieski, "Illegal Caravans Encouraged by Honduras and Soros" (October 8, 2018) at American Thinker https://www.americanthinker.com/articles/2018/10/illegal_caravans_encouraged_by_honduras_and_soros.html (accessed October 23, 2020).

103 Julie Shaw and Chris Palmer, "U.S. Attorney William McSwain slams DA Larry Krasner over fatal shooting of Cpl. James O'Connor IV" (March 16, 2020) at Philadelphia Inquirer https://www.inquirer.com/news/us-attorney-william-mcswain-district-attorney-larry-krasner-police-shooting-cpl-james-oconnor-20200316.html (accessed October 27, 2020).

104 Jim Kenny, "Mayor and Police Commissioner Release Statements on Police-Involved Shooting" (October 26, 2020) at City of Philadelphia https://www.phila.gov/2020-10-26-mayor-and-police-commissioner-release-statements-on-police-involved-shooting/ (accessed October 27, 2020).

105 Dom Calicchio, "Missouri couple who defended home have rifle seized during police search: report" (July 11, 2020) at Fox News https://www.foxnews.com/us/missouri-couple-who-defended-home-have-rifle-seized-during-police-search-report (accessed October 23, 2020).

106 Virginia Kruta, "Gov. Mike Parson: Over 100 St. Louis Murders Go Uncharged While Kim Gardner Charges McCloskeys" (July 25, 2020) at Daily Caller https://dailycaller.com/2020/07/25/mike-parson-100-st-louis-murders-uncharged-kim-gardner-charges-mccloskeys/ (accessed October 23, 2020).

107 Steve Pomper, "St. Louis Prosecutor Accused of Tampering with Evidence in McCloskey Case" (July 25, 2020) at National Police Association https://nationalpolice.org/st-louis-prosecutor-accused-of-tampering-with-evidence-in-mccloskey-case/ (accessed October 23, 2020).

108 Bryan Preston, "Breaking: McCloskeys Indicted by St. Louis Grand Jury" (October 6,2020) at PJ Media https://pjmedia.com/

news-and-politics/bryan-preston/2020/10/06/breaking-mccloskeys-in-
dicted-by-st-louis-grand-jury-n1012701 (accessed October 27, 2020).

109 Laura Ingraham, "George Soros pours $116K into pro-Kim
Gardner PAC" (August 3, 2020) at YouTube https://www.youtube.com/
watch?v=BGzDYJW1Oyg (accessed October 23, 2020).

110 Lauren Trager, "Indictments allege McCloskeys altered pistol
and 'obstructed prosecution'" (October 7, 2020) at KMOV4 https://www.
kmov.com/news/mccloskey-case-couple-indicted-by-grand-jury/arti-
cle_892b9ba4-0807-11eb-8750-b3b2937f7e0b.html (accessed October 7,
2020).

111 Marcy Oster, "Rudy Giuliani Says George Soros Wants to Destroy Government Due to His 'Sick Background'" (August 19, 2020) at
Jewish Journal, https://jewishjournal.com/news/united-states/320526/
rudy-giuliani-says-george-soros-wants-to-destroy-government-due-to-
his-sick-background/ (accessed October 23, 2020).

112 Cheryl K. Chumley, "George Soros, 89, is still on a quest to
destroy America" (January 25, 2020) at Washington Times https://www.
washingtontimes.com/news/2020/jan/25/george-soros-89-still-quest-de-
stroy-america/ (accessed October 23, 2020).

113 Devansh Lathia, "How Soros Broke the British Pound" (October
16, 2018) at Economics Review https://theeconreview.com/2018/10/16/
how-soros-broke-the-british-pound/ (accessed October 23, 2020).

114 Vanessa Romo, "Hungary Passes 'Stop Soros' Laws, Bans
Aid to Undocumented Immigrants" (June 20, 2018) at NPR https://
www.npr.org/2018/06/20/622045753/hungary-passes-stop-so-
ros-laws-bans-aid-to-undocumented-immigrants (accessed October 23,
2020).

115 Steve Balich, "Complete List of U.S. Organizations Funded by
George Soros" (January 11, 2020) at Will County News https://thewill-
countynews.com/install/index.php/2020/01/11/complete-list-of-u-s-orga-
nizations-funded-by-george-soros/ (accessed October 23, 2020).

116 Jim Hoft, "Judicial Watch: Tom Fitton Reveals Obama State
Dept. Worked Hand in Glove with Soros Operatives—Spent $9 Million
Tax Dollars in Albania" (October 10, 2018) at JWBlog Watch https://
blogwatch.judicialwatch.org/articles/judicial-watch-tom-fitton-reveals-
obama-state-dept-worked-hand-in-glove-with-soros-operatives-spent-9-
million-tax-dollars-on-albania (accessed October 23, 2020).

117 Jim Hoft, "Update: Soros Elevator Activist and Illegal Alien Ana

Maria Archila Made $178,071 in 2016 as a Far Left Activist" (October 6, 2018) at Gateway Pundit https://www.thegatewaypundit.com/2018/10/update-soros-elevator-activist-and-illegal-alien-ana-maria-archila-made-178071-in-2016-as-a-far-left-activist/ (accessed October 23, 2020).

118 Susan Price, "Soros, Obama and Hillary Clinton Are the Shadow Party" (October 11, 2018) at America Out Loud https://americaoutloud.com/soros-obama-and-hillary-clinton-are-the-shadow-party/ (accessed October 24, 2020).

119 Kevin Jackson, "Timeline of Obama's Treasonous Attempt to Get Trump" (July 6, 2020) at the Black Sphere https://theblacksphere.net/2020/07/timeline-of-obamas-treasonous-attempt-to-get-trump/ (accessed October 24, 2020).

120 Robert Kraychik, "Limbaugh: 'Deep State' is Obama's 'Shadown Government'" (February 19, 2017) at Daily Wire https://www.dailywire.com/news/limbaugh-deep-state-obamas-shadow-government-robert-kraychik (accessed December 8, 2020)

121 "An Online Database of the Left and Its Agencies" (2020) at Discover the Networks https://www.discoverthenetworks.org/ (accessed October 24, 2020). An

122 Benjamin Brown, "George Soros calls Obama 'greatest disappointment,' says he doesn't 'particularly want to be a Democrat'" (July 18, 2018) at Fox News https://www.foxnews.com/politics/george-soros-calls-obama-greatest-disappointment-says-he-doesnt-particularly-want-to-be-a-democrat (accessed October 24, 2020).

123 Eric Mack, "Fox News Host Apologizes for Silencing Newt on Soros Remarks" (September 17, 2020) at Newsmax https://www.newsmax.com/newsfront/conservative-shadow-ban-censorship-harris-faulkner/2020/09/17/id/987526/ (accessed October 24, 2020).

124 Jordan Davidson, "Twitter Labels Tucker Carlson's Expose on George Soros As 'Sensitive Content'" (September 22, 2020) at Fox News https://thefederalist.com/2020/09/22/twitter-labels-tucker-carlsons-expose-on-george-soros-as-sensitive-content/ (accessed October 24, 2020).

125 Robby Starbuck, "Why aren't we allowed to talk about George Soros's plan to remake America?" (September 19, 2020) at the Federalist https://thefederalist.com/2020/09/19/why-arent-we-allowed-to-talk-about-george-soross-plan-to-remake-america/ (accessed October 27, 2020).

126 Alex Newman, "Obama Urged Governors to Celebrate UN Day"

(October 26, 2012) at the New American https://thenewamerican.com/obama-urged-governors-to-celebrate-un-day/ (accessed October 24, 2020).

127 Mara Liasson, "Obama to Enlist Democratic Governors' Support" (February 21, 2014) at NPR https://www.npr.org/2014/02/21/280528586/obama-to-enlist-the-support-of-democratic-governors (accessed October 24, 2020).

128 John Hinderaker, "Why Does Obamacare Make Health Insurance So Expensive?" (October 29, 2013) at Powerline Blog https://www.powerlineblog.com/archives/2013/10/why-does-obamacare-make-health-insurance-so-expensive.php (accessed October 24, 2020).

129 Edmund Haislmaier and Doug Badger, "How Obamacare Raised Premiums" (March 5, 2018) at the Heritage Foundation https://www.heritage.org/health-care-reform/report/how-obamacare-raised-premiums (accessed October 3, 2020).

130 Amy Sherman, "No proof voter suppression kept Stacey Abrams from governorship, as Democrats said in Atlanta debate" (November 21, 2019) at Politifact https://www.politifact.com/article/2019/nov/21/no-proof-voter-suppression-kept-stacey-abrams-gove/ (accessed October 24, 2020).

131 Julian Zelizer, "Cory Booker, the 2020 race and Obama's legacy" (February 1, 2019) at CNN https://www.cnn.com/2019/02/01/opinions/cory-booker-obama-legacy-zelizer/index.html (accessed October 24, 2020).

132 Carol E. Lee, Kristen Welker, Josh Lederman, and Amanda Golden, "Looking for Obama's hidden hand in candidates coalescing around Biden" (March 2, 2020) at NBC News https://www.nbcnews.com/politics/2020-election/looking-obama-s-hidden-hand-candidate-coalescing-around-biden-n1147471 (accessed October 24, 2020).

133 Dan Merica, Kyung Lah, Jasmine Wright and Kate Sullivan, "Amy Klobuchar ends 2020 presidential campaign and endorses Joe Biden" (March 2, 2020) at CNN https://www.cnn.com/2020/03/02/politics/amy-klobuchar-ends-2020-campaign/index.html (accessed October 24, 2020).

134 Fox News, Eric Shawn, "Charges against 'New Black Panthers' Dropped by Obama Justice Dept." (May 29, 2009, Update: December 24, 2015) at Fox News https://www.foxnews.com/politics/charges-against-new-black-panthers-dropped-by-obama-justice-dept (accessed October

24, 2020).

135 ABC 12 News Staff, "Whitmer offers support to Trumps after positive coronavirus tests" (October 2, 2020) at ABC 12 News https://www.abc12.com/2020/10/02/whitmer-offers-support-to-trumps-after-positive-coronavirus-tests/ (accessed October 23, 2020).

136 "Editorial: Giving the Right Name to the Virus Causing a Worldwide Pandemic" (March 18, 2020) at Epoch Times https://www.theepochtimes.com/giving-the-right-name-to-the-virus-causing-a-worldwide-pandemic-2_3277200.html (accessed November 28, 2020).

137 ABC 12 News Staff, "FBI thwarted militia plot kidnap Whitmer, overthrow state government" (October 8, 2020) at ABC 12 News https://www.abc12.com/2020/10/08/fbi-thwarted-militia-plot-to-kidnap-whitmer-overthrow-state-government/ (accessed October 24, 2020).

138 Tyler Olson, "Dem governor mocked for pleading ignorance on Seattle anarchist takeover" (June 11, 2020) at Fox News https://www.foxnews.com/politics/dem-governor-mocked-for-pleading-ignorance-on-seattle-anarchist-takeover (accessed October 27, 2020).

139 Reid Wilson, "Measure making it easier to prosecute police for deadly force on Washington ballot" (August 30, 2020) at The Hill https://thehill.com/homenews/campaign/404381-measure-to-raise-police-deadly-force-threshold-on-washington-ballot (accessed October 24, 2020).

140 Lucas Acosta, "HRC Endorses Gov. Jay Inslee for Reelection" (June 25, 2020) at Human Rights Campaign https://www.hrc.org/news/hrc-endorses-governor-jay-inslee-for-reelection (accessed October 24, 2020).

141 "Join HRC as 'We Dissent' in this Supreme Court Confirmation Process" (2020) at Human Rights Campaign https://act.hrc.org/page/68193/petition/1?ea.tracking.id=or_gnr_hrc_SCOTUS0920?_ga=2.213425812.1693946403.1602181339-271652733.1602181339 (accessed October 24, 2020).

142 Paul Steinhauser, "Jay Inslee labels Trump a 'white nationalist' at debate" (July 31, 2019) at Fox News https://www.foxnews.com/politics/inslee-labels-trump-a-white-nationalist (accessed October 27, 2020).

143 Allen Kim, "It's no longer a crime in California not to help a police officer" (September 4, 2019) at CNN https://www.cnn.com/2019/09/04/us/california-police-help-trnd/index.html (accessed October 24, 2020).

144 Ian Schwartz, "IL Gov. Pritzker Asked about Wife Traveling to

FL during COVID: 'I'm just not going to answer that'" (May 4, 2020) at Real Clear Politics https://www.realclearpolitics.com/video/2020/05/04/il_gov_pritzker_asked_about_wife_traveling_to_fl_during_covid_im_just_not_going_to_answer_that.html (accessed October 24, 2020).

145 Rick Moran, "IL Governor Pritzker Threatens Local Police Who Don't Enforce His Edicts" (May 22, 2020) at PJ Media https://pjmedia.com/news-and-politics/rick-moran/2020/05/22/il-governor-pritzker-threatens-local-police-who-dont-enforce-his-edicts-n419040 (accessed October 24, 2020).

146 Ben Szalinski, "Pritzker Threatens Local Police Who Don't Enforce His Stay-at-Home Order" (May 21, 2020) at Illinois Policy https://www.illinoispolicy.org/pritzker-threatens-local-police-who-dont-enforce-his-stay-at-home-order/ (accessed October 24, 2020).

147 Mohamed Ibrahim, "Minnesota Gov. Tim Walz signs police accountability bill into law" (July 23, 2020) at the Globe and Mail https://www.theglobeandmail.com/world/us-politics/article-minnesota-gov-tim-walz-to-sign-police-accountability-bill/ (accessed October 24, 2020).

148 Jake Johnson, "Protests break out in Wisconsin after police shoot Black man in the back at point-blank range as kids watch from car" (August 24, 2020) at AlterNet https://www.alternet.org/2020/08/protests-break-out-in-wisconsin-after-police-shoot-black-man-in-the-back-at-point-blank-range-as-kids-watch-from-car/ (accessed October 24, 2020).

149 Jackson Danbeck, "Wisconsin police chiefs to Evers, Barnes: Stop making statements about Jacob Blake until facts are known" (August 27, 2020) at TMJ4 News https://www.tmj4.com/news/local-news/wisconsin-police-chiefs-to-evers-barnes-stop-making-statements-about-jacob-blake-until-facts-are-known (accessed October 24, 2020).

150 Austin Huguelet, "Former President Barack Obama endorses Nicole Galloway for Missouri governor" (September 25, 2020) at Springfield News-Leader https://www.news-leader.com/story/news/politics/elections/2020/09/25/missouri-governor-candidate-nicole-galloway-endorsed-by-president-obama/3533524001/ (accessed October 24, 2020).

151 Christina Wilkie, "Former President Barack Obama announces final 2020 candidate endorsements" (September 25, 2020) at CNBC https://www.cnbc.com/2020/09/25/barack-obama-announces-final-2020-candidate-endorsements.html (accessed October 24, 2020).

152 Christina Wilkie, "Barack Obama issues his first round of

2020 endorsements" (August 3, 2020) at CNBC https://www.cnbc.com/2020/08/03/barack-obama-issues-his-first-round-of-2020-endorsements.html (accessed October 24, 2020).

153 Ronn Blitzer, "Virginia Dems draft proposal to downgrade assault on police to misdemeanorhttps://www.foxnews.com/politics/virginia-dems-downgrade-assault-on-police-to-misdemeanor" (July 1, 2020) at Fox News (accessed December 8, 2020).

154 11Alive Staff, "Atlanta mayor hopes momentum of protests will carry over to voter turnout" (June 8, 2020) at 11Alive https://www.11alive.com/article/news/local/bottoms-voting-momentum-protests-atlanta/85-e4994681-4303-4b59-8329-58e9078cc918 (accessed October 24, 2020).

155 Elizabeth Chuck, "Baltimore Mayor Stephanie Rawlings-Blake Under Fire for 'Space' to Destroy Comment" (April 28, 2015) at NBC News https://www.nbcnews.com/storyline/baltimore-unrest/mayor-stephanie-rawlings-blake-under-fire-giving-space-destroy-baltimore-n349656 (accessed October 24, 2020).

156 Rich Lowry, "William Techumseh Sherman: A Warrior in Full" (August 6, 2020) at National Review https://www.nationalreview.com/magazine/2020/08/24/a-warrior-in-full/#slide-1 (accessed October 24, 2020).

157 Jonathan Raymond, "Bottoms on defunding police: Matter of 'reallocating funds' which Atlanta is 'ahead of the curve' on" (June 10, 2020) at 11Alive https://www.11alive.com/article/news/local/protests/atlanta-mayor-bottoms-on-defunding-police/85-bd8370a6-2a9b-48c5-a1ca-7d4cd85f37b4 (accessed October 24, 2020).

158 WCVB5 ABC, "Salem police investigating 'completely inappropriate tweet' sent from department's Twitter account" (June 1, 2020) at WCVB5 https://www.wcvb.com/article/salem-police-completely-inappropriate-tweet-departments-twitter-account/32731821 (accessed October 24, 2020).

159 Chris Pleasance, "Riot is declared in Portland as BLM mob 'celebrates' Mayor Ted Wheeler's 58th birthday by setting fires outside his home and chanting 'happy tear gas to you' on the 95th day of demonstrations" (September 4, 2020) at Daily Mail Online https://www.dailymail.co.uk/news/article-8684591/Protesters-celebrate-Portland-mayors-birthday-fire-street.html (accessed October 24, 2020).

160 Chattanoogan.com, "Berke Signs 4-Part Pledge from My Brother's Keeper Alliance" (June 5, 2020) at the Chattanoogan https://www.

chattanoogan.com/2020/6/5/410123/Berke-Signs-4-Part-Pledge-From-My.aspx (accessed October 24, 2020).

161 Meghan Mangrum, "Chattanooga mayor signs Obama's commitment-to-action, pledges to review police policies" (June 5, 2020) at Chattanooga Times Free Press https://www.timesfreepress.com/news/local/story/2020/jun/05/chattanoogmayor-signs-obamas-commitment-to-ac/524667/ (accessed October 24, 2020).

162 Sarah Grace Taylor, "Hamilton County officials defend use of tear gas, say assaulting police does not honor George Floyd" (June 1, 2020) at Chattanooga Free Press https://www.timesfreepress.com/news/local/story/2020/jun/01/hamilton-county-officials-defend-use-tear-gas-say-assaulting-police-does-not-honor-george-floyd/524282/ (accessed October 24, 2020).

163 Jacob Vaughn, "Mayor Wants City Employees to Feel Private Sector's Pain with Pay Cuts" (August 21, 2020) at Dallas Observer https://www.dallasobserver.com/news/dalla-mayor-city-staff-pay-11935208 (accessed October 24, 2020).

164 Andre-Naquian Wheeler, "San Francisco Mayor London Breed on Defunding the Police, White Activism, and Fighting for Her Community" (July 9, 2020) at Vogue https://www.msn.com/en-us/news/us/san-francisco-mayor-london-breed-on-defunding-the-police-white-activism-and-fighting-for-her-community/ar-BB16xIX8 (accessed October 24, 2020).

165 Bradford Betz, "San Francisco mayor says police will stop responding to non-criminal calls" (June 11, 2020) at Fox News https://www.foxnews.com/us/san-francisco-mayor-police-stop-responding-non-criminal-calls (accessed October 24, 2020).

166 Alex Corey, "DC Mayor Orders Removal of 'Defund the Police' Mural" (August 12, 2020) at Townhall https://townhall.com/tipsheet/alexcorey/2020/08/12/defund-the-police-mural-in-dc-ordered-to-be-removed-by-bowser-n2574233 (accessed October 24, 2020).

167 Will Vitka, "Black Lives Matter DC Criticizes Mayor Bowser's DNC Remarks" (August 19, 2020) at WTOP News https://wtop.com/dc/2020/08/dc-mayor-bowser-criticized-over-dnc-remarks/ (accessed October 24, 2020).

168 Peter St. Onge, "Revolutions Eat Their Parents" (January 12, 2015) at Mises Institute https://mises.org/library/revolutions-eat-their-parents (accessed October 24, 2020).

169 Katie Lauer, "San Jose Mayor Sam Liccardo unveils host of police accountability reforms" (June 24, 2020) at San Jose Spotlight https://sanjosespotlight.com/san-jose-mayor-sam-liccardo-unveils-host-of-police-accountability-reforms/ (accessed October 24, 2020).

170 "Pittsburgh Mayor Bill Peduto 'Livid' about Protester Arrest, Won't 'Tolerate These Tactics' in the Future" (August 18, 2020) at CBS Pittsburgh https://www.msn.com/en-us/news/us/pittsburgh-mayor-bill-peduto-e2-80-98livid-e2-80-99-about-protester-arrest-won-e2-80-99t-e2-80-98tolerate-these-tactics-e2-80-99-in-the-future/ar-BB184FEl (accessed October 24, 2020).

171 Bill Peduto, "It's hard to find the words" (August 17, 2020) at Twitter https://twitter.com/billpeduto/status/1295417406920196098 (accessed October 24, 2020).

172 MBKAP, "My Brother's Keeper Alliance Pledge" (2020) at PittsburghPA.gov https://pittsburghpa.gov/mayor/mbk/index.html (accessed October 24, 2020)

173 "My Brother's Keeper" (2020) at pittsburghpa.gov https://pittsburghpa.gov/mayor/mbk/index.html (accessed October 24, 2020).

174 "MBK Pittsburgh-Allegheny County Action Plan" (February 2018) at pittsburghpa.gov https://pittsburghpa.gov/mayor/mbk/action_plan.pdf (accessed October 24, 2020).

175 Matthew J. Hickman, "Department of Justice Owes the Seattle Police Department an Apology" (February 8, 2012) at the Seattle Times https://www.seattletimes.com/opinion/department-of-justice-owes-the-seattle-police-department-an-apology/ (accessed October 24, 2020).

176 Ian Schwartz, "Seattle Mayor Durkan: CHAZ Has a 'Block Party Atmosphere,' Could Turn into 'Summer of Love'" (June 12, 2020) at Real Clear Politics https://www.realclearpolitics.com/video/2020/06/12/seattle_mayor_durkan_chaz_has_a_block_party_atmosphere_could_turn_into_summer_of_love.html# (accessed October 24, 2020).

177 Eddy Rodriguez, "Seattle Police Chief Says 'Enough Is Enough' after 2 Teens Killed in CHOP Protest Zone" (June 30, 2020) at Newsweek https://www.newsweek.com/seattle-police-chief-says-enough-enough-after-2-teens-killed-chop-protest-zone-1514395 (accessed October 24, 2020).

178 Steve Pomper, "Seattle Busy Battling NYC and Portland for America's Stupidest City Crown" (September 27, 2020) at National Police

Association https://nationalpolice.org/seattle-busy-battling-nyc-and-portland-for-americas-stupidest-city-crown/ (accessed October 24, 2020).

179 WorldTribune Staff, "Reports: 'Baby Barack' Lived in Chaz/Chop" (June 21, 2020) at World Tribune https://www.worldtribune.com/reports-baby-barack-lived-in-chaz-chop/ (accessed October 24, 2020).

180 Erin Sirianni, "President Obama gives shout-out to Mercer Island" (October 12, 2015) at My Mercer Island https://mymercerisland.com/president-obama-gives-shout-out-to-mercer-island/ (accessed October 24, 2020).

181 Michael Patrick Leahy, *What Does Barack Obama Believe?* (Harpeth River Press, 2nd edition, 2008)

182 City of Seattle, Seattle City Council (2020) at Seattle.gov http://www.seattle.gov/council/ (accessed October 24, 2020).

183 Barnini Chakraborty, "Seattle City Council approves plan to defund police department, slashes jobs and salaries" (August 10, 2020) at Fox News https://www.foxnews.com/us/seattle-city-council-approves-defund-the-police (accessed October 24, 2020).

184 Dori Monson, "Dori: Socialist Alternative controls Kshama Sawant's every move" (January 9, 2019) at KIRO Radio https://mynorthwest.com/1236252/dori-socialist-alternative-controls-kshama-sawant/ (accessed October 24, 2020).

185 Ian, "Kshama Sawant calls for Socialist Revolution at Bernie 2020 rally" (February 25, 2020) at YouTube https://www.youtube.com/watch?v=fkclHPiO7Fw (accessed October 24, 2020).

186 Gary Horcher, "Seattle City Councilmember-elect shares radical idea with Boeing workers" (November 19, 2013) at KIRO 7 News https://www.kiro7.com/news/seattle-city-councilmember-elect-shares-radical-id/246045525/ (accessed October 24, 2020).

187 Essex Porter, "Kshama Sawant sued for defamation by Seattle police officers involved in shooting" (August 22, 2017) at KIRO 7 News https://www.kiro7.com/news/local/kshama-sawant-sued-for-defamation-by-seattle-police-officers-involved-in-shooting/596635068/ (accessed October 24, 2020).

188 Mike Carter, "Judge dismisses defamation lawsuit against Kshama Sawant filed by 2 police officers over 'brutal murder' comments" (March 1, 2019) at the Seattle Times https://www.seattletimes.com/seattle-news/crime/judge-dismisses-defamation-lawsuit-against-kshama-sawant-filed-by-2-police-officers-over-brutal-murder-comments/

(accessed October 24, 2020).

189 Ben Feuerherd, "Minneapolis City Council approves measure to abolish police force" (June 26, 2020) at New York Post https://nypost.com/2020/06/26/minneapolis-city-council-approves-measure-to-abolish-police-force/ (accessed October 24, 2020).

190 Bronson Stocking, "After Voting to Abolish Cops, Minneapolis City Council Members Hire Private Security" (June 27, 2020) at Townhall https://townhall.com/tipsheet/bronsonstocking/2020/06/27/after-voting-to-abolish-cops-minneapolis-city-council-members-hire-private-police-n2571462 (accessed October 24, 2020).

191 Valerie Richardson, "Report: Minnesota council members who voted to abolish police get taxpayer-funded private security" (June 28, 2020) at Washington Times https://www.washingtontimes.com/news/2020/jun/28/minneapolis-city-council-members-who-voted-gut-pol/ (accessed October 24, 2020).

192 Brandt Williams, "With violent crime on the rise in Mpls., City Council asks: Where are the police?" (September 15, 2020) at MPRNews.org https://www.mprnews.org/story/2020/09/15/with-violent-crime-on-the-rise-in-mpls-city-council-asks-where-are-the-police (accessed October 24, 2020).

193 Jackie Renzetti, "Obama: 'I'm urging every mayor' to reform use-of-force policies" (June 3, 2020) at Bring Me the News https://bringmethenews.com/minnesota-news/obama-im-urging-every-mayor-to-reform-use-of-force-policies (accessed October 24, 2020).

194 Associated Press, "Obama admin spent $36M on lawsuits to keep info secret" (March 14, 2017) at CBS News https://www.cbsnews.com/news/obama-administration-spent-36m-on-records-lawsuits-last-year/ (accessed October 24, 2020).

195 Associated Press, "Obama administration rejects FOIA requests from NYT, ACLU for 'targeted killing' papers" (June 21, 2012) at CBS News https://www.cbsnews.com/news/obama-administration-rejects-foia-requests-from-nyt-aclu-for-targeted-killing-papers/ (accessed October 24, 2020).

196 Jonathan Easley, "Obama says his is 'most transparent administration' ever" (February 14, 2013) at The Hill https://thehill.com/blogs/blog-briefing-room/news/283335-obama-this-is-the-most-transparent-administration-in-history (accessed October 24, 2020).

197 Charles Creitz, "AG Barr: The Soros-funded Dem prose-

cutor candidates will lead to increased crime, fewer police officers" (December 20, 2019) at Fox News https://www.foxnews.com/media/ag-barr-soros-funded-democratic-prosecutor-candidates-will-lead-to-increased-crime-police-department-vacancies (accessed September 26, 2020).

198 Jennifer Sinco Kelleher, "Bronx man who couldn't resist Hawaii's surf charged with violating state's strict coronavirus quarantine" (May 16, 2020) at New York Daily News https://www.nydailynews.com/new-york/ny-bronx-man-charged-violating-hawaii-quarantine-20200516-orhwvkr7ebexlkfjoljrjvi4iu-story.html (accessed September 26, 2020).

199 Jeffery Cook, Clayton Sandell, and Jennifer Leong, "Former police officer arrested in park for throwing ball with daughter due to coronavirus social distancing rules" (April 8, 2020) at ABC News https://abcnews.go.com/US/police-officer-arrested-park-throwing-ball-daughter-due/story?id=70032966 (accessed September 26, 2020).

200 Caleb Parke, "Idaho man arrested for not wearing mask at outdoor worship service: 'Unbelievable'" (September 25, 2020) at Fox News https://www.foxnews.com/us/coronavirus-idaho-arrest-mask-outdoor-worship-service-laura-ingraham-gabriel-rench (accessed September 26, 2020).

201 Amanda Prestigiacomo, "Veteran Bar Owner Commits Suicide Week after Special Prosecutor Indicts Him for Fatally Shooting Rioter" (September 21, 2020) https://www.dailywire.com/news/veteran-bar-owner-commits-suicide-week-after-special-prosecutor-indicts-him-for-fatally-shooting-rioter (accessed September 26, 2020).

202 Andrea Widburg, "Have we reached the point at which self-defense is a crime?" (July 3, 2020) at American Thinker https://www.americanthinker.com/blog/2020/07/have_we_reached_the_point_at_which_selfdefense_is_a_crime.html (accessed September 26, 2020).

203 Robert Kraychik, "Timeline: Jussie Smollett Hate Hoax Attack" (February 17, 2019) at Breitbart https://www.breitbart.com/entertainment/2019/02/17/timeline-jussie-smollett-hate-hoax-attack/ (September 26, 2020).

204 Stephanie Pagones, "Special prosecutor in Jussie Smollett investigation finds Kim Foxx's office mishandled case" (August 17, 2020) at Fox News https://www.foxnews.com/us/special-prosecutor-jussie-smollett-investigation-kim-foxxs-mishandled-case (accessed September 26, 2020).

205 CST Editorial Board, "Voters deserve full story, spelled out by Foxx, of what went down in Jussie Smollett case" (August 17, 2020) at Chicago Sun Times https://chicago.suntimes.com/2020/8/17/21372850/dan-webb-kim-foxx-jussie-smollett-states-attorney-suntimes-editorial (September 26, 2020).

206 David Jackson, Todd Lighty, Gary Marx, and Alex Richards, "Kim Foxx drops more felony cases as Cook County state's attorney than her predecessor, Tribune analysis shows" (August 10, 2020) at Chicago Tribune https://www.chicagotribune.com/investigations/ct-kim-foxx-felony-charges-cook-county-20200810-ldvrmqvv6bd3hpsuqha4duehmu-story.html (accessed November 29, 2020).

207 Joe Dougherty, "Chicago police union chief asks Feds to step in after Soros-funded prosecutor dismisses 25k felonies" (August 13, 2020) at BizPac Review https://www.bizpacreview.com/2020/08/13/chicago-police-union-chief-asks-feds-to-step-in-after-soros-funded-prosecutor-dismisses-25k-felonies-959743 (accessed October 24, 2020).

208 Ferlon Webster Jr., "Boston's New District Attorney Won't Be Prosecuting 15 Crimes—Including Resisting Arrest" (December 7, 2018) at mrcTV https://www.mrctv.org/blog/bostons-new-district-attorney-wont-be-prosecuting-15-crimes-including-resisting-arrest (accessed October 24, 2020).

209 Alejandro Serrano, "Obama gave a Suffolk DA candidate a shoutout in speech" (September 7, 2018) at Boston Globe https://www.bostonglobe.com/news/politics/2018/09/07/barack-obama-gave-suffolk-candidate-shoutout-today-speech/NCgFZZ9XJlYtbo1TEgEX4H/story.html (accessed October 24, 2020).

210 "National Police Association Files Bar Complaint against District Attorney-Elect Racheal Rollins" (December 28, 2018) at National Police Association https://nationalpolice.org/national-police-association-files-bar-complaint-against-district-attorney-elect-rachael-rollins/ (accessed October 27, 2020).

211 Heather Knight, "How Chesa Boudin, a public defender who never prosecuted a case, won SF D.A. race" (November 11, 2019) at San Francisco Chronicle https://www.sfchronicle.com/bayarea/heatherknight/article/How-Chesa-Boudin-a-public-defender-who-never-14826323.php (accessed October 24, 2020).

212 Steve Pomper, "What the New San Francisco DA Means for City's Cops" (November 15, 2019) at National Police Association https://nationalpolice.org/what-the-new-san-francisco-da-means-for-citys-cops/

(accessed October 24, 2020).

213 Allan Smith, "Parents guilty of murder and raised by radicals, Chesa Boudin is San Francisco's next district attorney" (December 16, 2019) a NBC News https://www.nbcnews.com/politics/elections/parents-guilty-murder-raised-radicals-chesa-boudin-san-francisco-s-n1101071 (accessed October 24, 2020).

214 Steve Lieberman, "Brinks: Cops, guard killed in 1981 robbery honored on 38th anniversary" (October 16, 2019) at IOHUD https://www.lohud.com/story/news/local/rockland/nyack/2019/10/16/brinks-robbery-two-cops-guard-killed-oct-20-1981-honored-38th-anniversa-ry/3983929002/ (accessed October 24, 2020).

215 Edward Guthmann, "For 11 years, Bernardine Dohrn and Bill Ayers were on the run from the FBI. In the film 'The Weather Underground,' the anti-war activists explain why they fought the law—and why they have no regrets" (July 21, 2003) at SF Gate https://www.sfgate.com/entertainment/article/For-11-years-Bernardine-Dohrn-and-Bill-Ayers-2564825.php (accessed October 24, 2020).

216 Bernie Quigley, "Obama and Bill Ayers Together from the Beginning" (September 24, 2008) at The Hill https://thehill.com/blogs/pundits-blog/presidential-campaign/32072-obama-and-bill-ayers-togeth-er-from-the-beginning (accessed October 24, 2020).

217 Monica Showalter, "First, the purges: Comrade Chesa Boudin fires prosecutors for… prosecuting" (January 14, 2020) at American Thinker https://www.americanthinker.com/blog/2020/01/first_the_purg-es_comrade_chesa_boudin_fires_prosecutors_for__prosecuting_.html (accessed October 24, 2020).

218 Michelle Malkin, "Radical Spawn Chesa Boudin: Nation's Most Toxic DA Candidate" (October 30, 2019) at Townhall https://townhall.com/columnists/michellemalkin/2019/10/30/radical-spawn-chesa-bou-din-nations-most-toxic-da-candidate-n2555557 (accessed October 24, 2020).

219 Gabe Greschler, "Why Did San Francisco's New District Attor-ney Fire Seven Prosecutors?" (January 12, 2020) at KQED https://www.kqed.org/news/11795676/why-did-san-franciscos-new-district-attor-ney-fire-seven-prosecutors (accessed October 24, 2020).

220 Joseph Curl, "Holy Crap! New 'Poop Map' Shows San Francis-co Literally Covered in Human Excrement" (April 23, 2019) at Gateway Pundit https://www.thegatewaypundit.com/2019/04/holy-crap-new-

poop-map-shows-san-francisco-literally-covered-in-human-excrement/ (accessed October 24, 2020).

221 Steve Pomper, "U.S. Attorney issues stinging rebuke of Philadelphia D.A. Larry Krasner" (March 22, 2020) at LifeZette https://www.lifezette.com/2020/03/u-s-attorney-issues-stinging-rebuke-of-philadelphia-d-a-larry-krasner/ (accessed October 24, 2020).

222 Jon Dougherty, "Soros-Funded Marxist 'Prosecutors' Overseeing Murder Spikes, Breakdown of Law and Order in U.S. Cities" (June 11, 2019) at the National Sentinel https://thenationalsentinel.com/2019/06/11/soros-funded-marxist-prosecutors-overseeing-murder-spikes-breakdown-law-and-order-in-us-cities/ (accessed October 24, 2020).

223 CBS3 Staff, "Philadelphia Police SWAT Officer James O'Connor Shot, Killed While Serving Warrant in Frankford" (March 13, 2020) at CBS3 Philly https://philadelphia.cbslocal.com/2020/03/13/james-oconnor-hassan-elliott-philadelphia-police-swat-officer-shot-killed-while-serving-warrant-in-frankford/ (accessed October 24, 2020).

224 Max Bennett, "Former Obama Official Named Philadelphia's First Assistant DA" (February 28, 2018) at Patch https://patch.com/pennsylvania/philadelphia/former-obama-official-named-philadelphia-as-first-assistant-da (accessed October 24, 2020).

225 Todd Herman Show (2020) at Facebook https://www.facebook.com/ToddHermanShow/ (accessed October 24, 2020).

226 "King County prosecutor endorses safe injection sites for drug users" (January 19, 2017) at KIRO 7 News https://www.kiro7.com/news/local/king-county-prosecutor-endorses-safe-injection-sites-for-heroin-addicts-/486013694/ (accessed October 24, 2020).

227 Steve Pomper, "Anti-Police City Officials Oppose the Law and Order They Are Obligated to Uphold in Court" (July 8, 2020) at National Police Association https://nationalpolice.org/anti-police-city-officials-oppose-the-law-and-order-they-are-obligated-to-uphold-in-court/ (accessed October 24, 2020).

228 Anthony Leonardi, "'We could have the summer of love!'" Seattle mayor says she doesn't know when CHAZ will conclude" (June 11, 2020) at Washington Examiner https://www.washingtonexaminer.com/news/we-could-have-the-summer-of-love-seattle-mayor-says-she-doesnt-know-when-chaz-occupation-will-conclude (accessed October 24, 2020).

229 "Business owners have mixed reactions to Dallas County DA's

new policies" (April 12, 2019) at Fox 4 KDFW https://www.fox4news.com/news/business-owners-have-mixed-reactions-to-dallas-county-das-new-policies (accessed October 24, 2020).

230 Lia Eustachewich, "California DA's new policy to consider looter's 'needs' before charging them" (September 2, 2020) at New York Post https://nypost.com/2020/09/02/das-policy-to-consider-looters-needs-before-charging-them/ (accessed October 24, 2020).

231 Black Futures Lab, "About: Our Allies" (2020) at Black Futures Lab https://blackfutureslab.org/our-allies/ (accessed October 24, 2020).

232 Fola Akinnibi, "Lawsuits over protest brutality pile up, adding to cities' police costs" (October 28, 2020) at Bloomberg CityLab https://www.bloomberg.com/news/articles/2020-10-28/protest-policing-lawsuits-are-costing-cities-money (accessed November 1, 2020).

233 "ACAB" (2020) at Anti-Defamation League https://www.adl.org/education/references/hate-symbols/acab (accessed November 1, 2020).

234 Ben Goad, "Holder taps ACLU lawyer to head civil rights unit" (October 15, 2014) at The Hill https://thehill.com/regulation/administration/220843-holder-taps-aclu-lawyer-to-head-dojs-civil-rights-unit (accessed November 1, 2020).

235 David Harsanyi, "Obama Lawsuit against North Carolina Isn't about Civil Rights. It's about Crushing Dissent" (May 10, 2016) at the Federalist https://thefederalist.com/2016/05/10/obamas-lawsuit-against-north-carolina-isnt-about-civil-rights-its-about-crushing-dissent/ (accessed November 1, 2020).

236 Chris Geidner, "Gupta on what #HB2 Does …" (May 9, 2016) at Twitter https://twitter.com/chrisgeidner/status/729766704293761025 (accessed November 1, 2020).

237 KATU Staff, "National Police Association asks court to rule against journalists in ACLU lawsuit" (July 22, 2020) at KATU2 ABC https://katu.com/news/local/national-police-association-asks-court-to-rule-against-journalists-in-aclu-lawsuit (accessed December 8, 2020)

238 National Police Association, "The National Police Association Takes on ACLU over Right of Police to Maintain Gang Database" (July 16, 2019) at Cision PR Newswire https://www.prnewswire.com/news-releases/the-national-police-association-takes-on-aclu-over-right-of-police-to-maintain-gang-databases-300884905.html?tc=eml_cleartime (accessed December 8, 2020)

239 NPA, "The National Police Association Takes on ACLU over

Right of Police to Maintain Gang Databases" (July 16, 2019) at Cision PR Newswire https://www.prnewswire.com/news-releases/the-national-police-association-takes-on-aclu-over-right-of-police-to-maintain-gang-databases-300884905.html?tc=eml_cleartime (accessed November 2, 2020).

240 "ACLU of [Oregon] Protest Legal Observer Training" (2020) at ACLU Oregon https://action.aclu.org/webform/aclu-protest-legal-observer-training (accessed November 3, 2020).

241 Dr. Susan Berry and Ezra Dulis, "Black Lives Matter Foundation Aims to 'Disrupt' Family Structure, Excludes Fathers from Vision of Community" (June 10, 2020) at Breitbart https://www.breitbart.com/politics/2020/06/10/black-lives-matter-foundation-aims-to-disrupt-family-structure-excludes-fathers-from-vision-of-community/ (accessed October 23, 2020).

242 *The Sopranos* (2020) at HBO https://www.hbo.com/the-sopranos (accessed October 23, 2020).

243 *Five Families of New York City* (2020) at fivefamiliesnyc.com http://www.fivefamiliesnyc.com/ (accessed October 23, 2020).

244 Lee Brown, "Seattle cop hit on head with baseball bat as 13 arrested in protests" (September 24, 2020) at New York Post https://nypost.com/2020/09/24/seattle-cop-hit-on-head-with-baseball-bat-as-13-arrested-in-protests/ (accessed October 23, 2020).

245 Elise Takahama, "Seattle police officer injured after man allegedly sets patrol vehicle on fire" (October 15, 2020) at the Seattle Times https://www.seattletimes.com/seattle-news/crime/seattle-police-officer-injured-after-man-allegedly-sets-his-patrol-vehicle-on-fire/ (accessed October 23, 2020).

246 Staff, "Two Los Angeles police officers shot in apparent ambush" (September 13, 2020) at NZHerald https://www.nzherald.co.nz/world/two-los-angeles-police-officers-shot-in-apparent-ambush/UYSF2O4U-VH44635E6LTIXWTMAI/ (accessed October 23, 2020).

247 Jack Davis, "Suspect Arrested after 84-Year-Old Trump Supporter Beaten in Savage Daylight Attack" (September 20, 2020) at the Western Journal https://www.westernjournal.com/suspect-arrested-84-year-old-trump-supporter-beaten-savage-daylight-attack/ (accessed October 23, 2020).

248 Jim Treacher, "Trump Supporter Shot Dead in Denver, Media Tiptoes around It" (October 12, 2020) at PJ Media https://pjmedia.com/news-and-politics/jim-treacher/2020/10/12/trump-supporter-shot-dead-

in-denver-media-tiptoes-around-it-n1038934 (accessed October 23, 2020).

249 "Omerta" (2020) at Bing.com https://www.bing.com/search?q=omerta&form=ANNNB1&refig=8ca51450f-27c4d94b0552ec745cc1089&sp=-1&ghc=1&pq=omer-ta&sc=8-6&qs=n&sk=&cvid=8ca51450f27c4d94b0552ec745cc1089 (accessed October 23, 2020).

250 Jennifer Bilek, "Who Are the Rich, White Men Institutionalizing Transgender Ideology?" (February 20, 2018) at the Federalist https://thefederalist.com/2018/02/20/rich-white-men-institutionalizing-transgender-ideology/ (accessed October 23, 2020).

251 Media Contact, "NYC Commission on Human Rights Announces Strong Protections for City's Transgender and Gender Non-Conforming Communities in Housing, Employment and Public Spaces" (December 21, 2015) at 1NYC.gov https://www1.nyc.gov/office-of-the-mayor/news/961-15/nyc-commission-human-rights-strong-protections-city-s-transgender-gender (accessed October 23, 2020).

252 Valerie Richardson, "Martina Navratilova slammed for calling out transgender 'cheating' in women's sports" (February 20, 2019) at Washington Times https://www.washingtontimes.com/news/2019/feb/20/martina-navratilova-slammed-calling-out-transgende/ (accessed October 23, 2020).

253 Susan Dorman, "J.K. Rowling slammed for defending concept of biological sex: 'It isn't hate to speak the truth'" (June 6, 2020) at Fox News https://www.foxnews.com/entertainment/jk-rowling-backlash-sex-gender (accessed October 23, 2020).

254 Trevor Loudon, "The Tides Foundation and Center: Brokers of Revolution" (October 2010) at Capital Research Center: Foundation Watch http://www.wnd.com/files/tides.pdf (accessed October 23, 2020).

255 Russ Choma and Monica Vendituoli, "Advocacy Fund Spends Millions to Lobby on Immigration" (July 22, 2013) at Open Secrets https://www.opensecrets.org/news/2013/07/tides-advocacy-fund/ (accessed October 23, 2020).

256 *Philanthropy: The Quarterly National Magazine of the Philanthropy Roundtable* http://www.philanthropyroundtable.org/topic/excellence_in_philanthropy/philanthropy_the_law_a_symposium (accessed October 23, 2020).

257 "Tides Foundation" (2020) at InfluenceWatch.org https://www.

influencewatch.org/non-profit/tides-foundation/ (accessed October 23, 2020).

258 "Tides Center" (2020) at InfluenceWatch.org https://www.influencewatch.org/non-profit/tides-center/ (accessed October 23, 2020).

259 "Tides Nexus" (2020) at InfluenceWatch.org https://www.influencewatch.org/organization/tides-nexus/ (accessed October 23, 2020).

260 "Tides Network" (2020) at InfluenceWatch.org https://www.influencewatch.org/non-profit/tides-network/ (accessed October 23, 2020).

261 Tim Haines, "New Gingrich Confused after FOX Hosts Ask Him Not to Talk about George Soros: 'It's Verboten?'" (September 17, 2020) at Real Clear Politics https://www.realclearpolitics.com/video/2020/09/17/newt_gingrich_confused_after_fox_host_asks_him_not_to_talk_about_george_soros_its_verboten.html (accessed October 23, 2020).

262 Allen Alley, "Hidden Surprises behind a BLM Donation" (June 22, 2020) at Oregon Catalyst https://oregoncatalyst.com/48196-allen-alley-hidden-surprises-blm-donation.html (accessed October 23, 2020).

263 AB Charities, "Cutting-Edge Fundraising Tools to Help Nonprofit Make an Impact" (2020) at ActBlue.com https://secure.actblue.com/abcharities (accessed October 23, 2020).

264 Jerry Dunleavy, "Black Lives Matter fundraising handled by group with convicted terrorists on its board" (June 25, 2020) at Washington Examiner https://www.washingtonexaminer.com/news/black-lives-matter-fundraising-handled-by-group-with-convicted-terrorist-on-its-board (accessed October 23, 2020).

265 Lila Thulin, "In the 1980s, a Far-Left, Female-led Domestic Terrorism Group Bombed the U.S. Capital" (January 6, 2020) at Smithsonian Magazine https://www.smithsonianmag.com/history/1980s-far-left-female-led-domestic-terrorism-group-bombed-us-capitol-180973904/ (accessed October 23, 2020).

266 "The Open Society Foundations Work to Build Vibrant and Inclusive Democracies Whose Governments Are Accountable to Their Citizens" (2020), at Open Society Foundations, https://www.opensocietyfoundations.org/ (accessed September 22, 2020).

267 "Democratic Principles" (2020) at Open Society Foundations https://www.opensocietyfoundations.org/what-we-do/themes/democratic-practice (accessed September 22, 2020).

268 "Higher Education" (2020) at Open Society Foundations https://

www.opensocietyfoundations.org/what-we-do/themes/higher-education (accessed September 22, 2020).

269 "Early Childhood and Education" (2020) at Open Society Foundations https://www.opensocietyfoundations.org/what-we-do/themes/early-childhood-and-education (accessed September 22, 2020).

270 "Human Rights Movements and Institutions" (2020) at Open Society Foundations https://www.opensocietyfoundations.org/what-we-do/themes/human-rights-movements-and-institutions (accessed September 22, 2020).

271 "Economic Equity and Justice" (2020) at Open Society Foundations https://www.opensocietyfoundations.org/what-we-do/themes/economic-equity-and-justice (accessed September 22, 2020).

272 "Information and Digital Rights" (2020) at Open Society Foundations https://www.opensocietyfoundations.org/what-we-do/themes/information-and-digital-rights (accessed September 22, 2020).

273 "Equality and Antidiscrimination" (2020) at Open Society Foundations https://www.opensocietyfoundations.org/what-we-do/themes/equality-and-antidiscrimination (accessed September 22, 2020).

274 "Journalism" (2020) at Open Society Foundations https://www.opensocietyfoundations.org/what-we-do/themes/journalism (accessed September 22, 2020).

275 "Health and Rights" (2020) at Open Society Foundations https://www.opensocietyfoundations.org/what-we-do/themes/health-and-rights (accessed September 22, 2020).

276 "Justice Reform and the Rule of Law" (2020) at Open Society Foundations https://www.opensocietyfoundations.org/what-we-do/themes/justice-reform-and-the-rule-of-law (accessed September 22, 2020).

277 "Grants, Scholarships, and Fellowships" (2020) at Open Society Foundations https://www.opensocietyfoundations.org/grants (accessed October 4, 2020).

278 Brooke Singman, "Obama State Dept Used Taxpayer Dollars to Fund George Soros Group's Political Activities in Albania, Watchdog Group Says" (April 4, 2018) at Fox News https://www.foxnews.com/politics/obama-state-dept-used-taxpayer-dollars-to-fund-george-soros-groups-political-activities-in-albania-watchdog-group-says (accessed on September 22, 2020).

279 "Civil Society 2.0" (2020) at U.S. Department of State https://2009-2017.state.gov/statecraft/cs20/index.htm (accessed October 24, 2020).

280 Glenn Beck, "The Documents for 'The Democrats' Hydra'" (November 17, 2019) at Glenn Beck https://www.glennbeck.com/research/the-documents-for-the-democrats-hydra (accessed October 27, 2020).

281 Sam J., "It's being done in YOUR name! Glenn Beck goes ALL the way back to 2014 in Ukraine thread and it's so DAMNING for Obama" (November 14, 2019) at Twitchy https://cutt.ly/ogndHzL (accessed October 24, 2020).

282 Rebecca Diserio, "Photo Proof … Obama and Soros Are Shaken Over 2020" (October, 2019) at National Insiders https://www.nationalinsiders.com/photo-proof-obama-and-soros-are-shaken-over-2020/ (accessed October 24, 2020).

283 Pierre-Antoine Louis, "Color of Change: Tackling Systemic Racism One Strategy at a Time" (September 5, 2020) at The New York Times https://www.nytimes.com/2020/09/05/us/Rashad-Robinson-color-of-change.html (accessed December 8, 2020).

284 "Color of Change" (2020) at InfluenceWatch https://www.influencewatch.org/non-profit/color-of-change/ (accessed October 24, 2020).

285 "Van Jones" (2020) at InfluenceWatch https://www.influencewatch.org/person/van-jones/ (accessed October 24, 2020).

286 Paul Grein, "Recording Academy Partners with Color of Change to 'Elevate Black Music Creators'" (July 7, 2020) at Billboard https://www.billboard.com/articles/business/9414328/recording-academy-color-of-change-black-music-creators (accessed October 24, 2020).

287 "63rd Grammy Nominees Announced" (2020) at Recording Academy (Grammys) https://www.grammy.com/recording-academy (accessed October 24, 2020).

288 Mark Tapscott, "What's Color of Change hiding about itself?" (April 12, 2012) at Washington Examiner https://www.washingtonexaminer.com/whats-color-of-change-hiding-about-itself (accessed October 24, 2020).

289 Victoria Taft, "Here We Go Again. Triggered Liberals Call for ANOTHER Boycott of Hobby Lobby" (September 7, 2020) at PJ Media https://pjmedia.com/news-and-politics/victoria-taft/2020/09/07/here-we-go-again-triggered-liberals-call-for-another-boycott-of-hobby-lobby-n902086 (accessed October 24, 2020).

290 Jessilyn Lancaster, "Chick-fil-A LGBT Boycott Backfires Again as New York Chains Boom" (May 1, 2016) at Charisma News https://www.charismanews.com/us/57166-chick-fil-a-lgbt-boycott-backfires-again-as-new-york-chains-boom (accessed October 24, 2020).

291 Megan Mcardle, "Boycotting Whole Foods" (August 17, 2009) at the Atlantic https://www.theatlantic.com/business/archive/2009/08/boycotting-whole-foods/23348/ (accessed October 24, 2020).

292 Charlie Spiering, "Donald Trump Mocks Failed 'Radical Left Smear Machine' Boycott of Goya Foods" (July 15, 2020) at Breitbart https://www.breitbart.com/politics/2020/07/15/donald-trump-mocks-failed-radical-left-smear-machine-boycott-of-goya-foods/ (accessed October 24, 2020).

293 Saul Alinsky, "Rules for Radicals" (1971) at Academia https://www.academia.edu/26028008/Rules_for_Radicals_Rules_for_Radicals_Rules_for_Radicals_A_Pragmatic_Primer_for_Realistic (accessed October 24, 2020).

294 Campaign Zero, "We Can End Police Violence in America" (2020) at Campaign Zero https://www.joincampaignzero.org/#vision (accessed October 24, 2020).

295 David Aaro, "Unrest over fatal police shooting in Lancaster results in 8 arrests, 4 from outside county" (September 15, 2020) at Fox News https://www.foxnews.com/us/unrest-over-police-involved-shooting-in-lancaster-prompts-8-arrests-4-from-outside-county (accessed October 24, 2020).

296 Heather MacDonald, "Protesters Demand Cops Let Themselves Be Stabbed or Shot" (September 14, 2020) at New York Post https://nypost.com/2020/09/14/protesters-demand-cops-let-themselves-be-stabbed-or-shot/ (accessed October 27, 2020).

297 "US Protests" (2020) at Fox News https://www.foxnews.com/category/us/us-protests (accessed October 24, 2020).

298 "Pennsylvania" (2020) at Fox News https://www.foxnews.com/category/us/us-regions/northeast/pennsylvania (accessed October 24, 2020).

299 *Superman: Tales of the Bizarro World* (DC Comics, 2003) at DC Comics https://www.dccomics.com/graphic-novels/superman-tales-of-the-bizarro-world (accessed October 24, 2020).

300 FaRaRi, "Leo Terrell Ripped Barack Obama: He Used a Funeral and House of Worship to LIE Just Like Al Sharpton" (July 31, 2020) at

YouTube https://www.youtube.com/watch?v=cIG6QviJ9kA (accessed October 24, 2020).

301 "Civil Rights Corps" (2020) at Influence Watch https://www.influencewatch.org/non-profit/civil-rights-corps/ (accessed October 24, 2020).

302 Samantha Ketterer, "Repeated bail for Houston man accused of murder, 6 felony convictions raises eyebrows" (September 10, 2020) at LMT Online https://www.lmtonline.com/news/houston-texas/crime/article/houston-man-bail-repeat-murder-felony-police-15556380.php (accessed October 24, 2020).

303 Alec Karakatsanis, "President Obama's Department of Injustice" (August 18, 2015) at the New York Times https://www.nytimes.com/2015/08/18/opinion/president-obamas-department-of-injustice.html?ref=opinion (accessed October 24, 2020).

304 Alec Kazakhstanis, "Why 'Crime' Isn't the Question and Police Aren't the Answer" (August 10, 2020) at Current Affairs https://www.currentaffairs.org/2020/08/why-crime-isnt-the-question-and-police-arent-the-answer (accessed October 24, 2020).

305 "Minnesota Freedom Fund, Simon Cecil, Founder" (2020) at Minnesota Freedom Fund https://cutt.ly/GgnfIDW (accessed October 24, 2020).

306 Kemberlee Kaye, "Celebrity-Backed Jail Bail Fund Has Spent Less Than 1% Bailing Out Protesters and Rioters" (June 18, 2020) at Legal Insurrection https://legalinsurrection.com/2020/06/celebrity-backed-jail-bail-fund-has-spent-less-than-1-bailing-out-protesters-and-rioters/ (accessed October 24, 2020).

307 David Ng, "Minnesota Freedom Fund Faces Scrutiny for Antifa and Soros Ties, Demands Defunding of Police" (June 9, 2020) at Breitbart https://www.breitbart.com/crime/2020/06/09/minnesota-freedom-fund-faces-scrutiny-for-antifa-and-soros-ties-demands-defunding-of-police/ (accessed October 24, 2020).

308 "Tonja Honsey—Native Rachel Dolezal" (2020) at Facebook https://www.facebook.com/Tonja-Honsey-Native-Rachel-Dolezal-105869631079262/ (accessed October 24, 2020).

309 Kyle Hooten "George Soros Associated with Effort To Spring Minnesota Rioters From Jail" (June 10, 2020) at Alpha News MN https://alphanewsmn.com/soros-associated-rioters/ (accessed December 8, 2020)

310 "Soros Justice Fellowships" (2020) at Open Society Foundations

https://www.opensocietyfoundations.org/grants/soros-justice-fellow-ships#:~:text=The%20Soros%20Justice%20Fellowships%20fund,the%20U.S.%20criminal%20justice%20system. (accessed October 24, 2020).

311 Patty McMurray, "BLM Supporters Call Out MN Freedom Fund Run by White, Female Ex-Con, for Only Spending $200K of Over $30 Million Collected to Bail Out Protesters: 'Where's the money?'" (June 16, 2020) at 100 Percent Fed Up https://100percentfedup.com/blm-support-ers-call-out-mn-freedom-fund-run-by-white-female-ex-con-for-only-spending-200k-of-over-30-million-collected-to-bail-out-protesters-whe-res-the-money/ (accessed October 24, 2020).

312 Bradley Betters, "Commentary: Antifa's Most Important Enabler Is Its Legal Arm the National Lawyers Guild" (March 10, 2020) at the Tennessee Star https://tennesseestar.com/2020/03/10/commentary-anti-fas-most-important-enabler-is-its-legal-arm-the-national-lawyers-guild/ (accessed October 25, 2020).

313 Jorge Arenas, "Over 40 Hollywood Celebrities Who Donated to Social Justice Causes Including Black Lives Matter and Minneso-ta Freedom Fund" (June 13, 2020) at Bounding into Comics https://boundingintocomics.com/2020/06/13/over-40-hollywood-celebri-ties-who-donated-to-social-justice-causes-including-black-lives-mat-ter-and-minnesota-freedom-fund/ (accessed October 25, 2020).

314 Craig Bannister, "Joe Biden's Staff Donated to, Kamala Harris Promoted, Group That Pays Bail for Those Arrested in Riot-Ravaged MN" (September 2, 2020) at CNS News https://www.cnsnews.com/index.php/blog/craig-bannister/joe-bidens-staff-donated-kamala-harris-pro-moted-group-pays-bail-those-arrested (accessed October 25, 2020).

315 Joshua Caplan, "Report: Minnesota Freedom Fund, Backed by Biden Staff, Released Hardcore Criminals" (August 11, 2020) at Breitbart https://www.breitbart.com/2020-election/2020/08/11/report-minneso-ta-freedom-fund-backed-by-biden-staff-released-hardcore-criminals/ (accessed October 25, 2020).

316 Reuters, "Biden Staff Donate to Group That Pays Bail in Ri-ot-Torn Minneapolis" (May 30, 2020) at US News & World Report https://www.usnews.com/news/us/articles/2020-05-30/biden-staff-do-nate-to-group-that-pays-bail-in-riot-torn-minneapolis (accessed October 25, 2020).

317 Rebecca Rosenberg and Bruce Golding, "NY released MS-13 gang member facing federal murder charges" (September 15, 2020) at New York Post https://nypost.com/2020/09/15/ny-state-freed-ms-13-

member-facing-federal-murder-charge-sources/ (accessed October 25, 2020).

318 Nicole Gelinas, "Embracing 'no-bail' law is Cuomo's first huge political mistake as gov" (January 5, 2020) at New York Post https://nypost.com/2020/01/05/embracing-no-bail-law-is-cuomos-first-huge-political-mistake-as-gov/ (accessed October 25, 2020).

319 Brendan Williams, "Cuomo's Nursing Home Fiasco Is Unforgivable" (May 23, 2020) at the Post-Journal https://www.post-journal.com/opinion/local-commentaries/2020/05/cuomos-nursing-home-fiasco-is-unforgivable/ (accessed October 28, 2020).

320 Joseph Spector and Jon Campbell, "Gov. Andrew Cuomo's COVID book hits shelves amid growing virus cases. Here's what he writes" (October 13, 2020) at USA Today https://www.usatoday.com/story/entertainment/books/2020/10/13/gov-andrew-cuomo-covid-book-new-york-pandemic/5977221002/ (accessed October 25, 2020).

321 Mairead McArdle, "Minnesota Freedom Fund Bails Out Violent Criminals along with Protesters" (August 11, 2020) at National Review https://www.nationalreview.com/news/minnesota-freedom-fund-bails-out-violent-criminals-along-with-protesters/ (accessed October 25, 2020).

322 "Media Matters for America" (2020) at Influence Watch https://www.influencewatch.org/non-profit/media-matters-for-america/ (accessed October 25, 2020).

323 "Media Matters Action Network" (2020) at Influence Watch https://www.influencewatch.org/non-profit/media-matters-action-network/ (accessed November 30, 2020).

324 Monica Showalter, "David Brock's Loathsome Media Matters accused of corruption—again" (April 25, 2020) at American Thinker https://www.americanthinker.com/blog/2020/04/david_brocks_loathesome_media_matters_accused_of_corruption__again.html (accessed October 25, 2020).

325 Amber Athey, "The left's real cause is muzzling its opponents" (February 2020) at the Spectator https://spectator.us/left-real-cause-muzzling-opponents-media-matters/ (accessed October 4, 2020).

326 "Power in Action" (2020) at MoveOn.org https://front.moveon.org/ (accessed October 25, 2020).

327 About MoveOn Political Action" (2020) at MoveOn.org https://front.moveon.org/about-moveon-political-action/ (accessed October 25,

2020).

328 "MoveOn Civic Action (MoveOn.org)" (2020) at Influence Watch https://www.influencewatch.org/non-profit/moveon-civic-action-moveon-org/ (accessed October 25, 2020).

329 "Police Unions Exposed" (2020) at MoveOn.org https://sign.moveon.org/partnerships/police-unions-exposed (accessed October 25, 2020).

330 James Rucker, "Demand justice for Elijah McClain and say NO to police unions" (2019) at MoveOn.org https://sign.moveon.org/petitions/aurora-co-it-s-time-to-say-no-to-police-unions (accessed October 25, 2020).

331 James Rucker, "Bob Kroll—leader of MPLS police union—is violent and racist. He has to go" (2020) at MoveOn.org https://sign.moveon.org/petitions/bob-kroll-leader-of-mpls-police-union-is-violent-and-racist-he-has-to-go-1 (accessed October 25, 2020).

332 "Citizen Engagement Laboratory (CEL)" (2020) at InfluenceWatch.org https://www.influencewatch.org/non-profit/citizen-engagement-laboratory/ (accessed October 25, 2020).

333 Alec Torres, "Citizen Engagement Laboratory" (November 18, 2016) at Capital Research Center https://capitalresearch.org/article/citizen-engagement-laboratory/ (accessed October 25, 2020).

334 "The Indivisible Project (Indivisible)" (2020) at Influence Watch https://www.influencewatch.org/non-profit/the-indivisible-project-indivisible/ (accessed October 25, 2020).

335 Phil Johncock, "Prosperity Now: The Next Chapter in CFED's History" (June 19, 2017) at Opportunity Alliance Nevada http://www.opportunityalliancenv.org/prosperity-now/ (accessed October 25, 2020).

336 Judicial Watch, "ACORN Operating under Different Name" (March 23, 2010) at Judicial Watch https://www.judicialwatch.org/corruption-chronicles/acorn-operating-under-different-name/ (accessed October 25, 2020).

337 MSN News, "Read the Transition Integrity Project's Full Report" (August 4, 2020) at MSN News https://www.msn.com/en-us/news/politics/read-the-transition-integrity-projects-full-report/ar-BB17x0w3 (accessed October 24, 2020).

338 "Transition Integrity Project Report" (August 21, 2020) at Judicial Watch https://www.judicialwatch.org/documents/transition-integri-

ty-project-report/ (accessed October 25, 2020).

339 Joshua Klein, "Transition Integrity Project Founder Suggested 'Military Coup' against Trump Days after Inauguration" (September 10, 2020) at Breitbart https://www.breitbart.com/politics/2020/09/10/transition-integrity-project-founder-suggested-military-coup-against-trump-days-after-inauguration/ (accessed October 24, 2020).

340 Natalie Winters, "Transition Integrity Project Founder Calls for EXECUTION of Former Trump Official" (September 21, 2020) at the National Pulse https://thenationalpulse.com/news/transition-integrity-project-execution/ (accessed October 25, 2020).

341 TEGNA, "'Joe Biden should not concede': Hillary Clinton sends warning about election day" (August 25, 2020) at WUSA9 https://www.wusa9.com/article/news/nation-world/hillary-clinton-tells-joe-biden-dont-concede/507-5f04d238-4fba-4804-bea9-6b0b9235d681 accessed October 24, 2020).

342 "Preventing a Disrupted Presidential Election and Transition" (August 3, 2020) at Judicial Watch https://www.judicialwatch.org/wp-content/uploads/2020/08/Transition-Integrity-Project-Report.pdf (accessed October 24, 2020).

343 Osita Nwanevu, "The Ridiculous War-Gaming of the 2020 Election" (September 14, 2020) at the New Republic https://newrepublic.com/article/159352/wargaming-2020-election-trump-biden (accessed October 25, 2020).

344 Onemoresmoke, "Transition Integrity Project Founder Dined With Soros and Biden Campaign Advisers, Offered Substantive Help" (September 8, 2020) at The Republic Post Informer (accessed December 8, 2020)

345 "John Podesta emails: Following up on conversation at Soros dinner" (May 5, 2015) at Wikileaks https://wikileaks.org/podesta-emails/emailid/42288

346 "Jake Sullivan" (2020) at Influence Watch https://www.influence-watch.org/person/jake-sullivan/ (accessed October 24, 2020).

347 Joe Hoft, "NO SURPRISE: The Transition 'Integrity' Project Is Working to Remove President Trump from Office No Matter What—Has Connections to China, Soros, Obama and Hunter Biden" (September 15, 2020) at Gateway Pundit https://www.thegatewaypundit.com/2020/09/no-surprise-transition-integrity-project-working-remove-presi-

dent-trump-office-no-matter-connections-china-soros-obama-hunter-biden/ (accessed October 25, 2020).

348 Michael Snyder, "Armies of Lawyers Stand Ready to Fight Long Legal Battle over 2020 Election Results" (August 27, 2020) at the Washington Standard https://thewashingtonstandard.com/armies-of-lawyers-stand-ready-to-fight-long-legal-battle-over-2020-election-results/ (accessed October 24, 2020).

349 Glenn Beck, "Civil War: The Left's Revolution Playbook Exposed" (September 22, 2020). At the Blaze https://www.theblaze.com/glenn-beck-special/the-lefts-color-revolution-playbook (accessed October 13, 2020).

350 BlazeTV, "Civil War: The Left's Revolution Playbook EXPOSED/ Glenn TV" (September 23, 2020) at YouTube https://www.youtube.com/watch?v=a0wWvV_KBXY (accessed October 25, 2020).

351 Lincoln A. Mitchell, *The Color Revolutions* (University of Pennsylvania Press, 2020) at University of Pennsylvania Press https://www.upenn.edu/pennpress/book/14990.html (accessed September 29, 2020).

352 Linda Goudsmit, "Color Revolutions Are Not about Color" (September 10, 2020) at Independent Sentinel https://www.independentsentinel.com/color-revolutions-are-not-about-color/ (accessed September 29, 2020).

353 Staff, "America's Own Color Revolution" (June 29, 2020) at Geopolitics https://geopolitics.co/2020/06/29/americas-own-color-revolution/ (accessed September 29, 2020).

354 Brian Niemietz, "Trump tells Rush Limbaugh he's cured and drug-free one week since admitted to Walter Reed" (October 9, 2020) at New York Daily News https://www.nydailynews.com/news/politics/us-elections-government/ny-coronavirus-trump-rush-limbaugh-20201009-24mpnthygngote4mk54ibbw2lu-story.html (accessed October 9, 2020).

355 The Wiz, "Professor: Probability of Biden winning given Trump's early lead is 'less than one in a quadrillion'" (December 8, 2020) at The Election Wizard (accessed December 9, 2020)

356 Colin Campbell, "Trump says troops love him even if Pentagon brass doesn't" (September 7, 2020) at MSN News https://www.msn.com/en-us/news/politics/trump-says-troops-love-him-even-if-pentagon-brass-doesn-t/ar-BB18NjeF (accessed October 25, 2020).

357 Staff (excerpt from Revolver), "Norm Eisen: Central Operative

in the 'Color Revolution' in the US" (September 9, 2020) http://www.ronpaulforums.com/showthread.php?549142-Norm-Eisen-Central-Operative-in-the-%E2%80%9CColor-Revolution%E2%80%9D-in-the-US (accessed November 30, 2020).

358 "Meet Norm Eisen: Legal Hatchet Man and Central Operative in the 'Color Revolution' against President Trump" (September 9, 2020) at Revolver News https://www.revolver.news/2020/09/meet-norm-eisen-legal-hatchet-man-and-central-operative-in-the-color-revolution-against-president-trump/ (September 29, 2020).

359 Ari Shapiro, "Norm Eisen Says He Drafted 10 Articles of Impeachment a Month before Inquiry" (July 27, 2020) at NPR https://www.npr.org/2020/07/27/895709528/norm-eisen-says-he-drafted-10-articles-of-impeachment-a-month-before-inquiry (accessed September 29, 2020).

360 Scott Morefield, "Tucker Carlson Breaks Down Every Police Shooting of Unarmed Black Suspects in 2019" (June 3, 2020) at Daily Caller https://dailycaller.com/2020/06/03/tucker-carlson-police-shootings-genocide/ (accessed October 25, 2020).

361 CNN Wire, "Fort Worth officer shot woman in her own home as she played video games with nephew" (October 14, 2019) at Fox59 https://fox59.com/news/fort-worth-officer-shot-woman-in-her-own-home-as-she-played-video-games-with-nephew/ (accessed October 25, 2020).

362 Ben Crump, "I believe black Americans face a genocide. Here's why I choose that word" (November 15, 2019) at the Guardian https://www.theguardian.com/commentisfree/2019/nov/15/black-americans-genocide-open-season (accessed October 25, 2020).

363 Zachary Halaschak, "Officals say Jacob Blake admitted to having a knife in his possession during Kenosha shooting" (August 26, 2020) at Washington Examiner https://www.washingtonexaminer.com/news/officials-say-jacob-blake-admitted-to-having-a-knife-in-his-possession-during-kenosha-shooting-officer-identified accessed October 25, 2020).

364 Jorge Fitz-Gibbon, "Officials release video of DC cops fatally shooting 18-year-old Deon Kay" (September 3, 2020) at New York Post https://nypost.com/2020/09/03/officials-release-video-of-dc-police-fatally-shooting-deon-kay/ (accessed October 28, 2020).

365 Sundance, "Riots Cancelled—Grievance Network Back Together Again—Former President Obama and Floyd Family Attorney, Ben Crump, Now Execute Phase Two" (June 3, 2020) at the Conservative Tree

House https://theconservativetreehouse.com/2020/06/03/riots-cancelled-grievance-network-back-together-again-former-president-obama-and-floyd-family-attorney-ben-crump-now-execute-phase-two/ (accessed October 25, 2020).

366 MJ Lee and Dan Merica, "Obama urges young black people to 'feel hopeful even as you may feel angry' after George Floyd's death" (June 3, 2020) at CNN https://www.cnn.com/2020/06/03/politics/obama-george-floyd/index.html (accessed October 25, 2020).

367 CBS News, Attorney Ben Brump (June 3, 2020) at Twitter https://twitter.com/CBSNews/status/1268248618768752643 (accessed October 25, 2020).

368 Hannah C., "Updated Autopsy Report: George Floyd Died of Heart Attack with Evidence of Fentanyl and Meth Use" (June 1, 2020) at Science Times https://www.sciencetimes.com/articles/25898/20200601/updated-autopsy-report-george-floyd-died-heart-attack-evidence-fentanyl.htm (accessed October 25, 2020).

369 Jenna Curren, "Leaked Documents suggest Breonna Taylor was managing ex-boyfriend's drug money—letting him use her address" (September 6, 2020) at Law Enforcement Today https://www.lawenforcement-today.com/leaked-documents-give-more-details-in-breonna-taylor-case/ (accessed October 28, 2020).

370 Sundance, "Everything the Media Claimed About Breonna Taylor's Death Was a Lie—Truth Surfaces—No Police Charged in Her Death" (September 23, 2020) at the Conservative Tree House https://theconservativetreehouse.com/2020/09/23/everything-the-media-claimed-about-breonna-taylors-death-was-a-lie-truth-surfaces-no-police-charged-in-her-death/comment-page-3/ (accessed October 25, 2020).

371 Malachi Tate, "North Hollywood Shootout—Best Cut, October 28, 2016" (February 28, 1997) at YouTube https://www.youtube.com/watch?v=dtyxCiPpkHQ (accessed October 25, 2020).

372 "Man Beheaded Co-Worker in Moore, Oklahoma, Workplace Attack: Police" (September 26, 2014) at NBC News https://www.nbcnews.com/news/crime-courts/man-beheaded-co-worker-moore-oklahoma-workplace-attack-police-n212396 (accessed October 25, 2020).

373 Danny Spewak, "Minneapolis police officers now banned from 'warrior-style' training" (April, 18 2019) at KARE11 https://www.kare11.com/article/news/minneapolis-police-officers-now-banned-from-warrior-style-training/89-240421f4-7d10-4034-853b-cfcbc410c0c5 (accessed

October 25, 2020).

374 Tristan Justice, "Virginia senate passes bill to reduce sentencing for assaulting police" (August 27, 2020) at the Federalist https://thefederalist.com/2020/08/27/virginia-senate-passes-bill-to-reduce-sentences-for-assaulting-police/ (accessed October 28, 2020).

375 WCVB5, "DA Rachael Rollins publishes list of 136 current, former police officers 'whose credibility is questionable'" (September 25, 2020) at WCVB5 https://www.wcvb.com/article/da-rachael-rollins-publishes-list-of-136-current-former-police-officers-whose-credibility-is-questionable/34169083 (accessed October 25, 2020).

376 Erica C. Barnett, "PubliCola TV: City Attorney Pete Holmes" (July 7, 2010) at Seattle Met https://www.seattlemet.com/news-and-city-life/2010/07/publicola-tv-city-attorney-pete-holmes (accessed October 28, 2020).

377 Erica C. Barnett, "'Surprised and Dismayed' City Attorney Rejects SPD Request to Prosecute Repeat Downtown Offenders" (August 21, 2013) at Seattle Met https://www.seattlemet.com/news-and-city-life/2013/08/surprised-and-dismayed-holmes-rejects-spd-request-to-prosecute-repeat-downtown-offenders-august-2013 (accessed October 25, 2020).

378 Maxine Bernstein, "Mayor Ted Wheeler bars Portland police use of loud warning sounds, signals 30-day moratorium on tear gas for protests" (June 6, 2020) at the Oregonian/OregonLive https://www.oregonlive.com/portland/2020/06/portlands-mayor-bars-portland-police-use-of-sonic-sound-boom-as-crowd-control-device-comes-under-scrutiny.html (accessed October 25, 2020).

379 KOIN 6 News Staff, "What is LRAD? PPB explain their 'sonic tone' device" (June 5, 2020) at KOIN 6 News https://www.koin.com/local/multnomah-county/what-is-lrad-ppb-explain-their-sonic-tone-device/ (accessed October 25, 2020).

380 Mark Chestnut, "Seattle Citizens on Their Own after City Council Bans Less Lethal for Cops" (July 30, 2020) at Tactical Life https://www.tactical-life.com/news/seattle-city-council-police-less-lethal/ (accessed October 25, 2020).

381 Kanishka Singh, "Judge exempts journalists, legal observers from Portland protest dispersal orders" (August 21, 2020) at Reuters https://www.reuters.com/article/us-global-race-portland-ruling-idUSKBN25H0MF (accessed October 28, 2020).

382 Maxine Bernstein, "Feds urge appeals court to throw out order exempting journalists, legal observers from dispersal orders during Portland riots" (September 17, 2020) at Oregon Live/The Oregonian https://www.oregonlive.com/crime/2020/09/feds-urge-appeals-court-to-throw-out-order-exempting-journalists-legal-observers-from-dispersal-orders-during-portland-riots.html (accessed October 28, 2020).

383 Nicole Gelinas, "Embracing 'no-bail' law is Cuomo's first huge political mistake as gov" (January 5, 2020) at New York Post https://nypost.com/2020/01/05/embracing-no-bail-law-is-cuomos-first-huge-political-mistake-as-gov/ (accessed on December 9, 2020)

384 John Boch via TTAG, "Attempted Murderer Released without Bail in NY, Goes On to Shoot 3 More People" (August 6, 1010) at Concealed Nation https://concealednation.org/2020/08/attempted-murderer-released-with-no-bail-in-ny-goes-on-to-shoot-3-more-people/ (accessed October 25, 2020).

385 Evie Fordhan, "Protesters show up at LA hospital treating ambushed cops, yell 'I hope they f------ die'" (September 13, 2020) at Fox News https://www.foxnews.com/us/protesters-hospital-los-angeles-sheriffs-deputies-ambushed (accessed October 25, 2020).

386 Vincent Barone, "Two Louisville cops shot amid Breonna Taylor protests" (September 23, 2020) at New York Post https://nypost.com/2020/09/23/louisville-cop-shot-in-citys-downtown-area/ (accessed October 25, 2020).

387 Hannity Staff, "'Attempted Murder': Portland Rioters Attack Police with Molotov Cocktails as City Explodes" (September 24, 2020) at Sean Hannity https://hannity.com/media-room/attempted-murder-portland-rioters-attack-police-with-molotov-cocktail-as-city-explodes/ (accessed October 25, 2020).

388 MOXNEWS, "Video Shows Protester Hit Seattle Police Officer in the Head with a Metal Baseball Bat!" (September 25, 2020) at YouTube https://www.youtube.com/watch?v=6HpFJflbhig (accessed October 25, 2020).

389 DB, "5 Police Officers Killed by Snipers at Scene of Dallas BLM Protest" (July 8, 2016) at Talking Points Memo https://talkingpointsmemo.com/news/police-officers-killed-dallas-shooting (accessed October 25, 2020).

390 CBS 17, "Las Vegas police officer shot in head" (June 2, 2020) at YouTube https://www.youtube.com/watch?v=OjgyrTeMpaw (accessed

October 25, 2020).

391 M. Dowling, "Antifa's Recruitment Video Is Aimed at Criminals, Criminal Aliens" (August 26, 2017) at Independent Sentinel https://www.independentsentinel.com/antifas-recruitment-video-is-aimed-at-criminals-criminal-aliens/ (accessed September 24, 2020).

392 Thomas Madison, "Antifa is openly recruiting and inciting the mentally ill to commit violence" (February 26, 2018) https://powderedwigsociety.com/antifa-mentally-ill/ (accessed September 24, 2020).

393 Ryan Ledendecker, "NFL Player Removes Name of Police Shooting Victim from Helmet after Learning All the Details of the Case" (September, 19 2020) at the Federalist Papers https://thefederalistpapers.org/us/nfl-player-removes-name-police-shooting-victim-helmet-learning-details-case (accessed September 24, 2020).

394 Paula Reed Ward, "Court filing: Drive-by victim told police that Antwon Ross II shot him" (March 1, 2019) at Pittsburgh Post-Gazette https://www.post-gazette.com/news/crime-courts/2019/03/01/Michael-Rosfeld-Antown-Rose-shooting-east-pittsburgh-drive-by-victim-tells-police/stories/201903010161 (accessed September 24, 2020).

395 David Boroff, "Police officer in Antwon Rose shooting admits he did not see a gun, charged with criminal homicide" (June 27, 2018) at New York Daily News https://www.nydailynews.com/news/crime/ny-news-police-officer-charged-antwon-rose-shooting-20180627-story.html (accessed September 24, 2020).

396 Jason Rantz, "Rantz: Sue Bird implies you're a bigot for not watching women's basketball" (October 20, 2020) at 770 KTTH/MyNorthwest.com https://mynorthwest.com/2246192/rantz-sue-bird-implies-bigot-wnba-womens-basketball/ (accessed October 25, 2020).

397 Mechelle Voepel, "Sue Bird: WNBA's growth mirroring NBA's" (July 20, 2017) at ESPN https://www.espn.com/wnba/story/_/id/20112760/sue-bird-seattle-storm-says-wnba-hurt-homophobia-racism-sexism (accessed October 25, 2020).

398 The Young Turks, "NFL Stars Do 'Hands Up, Don't Shoot' Protest during Game, Cops Furious" (December 1, 2014) at YouTube https://www.youtube.com/watch?v=NNhtEcA3gRw (accessed September 24, 2020).

399 Leia Idliby, "Obama Praises Player Protests in Response to Jacob Blake Shooting: 'It's Going to Take All Our Institutions to Stand Up for Our Values'" (August 26, 2020) at Mediaite https://www.mediaite.com/

news/obama-praises-player-protests-in-response-to-jacob-blake-shoot-ing-its-going-to-take-all-our-institutions-to-stand-up-for-our-values/ (accessed October 25, 2020).

400 ABC News, "Police bodycam footage shows officers asking man to put down knife" (July 3, 2019) at YouTube https://www.youtube.com/watch?v=kAMBdfnNvCU (accessed October 25, 2020).

401 Georgi Boorman, "Why Is Drew Brees Wearing the Name of an Alleged Rapist on His Helmet?" (September 2, 2020) at the Federalist https://thefederalist.com/2020/09/02/why-is-drew-brees-wearing-the-name-of-an-alleged-rapist-on-his-helmet/ (accessed October 25, 2020).

402 For Conservatives Only, "Herschel Walker Speech RNC Republican Convention 2020" (August 24, 2020) at YouTube https://www.youtube.com/watch?v=D_O7FdKsb2o (accessed September 24, 2020).

403 Jeremy Frankel, "Herschel Walker Slams BLM AS 'Anti-American,' 'Anti-Christian'" (September 19, 2020) at the Dan Bongino Show https://bongino.com/herschel-walker-slams-blm-as-anti-american-anti-christian (accessed October 25, 2020).

404 Scott Moorefield, "Burgess Owens Says 'BLM Inc. Is Nothing but a Marxist Organization'" (August 20, 2020) at Daily Caller https://dailycaller.com/2020/08/20/burgess-owens-black-lives-matter-marxist/ (accessed October 25, 2020).

405 Virginia Kruta, "Riot Declared in Portland As 73rd Day of Protests Results in Fire at Police Union Building" (August 9, 2020) at Daily Caller https://dailycaller.com/2020/08/09/riot-declared-portland-protests-fire-police-union-building/ (accessed October 25, 2020).

406 Andrew Mark Miller, "Burgess Owens responds after a white NBA coach catches flak for donating to his campaign" (September 12, 2020) at Washington Examiner https://www.washingtonexaminer.com/news/burgess-owens-responds-after-white-nba-coach-catches-flak-for-donating-to-his-campaign (accessed September 25, 2020).

407 Jim Hoft, "Sick: Salt Lake Tribune Reporter Andy Larsen Attacks Utah Jazz Coach for Donating to Black Republican Who Fought against Racism for Decades" (September 12, 2020) at Gateway Pundit https://newsla.localad.com/2020/09/12/sick-salt-lake-tribune-reporter-andy-larsen-attacks-utah-jazz-coach-for-donating-to-black-republican-who-fought-against-racism-for-decades/ (accessed December 8, 2020).

408 Meme Generator, "Aw Geez, Not This Liberal Bullshit Again," at Meme Generator https://memegenerator.net/instance/60551902/archie-

bunker-1-aw-geeze-not-this-liberal-bullshit-again (accessed September 25, 2020).

409 Heritage Foundation, "'We Are Trained MARXISTS': BLM's Leftist Agenda Has Little to Do with Black Lives/The Heritage Foundation" (June 30, 2020) at YouTube https://www.youtube.com/watch?v=-8J68p5l-gjQ (accessed October 25, 2020).

410 "Opal Tometi" (February 29, 2016) at TED Talk https://www.ted.com/speakers/opal_tometi (accessed October 25, 2020).

411 TED, "An interview with the founders of Black Lives Matter/ Alicia Garza, Patrisse Cullors, Opal Tometi" (December 20, 2016) at YouTube https://www.youtube.com/watch?v=tbicAmaXYtM (accessed October 25, 2020).

412 Cal Thomas, "The goals of Black Lives Matter and its radical ideology" (July 29, 2020) at Washington Times https://www.washingtontimes.com/news/2020/jul/29/the-goals-of-black-lives-matter-and-its-radical-id/ (accessed October 25, 2020).

413 Dave Boyer, "Blacks at Trump rally boo BLM, president says group is 'destroying Black lives'" (September 25, 2020) at Washington Times https://www.washingtontimes.com/news/2020/sep/25/blacks-trump-rally-boo-black-lives-matter-presiden/ (accessed October 25, 2020).

414 Jerry Dunleavy, "Who Is Black Lives Matter?" (July 23 2020) at Washington Examiner https://www.washingtonexaminer.com/opinion/who-is-black-lives-matter (accessed October 25, 2020).

415 Black Lives Matter, "Celebrating Four Years of Organizing to Protect Black Lives" (2013) at Google Drive, Black Lives Matter.pdf https://drive.google.com/file/d/0B0pJEXffvS0uOHdJREJnZ2JJYTA/view (accessed October 25, 2020).

416 Kurt Zindulka, "Exclusive Video: BLM Activists says white men are 'the common enemy', 'we need to get rid of them.'" (July 21, 2020) https://www.breitbart.com/europe/2020/07/21/watch-blm-activist-says-white-men-are-common-enemy/ (accessed December 8, 2020)

417 "Trooper Werner Foerster" (May 2, 1973) at Officer Down Memorial Page https://www.odmp.org/officer/4964-trooper-werner-foerster (accessed October 25, 2020).

418 Humberto Fontova, "BLM Thanked Fidel Castro for Sheltering FBI's 'Most-Wanted' Murderer/Terrorist Assata Shakur" (June 27, 2020) at Townhall https://townhall.com/columnists/humbertofontova/2020/06/27/

blm-thanked-fidel-castro-for-sheltering-fbis-mostwanted-murdererter-rorist-assata-shakur-n2571407 (accessed October 25, 2020).

419 Lizette Alvarez, "City Criticizes Police Chief after Shooting" (March 22, 2012) at the New York Times https://www.nytimes.com/2012/03/22/us/police-chief-draws-fire-in-trayvon-martin-shooting.html (accessed October 25, 2020).

420 Erik Wemple, "Why did New York Times call George Zimmerman a 'white Hispanic'?" (March 28, 2012) at the Washington Post https://www.washingtonpost.com/blogs/erik-wemple/post/why-did-new-york-times-call-george-zimmerman-white-hispanic/2012/03/28/gIQAW-6fngS_blog.html (accessed October 25, 2020).

421 AP, Tamara Lush in Sanford; and Kelli Kennedy, Suzette Laboy and David Fischer, "George Zimmerman cleared of all charges in shooting of Trayvon Martin, released by judge" (July14, 2013) at Fox News https://www.foxnews.com/us/george-zimmerman-cleared-of-all-charges-in-shooting-of-trayvon-martin-released-by-judge (accessed October 25, 2020).

422 Evita Duffy, "Communist, Anti-Semite Angela Davis Says Biden Can Be 'Effectively Pressured' by the Left" (July 14, 2020) at the Federalist https://thefederalist.com/2020/07/14/communist-anti-semite-angela-davis-says-biden-can-be-effectively-pressured-by-the-left/ (accessed October 25, 2020).

423 Associated Press, "Angela Davis Is Sought in Shooting That Killed Judge on Coast" (August 16, 1970) at New York Times Archives https://archive.nytimes.com/www.nytimes.com/books/98/03/08/home/davis-shooting.html (accessed October 28, 2020).

424 Ian Schwartz, "Angela Davis: Biden the 'Candidate Who Can Be Most Effectively Pressured'" (July 4, 2020) at Real Clear Politics https://www.realclearpolitics.com/video/2020/07/14/angela_davis_biden_the_candidate_who_can_be_most_effectively_pressured.html (accessed October 25, 2020).

425 Fox News, "Tucker Exclusive: Tony Bobulinski, ex-Hunter Biden associate, speaks out on Joe Biden" (October 27, 2020) at YouTube https://www.youtube.com/watch?v=2zLfBRgeFFo (accessed October 28, 2020).

426 Jerry Dunleavy, "Black Lives Matter fundraising handled by group with convicted terrorist on its board" (June 25, 2020) at Washington Examiner https://www.washingtonexaminer.com/news/black-lives-matter-fundraising-handled-by-group-with-convicted-terrorist-on-its-

board (accessed October 25, 2020).

427 "#DefundThePolice" (May 30, 2020) at Black Lives Matter https://blacklivesmatter.com/defundthepolice/ (accessed October 25, 2020).

428 Jack Cashill, "The Day Barack Obama Launched Black Lives Matter" (July 8, 2020) at World Net Daily https://www.wnd.com/2020/07/day-barack-obama-launched-black-lives-matter/ (accessed October 11, 2020).

429 Ben Shapiro, "Zimmerman Brother: George Supported Obama Wanted to End 'Club of White Men'" (February 6, 2020) at Breitbart https://www.breitbart.com/politics/2013/02/06/Zimmerman-brother-voted-Obama/ (accessed October 25, 2020).

430 "BLM Harass Restaurant Customers" search (2020) at DuckDuckGo.com https://duckduckgo.com/?t=ffnt&q=blm+harass+restaurant+customers&atb=v132-1&ia=web (accessed October 25, 2020).

431 Kenneth Garger, "BLM protesters accost white diners for not raising fists" (August 25, 2020) at New York Post https://nypost.com/2020/08/25/blm-protesters-harass-white-diners-for-not-raising-fists-in-dc/ (accessed October 25, 2020).

432 "Speading Resistance One Leaflet at a Time" (2020) at White Rose Movement https://www.whiterosestance.com/uploads/9/8/1/1/98112200/hitler-youth-toddler_3.jpg (accessed October 25, 2020).

433 Philip K. Dick, *The Man in the High Castle* (Berkley Book, 1962).

434 "Hitler Youth and Stalingrad" (2020) at White Rose Movement https://www.whiterosestance.com/hitler-youth-and-stalingrad.html (accessed October 25, 2020).

435 Kemberlee Kaye, "DC Mob Harasses White Diners, Demanding They Raise Their Fists in Solidarity" (August 25, 2020) at Legal Insurrection https://legalinsurrection.com/2020/08/dc-blm-mob-harasses-white-diners-demanding-they-raise-fists-in-solidarity/ (accessed October 25, 2020).

436 Kiro Evans, "'I FELT UNDER ATTACK' Brave diner who refused to raise fist because of mob is BLM supporter herself but said 'it didn't feel right' to join" (August 27, 2020) at the Sun https://www.thesun.co.uk/news/12512876/brave-diner-who-refused-to-raise-fist-because-of-mob-is-blm-supporter-herself-but-said-it-didnt-feel-right-to-join/ (accessed October 25, 2020).

437 Christopher R. Browning, *Ordinary Men: Reserve Police Battalion 101 and the Final Solution in Poland* (Harper Perennial, revised edition, 2017).

438 Maxim Lott, "How socialism turned Venezuela from the wealthiest country in South America into an economic basket case" (January 26, 2019) at Fox News https://www.foxnews.com/world/how-socialism-turned-venezuela-from-the-wealthiest-country-in-south-america-into-an-economic-basket-case (accessed October 25, 2020).

439 Hannity Staff, "JUSTICE: Woman Accused of Attacking Boy with 'MAGA' Hat Charged with Robbery, Hate Crime, Assault" (September 9, 2020) at Hannity.com, https://hannity.com/media-room/justice-women-accused-of-attacking-boy-with-maga-hat-charged-with-robbery-hate-crime-assault/ (accessed September 22, 2020).

440 Robert Jonathan, "Woman sprays mace on maskless couple at California dog park" (July 27, 2020), at BPR Business & Politics https://www.bizpacreview.com/2020/07/27/woman-sprays-mace-on-maskless-couple-at-california-dog-park-952203 (accessed September 22, 2020).

441 Carlie Porterfield, "'I'll Kill You': Tensions over People Not Wearing Mask" (July 25, 2020) at Forbes, https://www.forbes.com/sites/carlieporterfield/2020/07/25/ill-kill-you-tensions-over-people-not-wearing-mask-continue-to-boil-over/#55aed3697ed4 (accessed September 22, 2020).

442 Adam, "Karen: Definition" (September 22, 2020) at Know Your Meme, https://knowyourmeme.com/memes/karen (accessed September 22, 2020).

443 Anthony Gockowski, "Minneapolis BLM protesters chant: 'Shoot back at the police'" (October 28, 2020) at Alpha News https://alphanewsmn.com/minneapolis-blm-protesters-chant-shoot-back-at-the-police/ (accessed October 28, 2020).

444 Robby Soave, "Antifa Mob Viciously Assaults Journalist Andy Ngo at Portland Rally" (June 29, 2019) at Reason, https://reason.com/2019/06/29/antifa-andy-ngo-mob-milkshake-violence/ (accessed September 22, 2020).

445 Hank Berrien, "Watch: Portland Activists Block Truck, Demand Passenger Give Black Power Salute and Chant 'Black Lives Matter'" (September 21, 2020) https://www.dailywire.com/news/watch-portland-activists-block-truck-demand-passenger-give-black-power-salute-and-chant-black-lives-matter?itm_source=parsely-api&utm_source=cne-

mail&utm_medium=email (accessed September 22, 2020).

446 Sargon of Akkad, "Antifa and the Black Bloc Explained" (January 26, 2017) at the United Patriots of America https://www.unitedpatriotsofamerica.com/antifa/antifa-and-the-black-bloc-explained.html (accessed October 28, 2020).

447 Tristan Justice, "Exclusive: Homeland Security Secretary Says Antifa 'Absolutely' Meets Definition of Domestic Terrorist Group" (August 27, 2020) at the Federalist. https://thefederalist.com/2020/08/27/exclusive-homeland-security-secretary-says-antifa-absolutely-meet-definition-of-domestic-terrorist-group/ (accessed September 22, 2020).

448 "Revolutionary Abolitionist Movement" (December 16, 2017) at RAM, https://www.revolutionaryabolition.org/ (accessed September 22, 2020).

449 Wild Smile, "Antifa Evolves into RAM—Revolutionary Abolitionist Movement" (December 16, 2017) at YouTube, https://www.youtube.com/watch?v=T_EetJHYicY (accessed September 22, 2020).

450 Steve Doocy, "Antifa in their own words: Lara Logan breaks down the dangerous movement" (June 2, 2020) at Fox & Friends, https://video.foxnews.com/v/6161084023001#sp=show-clips (accessed September 22, 2020).

451 Hank Berrien, "WATCH: Portland Activists Block Truck, Demand Passengers Give Black Power Salute And Chant 'Black Lives Matter'" (September 21, 2020) at Daily Wire https://www.dailywire.com/news/watch-portland-activists-block-truck-demand-passenger-give-black-power-salute-and-chant-black-lives-matter (accessed December 9, 2020)

452 Ted Wheeler, "An eye-opening, inside look at nightly protests in our city" (2020) at Mayor Wheeler's Office https://mailchi.mp/portlandoregon/an-eye-opening-inside-look-at-nightly-protests-in-our-city?e=6b738fc28a (accessed October 28, 2020).

453 DHM Survey Results, "Oregon Voters Disapprove of the Ongoing Protests" (September 10, 2020) at DHM Research, https://www.dhmresearch.com/oregon-voters-disapprove-of-the-ongoing-protests/ (accessed September 22, 2020).

454 TRUEmedia Portland, "Antifa Study from Rutgers & the Big Picture" (September 16, 2020) at YouTube https://www.youtube.com/watch?v=ttJjIEUGoQE (accessed October 25, 2020).

455 Proud Boys, "The Proud Boys vehemently denounce hate

groups, much the same way @realDonaltTrump has done" (October 1, 2020) at Twitter https://twitter.com/i/status/1311643918912684032 (accessed October 25, 2020).

456 Carmen Gasbarro, "ANTIFA Fighters Recruited into Syria—Turkish National Police Academy Report" (September 19, 2020) at Quarter Master News https://qm.news/antifa-fighters-recruited-into-syria-turkish-national-police-academy-report/ (accessed October 25, 2020).

457 Ebony Bowden, "Trump to designate KKK, Antifa as terrorist groups in black empowerment plan" (September 25,2020) at New York Post https://nypost.com/2020/09/25/trump-to-designate-kkk-antifa-as-terrorist-groups-in-black-empowerment-plan/ (accessed October 29, 2020).

458 Christine Douglass-Williams, "Islamic Republic of Iran Stands with Antifa and BLM, Calls American Law Enforcement 'Vicious Dogs'" (June 4, 2020) at Jihad Watch https://www.jihadwatch.org/2020/06/islamic-republic-of-iran-stands-with-antifa-and-blm-calls-american-law-enforcement-vicious-dogs (accessed October 25, 2020).

459 Lee Kaplan, "Hamas and Black Lives Matter: A Marriage Made in Hell" (2020) at Israel National News https://www.israelnationalnews.com/Articles/Article.aspx/19482 (accessed October 29, 2020).

460 BDS "The Peaceful BDS Movement Will Prevail Over The Far Right Trump-Netanyahu Alliance" (2020) at BDS https://bdsmovement.net/ (accessed December 9, 2020)

461 Kristian Davis Bailey, "Dream Defenders, Black Lives Matter & Ferguson Reps Take Historic Trip to Palestine" (January 9, 2015) at Ebony https://www.ebony.com/news/dream-defenders-black-lives-matter-ferguson-reps-take-historic-trip-to-palestine/ (accessed October 25, 2020).

462 Rusty Weiss, "John Kerry Embarrassed after Video Surfaces of Him Declaring Peace in the Middle East Is Not Possible without Palestinians" (September 17, 2020) at the Political Insider https://thepoliticalinsider.com/john-kerry-embarrassed-after-video-surfaces-of-him-declaring-peace-in-the-middle-east-is-not-possible-without-palestinians/ (accessed October 25, 2020).

463 Lee Kaplan, "ISM Exposed: How the ISM Sucker-Punched the IDF Again" (April 24, 2012) at Save Israel Campaign http://www.saveisraelcampaign.com/atad/articles.asp?article_id=14020 (accessed October 25, 2020).

464 Donald Trump et. al., "The Abraham Accords Declaration"

(September 15, 2020) at Whitehouse.gov https://www.whitehouse.gov/briefings-statements/the-abraham-accords-declaration/ (accessed October 25, 2020).

465 Adela Suliman and Charlene Gubash, "Sudan formally recognizes Israel in U.S.-brokered deal" (October 23, 2020) at NBC News https://www.nbcnews.com/news/world/sudan-formally-recognizes-israel-u-s-brokered-deal-n1240839 (accessed October 29, 2020).

466 Tristan Justice, "Celebrities Bail Out Rioters in Virtueless Virtue Signaling" (June 1, 2020) at the Federalist https://thefederalist.com/2020/06/01/celebrities-bail-out-rioters-in-virtueless-virtue-signaling/ (accessed September 25, 2020).

467 Lauryn Overhultz, "Here Are the Celebrities Who Donated to Minnesota Freedom Fund, Which Bailed Out Several Allegedly Violent Criminals" (August 11, 2020) at Daily Caller, https://dailycaller.com/2020/08/11/seth-rogen-steve-carrell-celebrities-minnesota-freedom-fund-donations-george-floyd-protests/ (accessed September 25, 2020).

468 Ben Kew, "Alyssa Milano Pushes 'White Silence Costs Black Lives' Meme Following Breonna Taylor Grand Jury Decision" (September 24, 2020) at Breibart https://www.breitbart.com/entertainment/2020/09/24/alyssa-milano-pushes-white-silence-costs-black-lives-meme-following-breonna-taylor-grand-jury-decision/ (September 25, 2020).

469 TatumReport.com, "Breonna Taylor LMPD homicide Unit report" (April 2016 to Present) at yumpu.com https://www.yumpu.com/en/document/read/63943132/breonna-taylor-summary-redacted1 (accessed September 25, 2020).

470 Nate Day, "Alyssa Milano explains why police were called near her home" (September 23, 2020) at Fox News https://www.foxnews.com/entertainment/alyssa-milano-police-presence-california-home (accessed September 25, 2020).

471 Charmed Fandom, *Charmed Alyssa Milano* at Charmed Wiki https://charmed.fandom.com/wiki/Alyssa_Milano (accessed September 25, 2020).

472 Allie Gold, "'Defund the Police' Activist Alyssa Milano Calls Police on Teen" (September 23, 2020) at WOR 710 https://710wor.iheart.com/content/2020-09-23-defund-the-police-activist-alyssa-milano-calls-police-on-teen/ (accessed December 4, 2020).

473 Daily Mail Online, "Heavy police presence on scene near Alyssa Milano's house" (September 23, 2020) at Daily Mail https://www.daily-mail.co.uk/video/news/video-2254728/Video-Heavy-police-presence-scene-near-Alyssa-Milanos-house.html (September 25, 2020).

474 Jill Ishkanian, "EXCLUSIVE: 'Defund the police' activist Alyssa Milano calls 911 sparking massive police presence in her quiet California neighborhood claiming a gunman was on her property—but it was really a teen shooting at squirrels with an air gun" (September 22, 2020) at Daily Mail https://www.dailymail.co.uk/news/article-8756911/Defund-po-lice-activist-Alyssa-Milano-sparks-massive-police-presence-calling-911.html (September 25, 2020).

475 "Michael E. Novogratz" (2020) at the Bail Project https://bail-project.org/team/michael-e-novogratz/ (accessed September 29, 2020).

476 Frieda Powers, "Tucker calls out wealthy Dems behind 'Bail Project' after organization chairman reportedly ducks his show" (September 29, 2020) at BPR Business & Politics https://www.bizpacreview.com/2020/09/29/tucker-calls-out-wealthy-dems-behind-bail-project-af-ter-organization-chairman-reportedly-ducks-his-show-978524 (accessed September 29, 2020).

477 Jack Hadfield, "Bail Project Tied to Antifa U-Haul Received Millions from Bill Gates, UMG, Jack Dorsey, Among Others" (September 24, 2020) at National File https://nationalfile.com/bail-project-tied-to-an-tifa-u-haul-received-millions-from-bill-gates-umg-jack-dorsey-among-others/ (accessed September 29, 2020).

478 Sloan Rachmuth and Katie Jensen, "Black Lives Matter in Public Schools Is Turning Kids into Little Marxists" (July 8, 2020) at the Feder-alist https://thefederalist.com/2020/07/08/black-lives-matter-in-public-schools-is-turning-kids-into-little-marxists/ (accessed October 25, 2020).

479 Nikole Hannah-Jones, "The 1619 Project" (August 14, 2019) at New York Times Magazine https://www.nytimes.com/interac-tive/2019/08/14/magazine/1619-america-slavery.html (accessed Septem-ber 24, 2020).

480 Rich Lowry, "Historians Roast the 1619 Project" (January 3, 2020) at National Review https://www.nationalreview.com/2020/01/1619-project-top-historians-criticize-new-york-times-slavery-feature/ (ac-cessed September 24, 2020).

481 Jordan Davidson, "In Racist Screed, NYT's 1619 Project Found-er Calls 'White Race' 'Barbaric Devils,' 'Bloodsuckers,' Columbus 'No Dif-

ferent Than Hitler'" (June 25, 2020) at the Federalist https://thefederalist.com/2020/06/25/in-racist-screed-nyts-1619-project-founder-calls-white-race-barbaric-devils-bloodsuckers-no-different-than-hitler/ (accessed September, 23 2020).

482 Andrew Mark Miller, "Author of New York Times 1619 Project called white race 'barbaric devils' in unearthed letter" (June 26, 2020) at Washington Examiner https://thefederalist.com/2020/06/25/in-racist-screed-nyts-1619-project-founder-calls-white-race-barbaric-devils-bloodsuckers-no-different-than-hitler/ (accessed September, 23 2020).

483 Accuracy in Media Staff, "Head of NY Times' 1619 Project backs away from entire premise" (August 4, 2020) at Accuracy in Media https://www.aim.org/aim-column/head-of-ny-times-1619-project-backs-away-from-entire-premise/ (accessed September 23, 2020).

484 Randy DeSoto, "Several Urging Times and Post to Give Back Pulitzers for False Reporting on Russia Collusion" (March 25, 2019) at the Western Journal https://www.westernjournal.com/several-urging-times-post-give-back-pulitzers-false-reporting-russia-collusion/ (accessed October 25, 2020).

485 Robby Soave, "Public Schools Are Teaching the 1619 Project in Class, Despite Concerns from Historians" (January 28, 2020) at Reason https://reason.com/2020/01/28/1619-project-new-york-times-public-schools/ (accessed October 25, 2020).

486 John Sexton, "Nikole Hannah-Jones on Violence and 'Uprising' in Minneapolis" (May 29, 2020) at Hot Air https://hotair.com/archives/john-s-2/2020/05/29/nikole-hannah-jones-violence-uprising-minneapolis/ (accessed September 23, 2020).

487 History.com, "Four Black schoolgirls killed in Birmingham church bombing" (September 15, 1963) at History https://www.history.com/this-day-in-history/four-black-schoolgirls-killed-in-birmingham (accessed October 25, 2020).

488 Sam Dorman, "Chris Rufo calls on Trump to end critical race theory 'cult indoctrination' in federal government" (September 1, 2020) at Fox News https://www.foxnews.com/politics/chris-rufo-race-theory-cult-federal-government (accessed October 25, 2020).

489 Christopher F. Rufo, "The New Segregation" (October 19, 2020) at City Journal https://www.city-journal.org/seattle-race-segregated-diversity-trainings (accessed October 25, 2020).

490 Helen Pluckrose and James Lindsay, *Cynical Theories: How Ac-*

tivist Scholarship Made Everything about Race, Gender, and Identity—and Why This Harms Everybody (Pitchstone Publishing, 2020), 59-60.

491 Ibid., 60.

492 Tyler O'Neil, "Trump Takes Aim at Marxist Propaganda behind the BLM Riots" (September 7, 2020) at PJ Media https://pjmedia.com/news-and-politics/tyler-o-neil/2020/09/07/trump-takes-aim-at-marxist-propaganda-behind-the-blm-riots-n901392 (accessed September 23, 2020).

493 Ben Shapiro, "Critical Race Theory Explained & Obama's Relation to It" (September 24, 2020) at Western Revival: The Online Journal of Western Nationalism http://westernrevival.org/?p=170 (accessed September 24, 2020)

494 Joel B. Pollak, "Pollak: Eight Years Later, Andrew Breitbart Vindicated on Critical Race Theory" (September 6, 2020) at Breitbart https://www.breitbart.com/politics/2020/09/06/pollak-eight-years-later-andrew-breitbart-vindicated-on-critical-race-theory/ (accessed September 24, 2020)

495 Ben Shapiro, "Obama: 'Open Up Your Hearts and Minds' to Racialist Prof" (March 7, 2012) at Breitbart https://www.breitbart.com/politics/2012/03/07/buzzefeed-selectively-edits-obama-tape/ (accessed September 24, 2020).

496 Lachlan Markay, "Derrick A. Bell Visited the White House Twice in 2010" (March 8, 2012) at Breitbart https://www.dailysignal.com/2012/03/08/derrick-a-bell-visited-the-white-house-twice-in-2010/ (accessed September 24, 2020).

497 Leonard E. Egede, M.D., and Rebekah J. Walker, Ph.D., "Structural Racism, Social Risk Factors, and Covid-19—A Dangerous Convergence for Black Americans" (September 17, 2020) at the New England Journal of Medicine https://www.nejm.org/doi/full/10.1056/NEJMp2023616 (accessed October 25, 2020).

498 Tiffany Ford, Sarah Reber, and Richard V. Reeves, "Race gaps in COVID-19 deaths are even bigger than they appear" (June 16, 2020) at Brookings https://www.brookings.edu/blog/up-front/2020/06/16/race-gaps-in-covid-19-deaths-are-even-bigger-than-they-appear/ (accessed October 25, 2020).

499 Ibram X. Kendi, "The Day *Shithole* Entered the Presidential Lexicon" (January 13, 2019) at the Atlantic https://www.theatlantic.com/politics/archive/2019/01/shithole-countries/580054/ (accessed October

25, 2020).

500 Larry Buchanan, Quoctrung Bui, and Jugal K. Patel, "Black Lives Matter May Be the Largest Movement in U.S. History" (July 3, 2020) at the New York Times https://www.nytimes.com/interactive/2020/07/03/us/george-floyd-protests-crowd-size.html (accessed October 25, 2020).

501 LET Staff, "Broward schools sidestep state law on Promise program that lead to Parkland shooting" (May 20, 2019) at Law Enforcement Today https://www.lawenforcementtoday.com/broward-schools-sidestep-state-law/ (access October 25, 2020).

502 Andrew Mark Miller, "LA teachers union demands defunding the police and charter 'moratorium' before reopening schools" (July 11, 2020) at the Washington Examiner https://www.washingtonexaminer.com/news/la-teachers-union-demands-defunding-the-police-and-charter-moratorium-before-reopening-schools (accessed September 24, 2020).

503 Joseph Thompson, "Edmonds School Board cuts school resources officer contract" (June 25, 2020) at HeraldNet https://www.heraldnet.com/news/edmonds-school-board-cuts-school-resource-officer-contracts/ (accessed October 25, 2020).

504 Tim Pearce, "'Police Are a Real Risk': Washington School District Severs Ties with Law Enforcement" (June 25, 2020) at Daily Wire https://www.dailywire.com/news/police-are-a-real-risk-washington-school-district-severs-ties-with-law-enforcement (accessed October 25, 2020).

505 "Election 2020" (2020) at Scholastic Classroom Magazines https://classroommagazines.scholastic.com/election.html (accessed October 25, 2020).

506 David Marcus, "The Ugly Racism of the Associated Press Capitalizing 'Black'" (July 21, 2020) at the Federalist https://thefederalist.com/2020/07/21/the-ugly-racism-of-the-associated-press-capitalizing-black/ (accessed October 25, 2020).

507 Alex Newman, "Schools Using Fake 'History' to Kill America" (September 26, 2020) at the Epoch Times https://www.theepochtimes.com/schools-using-fake-history-to-kill-america_3514284.html (accessed September 29, 2020).

508 "Youth Activists Toolkit" (2020) at Advocates for Youth https://advocatesforyouth.org/wp-content/uploads/2019/04/Youth-Activist-Toolkit.pdf (accessed October 25, 2020).

509 "Law Enforcement Digests" (2020) at Washington State Criminal Justice Training Commission https://www.cjtc.wa.gov/resources/law-enforcement-digest (accessed October 25, 2020).

510 Advocates for Youth, "How to Get Police Out of Your School" (August 24, 2020) at YouTube https://www.youtube.com/watch?v=s0_DmgZJ-NU (accessed October 25, 2020).

511 Natalie D., "The Full List—Here Are the 269 Companies Who Are Supporting BLM & Antifa Riots" (June 6, 2020) at Conservative US https://conservativeus.com/the-full-list-here-are-the-269-companies-who-are-supporting-blm-antifa-riots/ (accessed October 25, 2020).

512 Matt Palumbo, "Facebook Is Censoring Conservatives—Again" (April 7, 2020) at the Dan Bongino Show https://bongino.com/facebook-is-censoring-conservatives-again (accessed October 25, 2020).

513 Adam Candeub, "Social Media Plaftorms or Publishers? Rethinking Section 230" (June 21, 2019) at the American Conservative https://www.theamericanconservative.com/articles/social-media-platforms-or-publishers-rethinking-section-230/ (October 6, 2020).

514 "47 U.S. Code § 230—Protection for private blocking and screening of offensive material" (April 11, 2018) at Legal Information Institute, Cornell Law School https://www.law.cornell.edu/uscode/text/47/230 (accessed October 25, 2020).

515 Kyle S. Reyes, "GoFundMe shuts down page for cop's legal expenses, allows ANTIFA to raise funds for criminals" (July 4, 2019) at Law Enforcement Today https://www.lawenforcementtoday.com/GoFund-Me-cancels-cop-fundraiser/ (accessed October 6, 2020).

516 "Rudoph Giuliani" (2020) at the Mob Museum https://themob-museum.org/notable_names/rudolph-giuliani/ (accessed October 25, 2020).

517 Barack Obama, "If you're looking to take action—or looking to educate yourselves ..." (August 28, 2020) at Twitter https://twitter.com/BarackObama/status/1299384486241730568 (accessed October 25, 2020).

518 "Anguish and Action" (2020) at Obama.org https://www.obama.org/anguish-and-action/ (accessed October 25, 2020).

519 Ryan Bomberger, "Top 10 Reasons I Won't Support the #BlackLivesMatter Movement" (June 5, 2020) at Townhall https://townhall.com/columnists/ryanbomberger/2020/06/05/top-10-reasons-i-reject-the-blm-n2570105 (accessed October 25, 2020).

520 Brie Stimson, "Kenosha police union gives its accounting of Jacob Blake shooting" (August 29, 2020) at Fox News https://www.foxnews.com/us/kenosha-police-union-gives-its-account-of-jacob-blake-shooting (accessed October 25, 2020).

521 Gabrielle Fonrouge, "This is why Jacob Blake had a warrant out for his arrest" (August 28, 2020) at New York Post https://nypost.com/2020/08/28/this-is-why-jacob-blake-had-a-warrant-out-for-his-arrest/ (accessed October 25, 2020).

522 Joshua Rhett Miller, "Seattle-based activists arrested in Kenosha after filling up gas cans" (August 28, 2020) at New York Post https://nypost.com/2020/08/28/activists-arrested-in-kenosha-after-filling-up-gas-cans-police/ (accessed October 25, 2020).

523 Monica Showalter, "Antifa's 'Riot Kitchen' Gets Busted" (August 28, 2020) at American Thinker https://www.americanthinker.com/blog/2020/08/antifas_riot_kitchen_gets_busted.html (accessed October 25, 2020).

524 "18 U.S. Code § 844 Penalties" (November 30, 2004) at Legal Information Institute, Cornell Law School https://www.law.cornell.edu/uscode/text/18/844 (accessed October 25, 2020).

525 GoFundMe, "RIOT KITCHEN Food Truck" (June 26, 2020) at GoFundMe.com https://www.gofundme.com/f/mental-health-support-for-blm-seattle-protests (accessed October 25, 2020).

526 Kyle S. Reyes, "GoFundMe shuts down page for cop's legal expenses, allows ANTIFA to raise funds for criminals" (July 4, 2020) at Law Enforcement Today https://www.lawenforcementtoday.com/gofundme-cancels-cop-fundraiser/ (accessed October 25, 2020).

527 Isabel Togoh, "Corporate Donations Tracker: Here Are the Companies Giving Millions to the Anti-Racism Efforts" (June 1, 2020) at Forbes https://www.forbes.com/sites/isabeltogoh/2020/06/01/corporate-donations-tracker-here-are-the-companies-giving-millions-to-anti-racism-efforts/#5c4ac87337dc (accessed October 25, 2020).

528 Yaron Steinbuch, "Black Lives Matter co-founder describes herself as 'trained Marxist'" (June 25, 2020) at New York Post https://nypost.com/2020/06/25/blm-co-founder-describes-herself-as-trained-marxist/ (accessed October 25, 2020).

529 Tyler O'Neil, "Conservative Journalist Andy Ngo Beaten Up and Hit with Cement by Antifa in Portland, Says Police Did Nothing" (June 29, 2020) at PJ Media https://pjmedia.com/news-and-politics/tyler-o-

neil/2019/06/29/quillette-editor-beaten-up-and-hit-with-cement-by-an-tifa-in-portland-says-police-did-nothing-n66732 (accessed October 25, 2020).

530 Brian Flood, "Reporter Julio Rosas says media 'trying to dismiss' ugly side Seattle's 'Autonomous Zone,' but he's seen it himself" (June 12, 2020) at Fox News https://www.foxnews.com/media/julio-rosas-me-dia-seattle-autonomous-zone-chaz (accessed October 25, 2020).

531 Jim Hoft, "Antifa Terrorists Attack Independent journalist in Portland—Beat Him Bloody" (September 9, 2020) at Gateway Pundit https://www.thegatewaypundit.com/2020/09/antifa-terrorists-attack-in-dependent-journalist-portland-beat-bloody/ (accessed October 25, 2020).

532 Silenceisconsent.net, "Journalist Infiltrates ANTIFA, Undercov-er Video Exposes Everything" (September 30, 2017) at Red Ice https://redice.tv/news/journalist-infiltrates-antifa-undercover-video-exposes-ev-erything (accessed October 25, 2020).

533 Chuck Goudie, "1,500 rioters arrested in Chicago; most not facing serious charges" (June 3, 2020) at ABC 7 News https://abc7chicago.com/chicago-news-riots-protests-looting/6228227/ (accessed October 25, 2020).

534 Sundance, "DOJ Begins Indicting Portland (and National) Rioters with Federal 'Civil Disorder' Charges" (September 3, 2020) at the Conservative Tree House https://theconservativetreehouse.com/2020/09/03/doj-begins-indicting-portland-and-national-riot-ers-with-federal-civil-disorder-charges/ (accessed October 25, 2020).

535 Jonathan Levinson and Rebecca Ellis, "Portland area officers will remain federal deputies through end of year" (September 29, 2020) at OPB https://www.opb.org/article/2020/09/29/portland-area-officers-will-remain-federal-deputies-through-end-of-year/ (accessed December 4, 2020).

536 Zachary Stieber, "DOJ Labels Portland, Seattle, NYC As Ju-risdictions That Permit Anarchy, Violence, Property Destruction" (September 21, 2020) at the Epoch Times https://www.theepochtimes.com/portland-seattle-nyc-permitted-violence-destruction-of-proper-ty-doj_3507973.html (accessed October 25, 2020).

537 Dom Callcchio, "Suspect in Portland fatal shooting killed as fed-eral task force moved in" (September 4, 2020) at Fox News https://www.foxnews.com/us/suspect-in-portland-fatal-shooting-has-been-killed-re-ports (accessed October 25, 2020).

538 Jean-Jacques Rousseau (ed. Jonathan Bennett 2017), *The Social Contract* (1762) at https://www.earlymoderntexts.com/assets/pdfs/rousseau1762.pdf (accessed October 25, 2020).

539 Andrea Widburg, "Nancy Pelosi calls federal law enforcement officers 'stormtroopers'" (July 19, 2020) at American Thinker https://www.americanthinker.com/blog/2020/07/nancy_pelosi_calls_federal_law_enforcement_officers_stormtroopers.html (accessed October 25, 2020).

540 Tobias Hoonhout, "Obama Sees Protests as 'Tailor-Made' to Help Biden's Election Chances: Report" (June 29, 2020) at National Review https://www.nationalreview.com/news/obama-sees-protests-as-tailor-made-to-help-bidens-election-chances-report/ (accessed October 29, 2020).